Turkey Tails and Tales from Across the USA

Volume 5

By Tom "Doc" Weddle

Signed copies of this book and other volumes in the series can be purchased directly from me. Hardcovers are $39 and paperbacks $29. I'll take care of postage. The easiest way to send funds is via PayPal, using either of my email addresses: tdocweddle@comcast.net, or tdocweddle@gmail.com. Be sure to use their "send money to friends and family" option, so they don't deduct fees on my end. Also, please leave me your mailing address in the notes section, and let me know to whom the books should be signed. You can also send checks or money orders to:

Tom Weddle
PO Box 7281
Bloomington, IN 47407

© 2025 Tom Weddle
All rights reserved.

No part of this publication may be reproduced, stored in a retrieval system, or transmitted, in any form or by any means, electronic, mechanical, photocopying, recording or otherwise, without the written permission of the author.

ISBN: 978-1-7354419-8-6

Printed in the United States of America

Volume 5 is dedicated to my nephew, Daniel Thomas Hartley, who died May 14, 2025. Dan was the best our family had to offer, and an inspiration to me from the time he was old enough to walk amongst the wilds and woodlands. Every soul he touched along his too-short life's path felt the same way. His strong connection to the earth is only one of many we shared, and now my beloved nephew is free to wander where he always most wanted to be.
Cancer sucks!

Contents

Ephemera 6

Chapter 1
The U.S. Wild Turkey Super Slam 9

Chapter 2
2019 13

Chapter 3
2020 45

Chapter 4
2021 90

Chapter 5
2022 128

Chapter 6
2023 166

Chapter 7
2024 193

Chapter 8
2025 240

Chapter 9
Recollections from a Turkey Hunter of a Certain Age 278

Epilogue 285

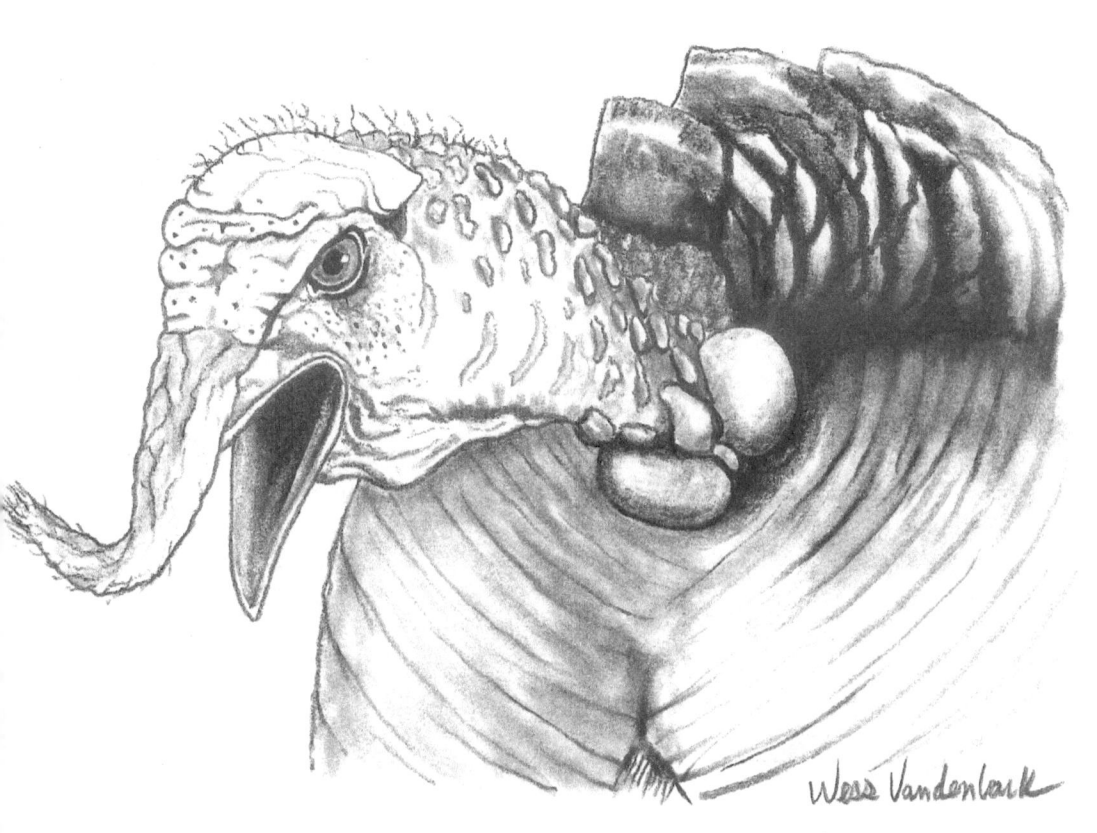

Ephemera

My first four books covered the initial 35 years of an ongoing and near-fanatical pursuit of the wild turkey: 1983 through 2018. This one continues that record, as taken from both the indelibly etched memories in my brain, as well as notes recorded in the journals which I've diligently kept since my very first turkey hunting season some 43 years ago. It's now June of 2025, and the completion of this volume has basically "caught up" to the journal entries. I've also included a lot of photos in this book, if only because I just like looking at them. Those "snapshots from my past" tell a tale in many ways equal to or greater than any written word I'm capable of putting in print, but they also serve as a way to personally whisk me right back to those earlier times of glory captured on film. Photographs are like time machines, in that regard, and I value them greatly. I only wish that it were possible to record my numerous missed opportunities and screw-ups on film, as well, for the simple truth of the matter is that it's those oh-so-regrettable instances of failure which are the recollections most seared into my gray matter. Every single one of them lingers there in vivid, living color, as if they happened only yesterday. I would welcome the opportunity to dredge up and convey the deep-seated emotions and mental turmoil which each one initially induced, too. The reason for bringing them back to fore would be that those bad times are as much or more a part of my growth as a turkey hunter, as were the times of glory. However, each painful miss or turkey boogered into the next county will remain my own personal burdens to bear; similar, I'm sure, to those mind-demons which all of us carry.

While most of the photos in this book were taken by yours truly, I want to thank Stephen Spurlock and Joe Ross for their quality ones which are sprinkled throughout these pages. Both of those guys actually know what they're doing behind the camera lens, and you can easily ascertain such in comparing any of their images to my own. I would also like to profoundly thank Stephen for allowing me the use of a couple of blog entries that I originally wrote for his Chasing 49 webpage. They are included here as chapters 1 & 9. I took the time to clean them up a little and make edits as I felt they needed, but the basic thoughts and ideas are the same as when first published. And, of course, I would be terribly remiss if I didn't thank Kevin Rhoades once again. His work on the cover and interior layout/design of this book and others before it has been substantial and invaluable. I so very much appreciate his talents and professionalism, and I would encourage anyone intending to write a book of their own to get ahold of him for help. Furthermore and as always, I'd also like to profoundly thank Wess Vandenburg for allowing me the use of his splendid drawings of turkeys at the beginning and ending of this volume. Wess's talents have been a steadying force in every single one of my books, and I am honored beyond limits that he has continued to allow me the usage of his visuals. They are magnificent, and he is a fine man for allowing me the privilege of putting them in print. Also too; my Mom's contributions remain steadfast, with her drawings gracing the pages of every new chapter heading. Mom's a great artist, with a keen interest in watercolors. I'm so lucky to be her son.

Once again, I have only myself to blame for the (lack of) editing on this book. I am cursed with an attitude of "anything you can do, I can do better," and this book should, if nothing else, serve as proof eternal that I may very well have that assumption all wrong. However, at this point it is how it is and I am who I am, so I will just say that I've tried my best to make the danged thing fairly readable and moderately coherent. If I've failed, so be it. Along with becoming older I've also grown much more tolerant, especially so of my own shortcomings and failings, so I can live with the way it's turned out.

Other than the thanks and what-nots, I don't believe there's a whole lot else to say before we embark down the turkey trails one more time. I'm not at all sure if this might-could be the final book in this series, but it will certainly be the last one for a while. I figure that it will take at least a half-dozen more years to acquire enough materiel for a follow-up edition, and given the health issues that I've faced of late and the uncertainty of life itself, who knows if I'll even be around long enough to notch that many more days afield. Heck; none of us are guaranteed even another single morning, so all I can do is keep on keepin' on, enjoy every single minute of every single day that I'm still walking upright, and focus on fully appreciating every gobble that I'm given the opportunity to hear. The truth of the matter is that I look at each one of those thunderous ovations as being the grains of sand in my life's hourglass, and while I hope they continue to trickle down for a long, long time, we shall see what we shall see…

And so, without further ado, let's get started on Volume 5:

Dreaming and scheming by lamplight at our Florida turkey camp.

Chapter 1

The U.S. Wild Turkey Super Slam

The U.S. Wild Turkey Super Slam: What is it, and why are so many hunters trying to attain one?

Well, the short answer to the first part is that by killing a turkey in all 49 states where they can legally be hunted (Alaska standing alone as the only missing entry from the list) an individual has accomplished what's called the U.S. Wild Turkey Super Slam. In short, this lofty goal ain't an easy thing to do, nor cheap, and it entails great effort and multiple hardships suffered over a long period of time. Only the most dedicated of turkey hunters would ever even dare to begin the challenge. Or, maybe only those who are crazy as bedbugs. As someone who just finished up his fifth, I'm still not so sure which of those qualifiers are the most accurate, but I would lean towards the latter....

Turkey hunting is addictive. We all know that. It's also a sport unlike any other type of hunting, insomuch as it's open to the masses. You might even call wild turkeys the "Every-Man's Big Game," because you don't need to be rich in order to hunt them. Licenses are relatively cheap, it doesn't take much of an initial expenditure to get into the sport, and turkeys fill nearly all of the suitable habitat found across this big, beautiful country of ours. If you've got a gun and ammo, a little camo, and a call or two, almost anyone can get started down the road to becoming a turkey hunter.

The gobble of the wild turkey (or, for that matter, simply seeing one strutting for his hens) generates such a high level of excitement in my own heart that it's a wonder to me why every person in America isn't crowding into the springtime woods. Fortunately, we're all different in our motivations and passions in life, and so, as hard as it may be to comprehend for anyone so addicted to this sport as I am, there are some poor souls in this country thrilling to other endeavors when the buds have begun sprouting from tree limbs: things like fishing, hiking, biking, etc. No complaints here, though! That just makes the woods less crowded. Well, at least it does, in theory. The Covid 19 pandemic of the 2020 season changed all of that and ever since then we've seen an explosion in hunter numbers and participation.

That love of the gobble is a driving reason for why so many turkey hunters these days choose to state-hop beyond their home turf. After all, there are only so many days of opportunity in every spring season, and hunting in other places allows the gobble-crazed addict to experience more time afield during the all-too-brief window of spring. The craziest amongst our ilk take this turkey hunting passion even further, and set their goals quite a bit higher, by pursuing a U.S. Super Slam. What motivates a man, or a woman, to forsake any semblance of sanity and devote so much time, effort, and money (not to mention the blood, sweat, and tears expended) to accomplish such a difficult goal? Is it looking forward to the long days and too-short nights of restless sleep which keep us wandering around all spring long looking like zombies? The quest for fast-food or processed meat products, granola bars, and peanut butter? Incurring the ire of family members and employers as we forsake duties and responsibilities back home? Any of these? All of them? None of the above?

There is something deep within a "Slammer's" soul; something that drives them beyond rhythm or reason. Something that's hard to put a finger on as being THE reason why, but yet, something which motivates each and every single one of us to keep plugging along far beyond what any ordinary, sane person might endure.

Perhaps the reason can be found during that magical, final hour before daylight, after having already arisen long before then in order to climb a steep unknown ridge to its highest point merely to gain the listening advantage which elevation provides. Sitting there cooling down from the exertion, as random sounds of night creatures fill our brains with musings both good and bad, one might begin to understand the wonder of that peaceful, tranquil feeling coming from watching a new day form on the horizon, as slowly, almost imperceptivity, the dark corners and folds of the valleys below fill with the misty haze of dawn. Anxiousness for the day's first gobble almost makes one's skin vibrate in anticipation of that much-anticipated pronouncement which will prove beyond worried doubts that our beloved opponents haven't all died during the night, and will soon again be crying out in eagerness for battle. Could the final proof of why we're here lie simply in the chills and goosebumps which rake up and down our spine when that glorious sound finally does echo out from so close that we can feel its rumble in our chest?

Maybe it's none of these things, after all. Perhaps the reason is simply a longing for the thrill of the hunt that will occur after our opponent has flown to ground, and the nervousness of the unknown outcome thence waiting in the wings. Or, it could be as simple as the mere hope of just "talking the talk," and "playing the game" with one of nature's most wild and fascinating creatures. It might even be the surprise and amazement which well up inside our hearts when an old tom actually answers something that we've said in his own language. But, then again, what about those long periods of silence which often then ensue, when we know not whether the old monarch is coming in, or going away, and the palpable feelings of building tension coursing through our veins like steam in a boiler?

What is it that drives our souls? I know: it's got to be the low, building hum that starts out merely as a question mark back in some hidden corner of our brain, but which eventually builds into that recognizable and most glorious of sounds in all of turkeydome...the drumming of a tom in full strut! Or, maybe not. It could just as easily be the shocked blast excitement that occurs when a gobble suddenly erupts from right behind our setup! That is a time when feelings of urgency and panic make your brain feel like it will explode into a million tiny pieces if *something* doesn't happen...and happen, SOON!

And then, you catch the first peek of a rounded tail-tip moving up above the land's contour out in front of your setup, or maybe just a fleck of bright white skull-cap peering out from behind a distant tree where moments ago there was nothing. A simple splash of crimson red or jet black in a mosaic of browns and greys might be all that it takes. What comes next, but the glorious personification of regal beauty and pageantry itself, as that master of the unknown finally steps plainly into view for the first time and we are once again privileged beyond all reason to lay witness to the majesty of his entire glorious splendor!

Walking up to our fallen opponent a minute or three hours later, we gaze in wonder at those gorgeous feathers laying so perfectly aligned on that magnificent, streamlined body, radiating every color of the rainbow and shimmering like a new penny in their pure exalted splendiferousness. That's a time when emotions run amuck: joy; elation; awe. And yet, at the same time: sorrow; remorse; even, sadness. But always: thankfulness; wonderment; respect.

And an unbinding, unilateral, driven desire to do it all again. Tomorrow. In someplace new and as-yet unexplored.

Chapter 2

2019

The 2019 season began in Florida, as nearly every spring season has done for me since 1988. During the preceding winter I'd acquired a new property on which to conduct some of my guided hunts, and it looked to be a doozy of a spot. Originally, those 80 acres had been part of a much larger 2500-acre ranch, but the owner's tragic death had placed his surviving family members in the very difficult position of maintaining his vast operation. They'd eventually found it too hard to handle, and were forced to sell off most of the land in order to pay back taxes and such. Only this smaller chunk of ground where they now lived and ran a micro-farming operation remained of the old ranch.

My first client that I took there was a young fellow who wanted to kill two birds…with his bow! I don't ordinarily agree to take bow hunters, for the simple fact that my hunts are conducted with a guarantee of a shot *opportunity*, and once that arrow is released from string, I've technically done my job and am owed the full amount of the fee; no matter the results. There are just short of a bazillion reasons why things can go wrong when attempting to kill a wild turkey with a sharp stick, and only the best of those bad results is a complete miss. Crippled toms are the very worst scenario, and that possibility alone is what makes me so reluctant to guide bow hunters. In my mind it's really quite simple: I just feel like the wild turkey deserves so much more than dying a slow death from an errant arrow. Administering a quick, humane kill on these magnificent birds is what I strive for myself, and demand of my clients, and that is never a foregone conclusion when bow hunting. Not to say that a well-placed arrow won't get the job done extremely efficiently, but I've just seen too many times when the end result was less than stellar, and it's those kinds of results which make me toss and turn at night from worry, regret, and sorrow.

Well, when a small flock of jakes arrived on the scene soon after sunrise, Jason told me that he'd be more than happy to take one of those youngsters home with him. Little did either of us anticipate what would happen next, for when his arrow passed through the first turkey, it veered off at a wild angle and struck another bird standing off to the side. The targeted jake went down right away, and the second one ran off about a hundred yards before piling up in a heap. Just like that, Jason had his two birds, and with only one arrow! He was thrilled.

The next day I sent a second hunter named Darrell back to this same farm by himself while I took another pair of guys to a small piece of ground nearby that is only accessible by boat. A client from several years earlier had dubbed Captain Billy's airboat ride out to his property "The Love Boat Cruise," and once again it afforded us a magnificent hunt featuring gobbling birds aplenty. By 8 o'clock both Jeff and Andy had their toms in-hand, and a text message from Darrell confirmed that he'd scored, as well.

These three rapid successes over the course of opening weekend freed me up to carry a gun for myself at Green Swamp WMA, but as per normal, that

Jeff and Andy with their toms from The Love Boat Cruise.

hainted and wicked place kicked my behind for the following couple of days. Public land turkey hunting in Florida is NOTHING like what's to be found on private ground!

My next client was Eric Brinser, who arrived in early afternoon. I took him to another new property which I felt held much promise. The landowner there had built a raised road back through a deep swamp behind his house, which came out into a massive pasture owned mostly by the neighboring cattle farm. However, we had access to about 30 acres along the near edge. Staying back from the pasture far enough to keep concealed, I spotted a pair of hens way out in the middle of the neighbor's land, and as we were trying to get as close as possible to them by easing along the woodline's edge, I noticed a tom strutting even further beyond them. When we had progressed as far as we could go and thus minimalized the distance between us and the turkeys, I called loudly on a glass pot and both hens cutt and yelped in response. Then, they immediately began moving towards us. Not only did the tom diligently follow along behind, but a few more turkeys emerged from the swamp on the far side of the pasture. Continued calling from me got the tom so fired up that he would answer even the lightest little clucks, purrs, or pitts coming from my pot call, despite the long distance between us. I mean to tell ya, he was on fire as he raced right past the original pair of hens to seek out one more unseen-but-highly-desired gal in the bushes (me). That was a very bad decision on his part, because Eric had no intentions of letting that gobbler get close enough to do to us what he'd been promising all the way across the pasture. Only one hour after we'd met and begun our hunt, Eric had himself a fine Osceola under foot!

After blanking again while hunting by myself at Green Swamp, my next trio of fellas showed up and I took them to yet another new property the following day. A flurry of gobbling activity at dawn was an encouraging way to start out, but it wasn't until 9:30 in the morning before I could finally coax a pair of toms and several hens close enough for the shot. Funny thing about guiding: you can do everything within your powers to provide the client(s) an ideal situation for their kills, but once the shooting begins things can go sideways in a hurry. I was tucked into some greenbriers off to the side of the blind in order for all three fellers to fit inside it, so at the moment of truth I was thus unable to witness with my eyes exactly how things went down, but my ears can attest to at least eight shots being fired before there were two fine Osceola toms flopping around in the sandy soil!

Eric Brinser struck quickly on his first trip to Florida.

The next morning the third member of their party and I failed to strike a bird on that same ranch, so I took him to the very first farm where I'd ever guided in Florida…a wonderland of a turkey property located way back off of any roads and only accessible by a long series of two-lane dirt tracks. It had been about 18 years since I'd hunted there, and I'm here to tell you that it sure felt good to come back again! My hunter and I spent several hours of the afternoon jaw-jacking with the landowner instead of venturing out into the blazing hot sun and blustering winds, but as things cooled down near sunset, we snuck into a hidden back pasture and heard several birds fly up to roost near us. Then, by using my natural voice to owl hoot, I forced a gobble from a tom all the way back in the corner, along the swamp edge.

Our hunt at dawn couldn't have progressed any more smoothly. The tom was roosted about 250 yards away from where I'd set up near the hens, and after he flew down really early, he strutted all the way to us by cutting diagonally across the wide open pasture. The only hiccup occurred when I failed to press the "play" button on Dan's video camera and thus got exactly none of "the dance" and subsequent kill shot recorded for posterity. I felt really bad about that, but as I explained afterward, he'd hired a turkey guide…not a videographer!

A pair of fellow Hoosiers were my next clients, and I got them both birds on their very first day…one in a conventional morning hunt on an old standby property where I'd been guiding for years, and the other by using a totally unorthodox method during an afternoon hunt conducted at the same farm where Eric had scored a week earlier. We'd arrived at that farm about 2:30 p.m., so I was worried that there would already be turkeys in the huge pasture, and I was right. We *really* needed to get closer to the distant birds, so I devised a plan which I felt might work; something similar to what I'd done during a long-ago hunt of my own on a big, wide-open sod farm. I wrote about it in a previous book.

Erecting my pop-up blind back out of sight of the four turkeys (three hens and a strutting tom), the three of us hunters then climbed inside and lifted the whole thing up off the ground before walking it down along the edge of our woods. We went slowly, so as to try and not be noticed, on a path which took us sort of diagonally closer and closer to the birds in the field. My guys were definitely doubtful of this crazy scheme working, but I had faith, and sure enough, we eventually eased our way to the same spot where I'd called in Eric's bird. This put us about 400 yards from the strutter and his girlfriends, who continued to peck around contentedly as if nothing was amiss. Then, just as I'd done so long ago at the sod farm, I set up a decoy beside our feet before lifting the blind up and over it. Slowly moving another 10 yards, we repeated the sequence, and then we did it one more time. After I had my three decoys safely set out, we eased our blind back away from them another 20 yards and settled in beside a patch of blackberry canes. There was absolutely no tree cover nearby...we were just right out there in the wide open field and baking in the sunshine of a hot Florida afternoon.

However, those turkeys out across the pasture hadn't given us so much as a sideways glance, and when I called real loud on a glass call we could visually see the tom thrust out his neck to gobble. We couldn't hear him, though. Florida is funny like that. I can't tell you how many times I've had turkeys standing at short range in a wide open pasture, and yet not been able to hear them gobble. Fortunately, this one also began moving towards us immediately, and once he was within 200 yards we could hear him loud and clear. Then, as the range between us shrunk to where our hopes were soaring and it was nearing time to flip off the safety, a pair of rambunctious calves ran up and chased our tom back out to about 150 yards away, where he stayed strutting and gobbling for the next two solid hours! I felt certain that the tom would eventually come back to us, but meanwhile, we were left sweating in the hot blind.

That's when I heard gobbles coming from a different direction, and turning my attention to the south-facing window, I saw three longbeards racing onto the scene. They weren't the bird we had intended to kill, but they were all dandy gobblers in their own right and our excitement level spiked through the roof. Then, at about the same spot as where the calves had interfered earlier, all three toms began putting and running around helter-skelter. At first I couldn't figure out what was going on, but that was before a coyote came dashing across the pasture in an attempt to catch one of our gobblers for his dinner!

At that point I was getting a little bit discouraged and wondered aloud what else could possibly go wrong. However, after the 'yote failed miserably, subsequently winded us, and ran off, the three lovelorn lotharios eventually calmed down from their fright and started thinking about that thing which male turkeys think about so often in the spring….girl turkeys! It didn't take them long after that before they'd decided to check out my pretty Dave Smith hens, and that ended up being a very bad decision on their part; especially-so for one of them who received much more than he bargained for in the deal.

My last client was a wealthy man with lots of hunting experiences all around the globe, and for all sorts of wild game. Throughout the day he graced me with tale after tale of his wondrous adventures, to the point where after a while it just sounded like bragging, and I eventually got tired of hearing about his great exploits and conquests. However, I continued to work hard to provide yet another story for this guy to add to his life's tally, and it eventually happened late in the afternoon when I called in three longbeards and four jakes to the gun. The big tom he shot ended up being an absolute stud of an Osceola, destined for the taxidermist, yet after I caped him out back at camp and it came time to pay my fee for the hunt, the guy tipped me absolutely nothing extra…not a dime….zilch.

I bring this up not out of sour grapes or any whining on my part, but simply because this same sort of thing happens often enough to be considered problematic. Now, most folks leave me quite generous tips, but some clients seemingly see only the dollar amount charged for the hunt while failing to comprehend just how much effort goes into making that experience happen. Standard procedure in most American service industry jobs is to tip 15-20% for exemplary effort beyond that which is required, and I certainly feel like I go far above and beyond what's considered as standard for my clients. I've always tried to bust my hump in order to make these adventures something truly special for my guys and gals, and whenever possible, to teach them some things along the way, as well. Basically, there are two things which propel me forward as I conduct my hunts: to get the birds killed, and to put as much money in my landowner's pocket as I can. If at the end of the day I can say that I've accomplished both of those things, then I know in my heart that I've done right and I'll be rewarded in more ways than monetarily. For instance, I get to experience the thrill of the kill without actually pulling the trigger myself, and I will also have been afforded the chance to meet new friends, which, most of the time, is a true blessing. Only lastly do I ever concern myself with whether or not I've put a little money in my own pocket, although I will say that anything I make sure comes in handy in helping to offset the expenses of being a hopelessly addicted traveling turkey hunter!

But, as I said, my main motivation has definitely never been about the money. I pride myself on a strong work ethic which steers me toward never shying away from doing the hard work necessary to achieve success, and that last hunt of 2019 in Florida was no exception. To then be stiffed completely just didn't sit very well with me. It left me feeling underappreciated and wondering if perhaps I'd done something wrong, even though I knew in my heart that I hadn't. Heck; the guy even told me that it was one of the best hunts of his lifetime! Oh, well…like I also said, I don't mean to bitch about it here, but I just had to get that off my chest and blow off a little steam. Hence, you won't be seeing this guy's picture on these pages.

I next hosted a camera crew who followed me around in Green Swamp for a couple of days. Stephen Spurlock of Chasing 49 had recently read my first book and was sufficiently intrigued by my lifestyle and focus on the wild turkey as a major part of my existence that he wanted to feature me in a short film. His vision wasn't to create your typical "shoot-em-up" hunting video, but rather, to tell a story via film. In this case, it would be focused on what drives a man to spend so much time and effort in quest of the wild turkey, and the motivations and aspirations which propel someone towards taking multiple turkeys in all 49 states offering a springtime hunting season. The conquering of that quest had recently been dubbed the "U.S. Super Slam," and there had been a noticeable uptick in interest nationwide amongst the turkey hunting legion in pursuing that goal. Tom Pero had even gone so far as to write a complimentary pair of books (Turkey Men; Volumes 1 & 2) detailing the lives and aspirations of 12 men who had done this crazy thing, and I had been honored to be among those included. Dave Owens and I shared a chapter in the second volume, and as an added bonus to anyone purchasing the book, Tom had included a CD of Dave and I talking about turkey hunting and demonstrating a few calls. We'd recorded the session at a world famous sound studio in Indianapolis, Indiana after Tom and Dave had flown there from the west coast (Tom) and Georgia (Dave). I only live 50 miles to the south of Indy, so I drove up to meet them there. Afterwards, the three of us traveled back to my hometown of Bloomington and shared a wonderful steak dinner at Janko's Little Zagreb…the best danged steakhouse that I've ever eaten at! The next day we did the interviews for Tom's book at my house nestled in the middle of state forest lands just outside of town.

That whole process of the Turkey Men book had been a real cool experience, and now here was Stephen wanting to make a movie about me. I found all of it rather counter-intuitive to the low-profile, behind the scenes and out of the limelight kind of existence which had always been my preferred modus operandi, but I eventually agreed to go along with the plan. I'm glad that I did, too, as I think his film; "The Doc" turned out magnificently…despite the subject matter.

Stephen's short movies seldom (if ever) include actual footage of a turkey being shot, and that is intentional on his part. The focus of his films is on the story being told, and not the kill. In keeping with that intent, no turkeys were harmed during the three days of filming in Florida, nor in the subsequent three days doing likewise in Pennsylvania later on in May, but believe me, that wasn't by design. If I could've persuaded a gobbler to cooperate in either place, I would've hammered him forthwith and then let Stephen edit out the kill as he saw fit, but for the life of me, I couldn't make a turkey cooperate. I guess, like me, my feathered adversaries were reluctant to become "movie stars."

At least so far as Florida's public land was concerned, failing to call in any toms was basically standard operating procedure, and even after Stephen, Ty Eubanks (cameraman extraordinaire) and Gabe Cuomo (director of the movie) left our camp, those hainted Osceolas of Green Swamp continued to evade me. I eventually did kill a tom on private land, but spent a total of 15 days in the WMA without denting a primer. Heck; I only called in two birds during that whole timeframe and neither one presented a good killing-shot opportunity.

There had, however, been a number of successes achieved by our friends and compadres back in camp: Bill George had killed on opening day, along with Eddie Parker, Doug Pickle, Rick Brown, and Charlie Parrish. Trevor Bays had brought in a fine gobbler on Day 2, and a total of five more were laid out on the butchering table on Day 7 alone. However, the management area itself had proven once again to be a reluctant host, at best, with her 51,000 acres yielding only 26 turkeys in total for the season; this, despite very heavy hunter numbers. In contrast, our camp tally board (with my 12 guided birds boosting the total) showed 31 kills. Some of those came out of The Swamp, but the majority were taken on private land, which is always MUCH more productive. For instance, those 12 clients of mine had each killed their bird in only eight total days of hunting, whereas the man-days per kill on the WMA was something like 4,000:1 (just kidding…I don't know the exact true figure, but it's pretty dismal.)

However, camp life had (as always) been phenomenal. Bill George's continual quest to build it up and improve it every year had really kicked in that spring, with our "under tent" acreage now totaling 1000 square feet: two 20' x 20' "circus awnings" tied together as the main gathering space, with another 10' x 20' kitchen area attached on the west side featuring a grill, a propane stove with oven (for baking brownies and such), a sink, and even a shower with hot water on demand. There were also numerous stainless steel storage units for food and cooking utensils, tables and chairs

Some of the "Swarp Camp" crew.

enough to comfortably seat 30 friends or more, a flagpole sporting the colors of our nation and a "Turkey Time" flag, and LED lighting throughout. The power source for all of our lighting and electronics were a number of deep cycle batteries which Bill would periodically charge up at his house, since we don't allow generators in camp…too noisy for our intended peace of mind. Taken as a whole, I believe this setup is the best danged "primitive" turkey camp in the country, but the real reason for its greatness is due to all of our friends and camp "family" who have been a part of it so for many years. We eat great, tell stories, and *always* have a blast!

The weather had been exemplary in Florida for the duration of my stay, with mild temps and very little rain; changing only during the final four days, when it turned brutally hot. With no moisture to speak of, the bugs had been negligible, as well. However, all good things must eventually pass, and the time had come to head on out of Florida and travel over to a state where mosquitoes always seem to be rampant…Mississippi. My two previous trips to the Magnolia State had yielded a total of four nice toms, but every single one had been earned through lots of hard work. I really wanted to kill at least one more bird there in order to eventually reach a self-imposed goal of conquering five U.S. Super Slams, but Mississippi is typically a serious test of a hunter's wits and endurance, and I was expecting nothing less than a difficult battle.

A close encounter on the first day there buoyed my hopes, but the weather then turned bad and the next few days saw a mixture of heavy rain and wind, with hot temperatures. Any one of these were problematic, but when combined they threatened to squash my hopes and dreams. Plus, I blew a couple of chances early-on by making bad moves at inopportune times and running off willing toms before I had a chance to pull the trigger.

Then, late in the evening of my fourth day, the weather pattern broke and the temperature plummeted. The skies also cleared, and the heretofore horrendous wind finally decided to abate. The next day dawned an absolutely perfect 38 degrees (warming only to about 70 by 4 o'clock in the afternoon) with zero wind, no clouds, and low humidity. I couldn't have dreamed up a more ideal day, and I vowed to "tune in and tighten up" by hunting smart. "No more mistakes!" was my mantra.

The only bird I heard gobbling that morning was a long way off, so I headed out after him and eventually closed in. However, by then he'd already flown to ground and I was forced to stop short and set up at about the 200 yard mark. Furthermore, a couple of his hens had begun yelping in between the tom and myself, so I didn't want to keep going and risk spooking them. An answering gobble to the first call from my glass pot was a little bit delayed in coming, but the hens were definitely excited by what I had to say and they soon headed towards me in a trot. I assumed that the tom would follow along, but I was wrong, and even after the girls were parading all around me at short range, he stayed put and never moved. Not even their sharp cutts and yelps could break the stalemate, and after the girls eventually lost interest and walked off in another direction, the tom did, too. Just as soon as the hens were out of sight, I arose and hot-footed it in pursuit of that fickle gobbler.

I caught up to him easily enough, though, as he'd begun ripping it good from the next ridgetop along his departure path and I once again set up in what I thought to be excellent position. However, despite answering another of my yelps, he held pat and merely continued to gobble from his new "chosen" spot sporadically. I only called three times in total over the next 20 minutes: he answered two of them, and the other was a yelp which I cutt into the back end of *his* gobble…a tactic I like to use that mimics what an excited hen is very likely to do. But, despite his obvious interest in me, we found ourselves locked in a standoff of stubbornness for a very long time. That is, until another bird gobbled on the next finger ridge to the east of us, and a hen beside that tom yelped quietly in answer.

At that point I began directing my calls to the new girl on the block, and whereas for the last hour I'd been mostly subtle and demure, now I change it up. Oh; I still kept my calls on the diaphragm rather low in volume, but now I focused on trying to put some real urgency and a demanding tone into them. And, do you want to know what happened? Well; it worked! As the late arrivals on the scene began easing over towards me, I could sense a jealous rage building in the original tom. His increased gobbling now took on a much-more animated and desperate tone, so I pointed my gun in his direction and clicked off the safety; confident that he'd beat the other birds to me.

When the solo gobbler slipped into range a few minutes later and periscoped his head up into the perfect "shoot me now" posture, I went ahead and ended the battle. Funny thing about this turkey, though…while I've always hustled out to a fallen adversary and put a boot on their neck, when I did that this time, there was no customary flopping of wings and flailing of the earth. Instead, the tom just immediately died without so much as another flutter or quiver. As for me and my emotions, I felt like I'd hunted extremely well and performed appropriately as the events dictated, and I was very pleased with how the battle had transpired. It was, indeed, a good day to be a turkey hunter, and I was both proud and confident.

When my seven-day hunting license expired three days later with nary another bird to show for the hard work that I'd been putting into the effort, I wasn't so sure about that and decided to move on. Yes; I could've stayed, bought another license, and tried to rekindle some positive vibes, but more bad weather was predicted to arrive the following day and at the very least, I had accomplished what I'd come to Mississippi to do. A fifth Magnolia gobbler was now riding around in the cooler, and although I was looking at a long drive to get there, I felt like Maryland was now calling my name.

It did, indeed, turn into a long drive, and coupled with some difficulties in the procurement of my hunting license at Walmart, I arrived a little later than anticipated. In fact, it was well-after prime gobbling time before I pulled into the WMA where I wanted to start. Lo and behold, there was already a truck in the parking lot, which caused my heart to sink because I'd been eager to come back to this spot ever since initially finding it two springs earlier. Back in 2017 the entire leaf-covered parking area looked like a whole flock of turkeys had been scratching it to pieces, and I'd subsequently killed a great tom the following morning only 60 yards from my van. I'd been counting the days to this return ever since.

Now, someone had beaten me there fair and square, and that changed everything. Oh, I could've just gone ahead and walked on into the WMA, since it was a fairly large chunk of public ground serviced only by the one parking area, but in my mind that would've been the wrong thing to do. That's not the way I was raised, and that's not the way I conduct myself in the turkey woods. In fact, crowding in on another hunter would've gone against everything that I most fervently believe in, and it would've sullied the dignity with which I think we should all conduct ourselves. The truth of the matter is that you couldn't have paid me to go in there and potentially mess up that other guy's hunt. However, reaching another WMA would've entailed a long drive, so with the sun already up, I decided to just pull out a chair and sit beside the van to listen. Besides that, I was road-weary and really needed a nap. Maybe if I just hung around I might even hear the other guy working a bird, or the gunshot of him killing one, and if so, I was prepared to offer my sincere congratulations when he carried his tom out of the woods.

Well, as luck would have it I heard no gunshot, but I did indeed hear a tom gobbling a few minutes later. He wasn't too far away, either, but that didn't matter one bit; I still had no intentions of being "that kind" of hunter who would horn-in on a bird which another other guy might, or might not, be working. I probably could've killed that tom, too, because he proceeded to walk right up to the very same spot where I'd found success two years earlier and begin gobbling from what had to be mere yards of the natural brush blind I'd built in that locale. I never did hear the other guy calling, but again, that mattered not one iota: if someone were seated a hundred yards from me on most of my own days afield, they might not hear me calling, either. A good deal of my technique is to be quiet and demure, and sometimes I don't even touch a call for very long periods of time.

After a while I realized that the all-night drive to get there had really taken a toll on me, and my eyelids grew heavy. Crawling into my van, I stretched out to get a little shut-eye, and obviously I needed it, because I slept a little harder and longer than intended. In fact, when I woke up my vehicle was the only one in the parking lot…the other guy had already come out of the woods and then headed for home! But, my phone showed that it was still only 9 o'clock, so I quickly got my hunting gear together and eased out to the ridgelet where the tom had been carrying on earlier. My old brush blind from two years prior was indeed still there, and so were a bunch of fresh scratchings. Right there in the middle of all that sign lay a big, still-wet gobbler turd!

For the next two days I hunted that WMA hard and never saw another hunter, but I also never saw that turkey. Oh, I heard some gobbling, but the weather had turned atrocious, with howling wind and relentless rain. Then, on Sunday I was forced to go hunt in another county altogether, because only select ones were open for hunting on the Sabbath in Maryland. I came close to killing a bird in that new spot too, but since I was sharing the woods with just about every other turkey hunter for many, many miles around, the odds of having a bird all to myself long enough to make the kill were low. That was verified when a guy came ambling through my setup and spooked my bird when he was only 60 yards away and coming in like a hooked crappie.

Rather than returning to my original WMA on Monday, I then began exploring other tracts close to it. However, besides a few more "almost's" and "what if's" over the next few days, that strategy proved ineffective for the most part. It wasn't that I couldn't find any turkeys, but rather, the biggest factor affecting my lack of tangible success was the persistent weather pattern of rain, rain, and ever-more rain which flooded that flat countryside and threatened to douse my spirits. Any time spent walking around basically turned into a mid-calf deep wade, and although I always rotate through several pair of hiking boots on my hunting trips, by the end of the first week all of them were soaked through and still wet, since the sun refused to shine long enough to dry any of them out back at camp. I finally resigned myself to going into town and buying a pair of knee-high rubber boots. I don't enjoy wearing rubbers, but I was simply sick and tired of continually having "pruned" feet and toes!

On the eighth day of the hunt I found a new WMA which intrigued me a lot. That first morning there I heard at least six different gobbling birds, and quickly decided to make a stand and hunt it hard. In hindsight, perhaps I shouldn't have gotten so stuck in a rut and forsaken any other properties, but this place just felt "right" to me. Sometimes in life, infatuation steers our course no matter what sense it doesn't make, and we end up with the wrong partner when it would've been best for all concerned to just "love it and leave it." Perhaps that was the case here, although this property had a lot of the intangibles which really appealed to me: things like isolation from any larger towns or busy highways, terrain which was very "user friendly" and had a welcoming feel to it, and it was bordered by cattle farms. And, did I mention that it was home to a good population of turkeys?

Well, that supposed new mistress of mine turned out to be an evil, tired bitch. She used me, abused me, and beat me up like a redheaded stepchild. Every time I thought things were going to turn in my favor, something ugly and unexpected would rear up and booger everything. As days passed it felt like I was destined for failure, but if there's one thing that I can pride myself on, it's in being stubborn and very reluctant to give up without a fight. Still, as day after day of failure rained down on my psyche like the continued patter of raindrops on my head, I began to feel like I was fighting a losing battle. In fact, I finally reached the point where I had resigned myself to giving up and walking away to battle another day; maybe in another year entirely. Enough had finally become enough. For nearly two weeks I'd suffered through horrendous weather, bad luck, and mental errors in judgement resulting in zero tags filled. All this was made even more painful because seemingly every one of my friends from all across the country had been blowing up my phone with tales of glory and triumph. I had certainly reached my fill and was more than ready to move on. Even a stubborn, hard-headed turkey hunter such as myself can only take so much!

The one constant in my time afield had been dawn's roost gobbling, for at least I had heard birds announcing their presence every single morning since my arrival. But, that streak ended on the 13th day, and by 10 o'clock I was basically going through the motions as I traipsed around the network of grassy roads which bisected the WMA, hoping against hope of garnering something positive from the miles put on my boot soles. To be honest, I had already mentally given up and my mind was somewhere else as I worked back towards the van, facing the fact that I had failed in an epic manner. I was mad at myself, mad at the entire state of Maryland, and mad at every turkey which had made me look like a danged fool. I hadn't had a shower in nearly two weeks, and my attitude had tanked to about as low as it could go. I was, without a doubt, ready to tuck tail and head on down the road.

Then, as I carefully eased into a four-way intersection of grassy roadways, moving east towards the parking lot only a half-mile ahead, I looked to the south and saw nothing. But, when I turned to the north, just about as far in that direction as I could see, I spotted a black blob. It was either a bear or a turkey, and the trusty old Swarovski mini's which I always wear around my neck quickly revealed that it was nothing other than the object of my grandest desires…a big old gobbler strutting along in all his glory. Not only that, but he was alone and making his way slowly in my direction!

Slinking back into a grove of young pines tangled with greenbrier, I sat down with my gun comfortably resting across the lowest limb of the tree in front of me and pointed towards the roadway. The only bad part of my setup was that I could only see down that grassy path for about 25 yards. I wouldn't know if the tom was continuing to advance towards my position until he was right there in front of my gun, and as I sat there in silence, I was fully cognizant of the fact that the past two weeks had conditioned me to expect the worst case scenario in every turkey encounter. Surely this one would end in failure, too, with either the tom reversing his direction of travel, or else venturing off into the woods on either side of the trail. Or, some scallywag of a skanky old hen would intercept him long before he reached me and they would vanish into the ethrid.

The urge to stand up and venture a peek down the path was almost overpowering, but somehow I resisted. And then, after what seemed far too little time for the tom to have covered the ground between us, a ferocious gobble erupted from just to the right of my area of vision. I nearly jumped out of my skin! Only moments afterwards, the tom emerged from behind the cover of the thick briars surrounding me and stopped with his head directly in line with the sight beads on my shotgun. I didn't even need to adjust my aim; one simple pull of the trigger and the tom piled up in a heap exactly 21 yards away.

I've killed a lot of turkeys after difficult hardships endured over long periods of time, but the death of that bird brought a greater sense of jubilation awash with relief than just about any of them. Finally, after 13 soggy days of toil and torture, the turkey gods had decided that the joke on me was all played out and they'd tossed me a bone! I was grateful beyond measure, and grinned like a Cheshire cat the whole way back to my van. So what if I'd never even uttered so much as a single call after spotting this tom? I was proud as a peacock to have brought him to bag!

The next day proved just how lucky I'd been the day before, when a pair of seemingly hot toms ignored my finest calling prowess and vanished into thin air. I took that final failure as a sign to get out while the going was good, and soon thereafter I began the long drive out to Iowa.

A Maryland "gift-gobbler." Deserved? Who's to say? Appreciated? You betcha!!

Iowa: easily one of my favorite states. This was to be my fifth time hunting there, and I was really looking forward to it. And, for good reason, since I've always experienced lots of turkeys amongst her rolling, forested hills. Unfortunately, Iowa is a state that charges a lot of money for the privilege of a non-resident acquiring a hunting license. Otherwise, I would try to visit it every spring. The turkey hunting can be that good.

2019 was no exception to the rule. Sneaking up onto the sandy hogback ridge where I traditionally like to begin my hunts, I spotted a bird roosted in a burr oak tree ahead of me in the gloomy haze of half-light. After glassing it over with my binoculars I decided that I was looking at a hen, even though her head was still tucked up under a wing and I couldn't be positive. She must've been really tired too; because I then pussyfooted right up underneath her undetected and then set up 40 yards on the other side of the roost tree. I'd shot a tom several years earlier in that exact same spot, and my previously used setup tree was both really comfortable and offered a great panoramic view of the surrounding area.

Normally, I could count on this wooded ridgeline to be ringing with gobbles at daylight, but it was rather subdued on that day. In fact, I could only hear three in total, with two of those being a pair of jake buddies which I called in to about a dozen yards soon after flydown. The third bird was about a bazillion miles away, and he only gobbled a few times before hushing up. As for the hen, she ended up being one of those loudmouthed gals a turkey hunter dreams about, but despite her best and most concerted efforts (including a couple of calls which I can only describe as the "wildcat" call referred to in some of the earliest turkey hunting literature written by Johenning, McClure, Bland, and others), neither her nor I could get a longbeard fired up. I eventually arose, ran her off, and continued on out the hogback another mile or so, to a cedar-bough blind which I'd built the season before. It was now brown as toast, but still in good shape structurally, so I climbed in and settled down to await developments. This particular spot along the hogback is *always* a place where turkeys just naturally venture through, cross over, or hang out, and with no gobbling going on within earshot, it was as good a place to sit as I could think of.

Sure enough, about an hour later a tom fired up all on his own from about 400 yards away, and after he answered a couple of my calls from the glass pot, I felt confident of him coming over to seek me out. It took about another hour before I heard that low, adrenalin-causing hum of a tom drumming close-by, and then a few minutes later he waltzed into my life in glorious fashion. After killing him, I lingered for quite a while up on that picturesque hog backed ridge in order to fully absorb the majesty of the hunt and the very special tom with which I'd been graced. If I never make it back to that spot, I wanted to burn the images into my brain for all time.

A cedar bough blind built the previous year proved itself once again.

One of my favorite turkey places and a magnificent Iowa tom.

My next stop was another favorite destination of mine: Minnesota. Previous years in that lush emerald-green landscape had provided lots of gobbling birds and few competing hunters on a particular chunk of public land where I liked to hunt, but I was in for a few shocking changes in 2019. Oh, the birds were still there in similar numbers, but now it seemed like there were a couple of other hunters after each one of them! I HATE a crowded turkey woods, so I got out of there mid-morning and took a long, circuitous drive to reach the other side of the river, where I'd heard at least two birds gobbling at dawn.

It was a fortuitous move on my part, because the only people I saw over there were a group of 15 folks riding horseback on the trail where I'd just found one of those heretofore gobbling toms. Luckily for me (not-so-much for the tom), they came riding through my setup just *after* I'd already killed and tagged the turkey! We talked for a bit while they admired my bird, and then I anxiously made the drive to Kellogg, Minnesota solely for the pleasure of eating pie at the Town and Country Diner. Patty's Mom Thelma started this place many years ago, and well into her 90's she was still picking the rhubarb for their delicious Custard-Rhubarb pie. Patty herself is a huntress with a full-mount bear displayed in the restaurant and numerous turkeys under her belt. They make a variety of fresh pies three times per week, and I can personally vouch that they are *all* amazing! That Rhubarb is a favorite, but the Butterscotch-Walnut is absolutely phenomenal, too. I always stop in to buy a pie or two whenever I'm close by, and I willingly confess to having driven a rather long way out of my way several times in order to visit. I highly recommend this place to all of my friends who like to eat good food, and especially delicious pie!

My Minnesota tom taken on a horse riding trail.

The fact that I'd just killed three birds in the previous four days of hunting might make a fella think that the bad-luck streak suffered in Maryland was an aberration, but I knew better than to trust in such foolish thoughts. Turkey hunting can be a streaky thing, and a stretch of good luck has absolutely zero bearing on anything, other than the fact that you know in your heart that it will eventually come to an end. It's not even a matter of "if," but "when."

Still, I had moderately high hopes on my drive to Ohio. There's a sign as you enter Vinton County which claims it to be the wild turkey capital of the state, and previous hunting trips there had proven that its public lands could, indeed, be pretty good. But, in the back of my mind I was still smarting from the ass-whooping I'd been given in Maryland, and despite those recent glowing successes in IA and MN, I was still feeling leery of how things might go. Hence, it didn't really surprise me at all when I heard no gobbling on the first morning there, and after hiking an estimated 14 miles that day without hardly cutting a track or finding much fresh sign, my apprehension grew. Covering that much ground in uncomfortably hot weather conditions had also subjected me to an unpleasantry of a rather serious nature: I'd become badly "galled." Now, if you've never had that condition, consider yourself very lucky. My nut sack and inner thighs were chaffed raw and were so sore that merely walking was excruciating. I had to stretch out bow-legged to keep any important parts from touching! Thankfully, there is a minor-miracle of a product available over the counter at any drugstore or Walmart called "Gold Bond Medicated Powder," which generally works overnight, and while I was still mighty tender the next day, at least I could ease around and hunt at a leisurely pace. I didn't cover nearly the acreage of the day before, but I didn't need to, as I had an ace-in-the-hole...

You see; a kind-hearted female wildlife biologist for the state forest where I was hunting had suggested some areas to try that were both new to me and close to the road, and sure enough, up on one of those ridges I found a hard-gobbling bird. He and I ended up having an absolutely classic battle, in a splendidly beautiful spot, and which eventually resulted in me proudly wrapping a tag around his long spurred and scaly leg. I then sat there on a log for quite a while and basked in the glory of it all and the memories made. The hunt itself had progressed smoothly as silk, like one you would read about in a textbook, and I distinctly remember the sense of appreciativeness I beheld afterward. So many times in this sport the outcome is anything other than predictable, so I knew that this one would remain a treasured keepsake in my brain trust forever.

Then, almost immediately from that moment onward, the bottom fell out once again and I suffered through another six days of heartache and sorrow. Some of that woe was of my own making, of course, but more than a fair share of it was due to inclement weather, uncooperative toms, or simple bad luck. And, let's never forget to mention hens. They were running interference seemingly every time I set up on a gobbling tom, and invariably they stole away several which might've otherwise cooperated. After one too many of those hussies had ruined my chances of filling a second tag, I finally reached the limit of tolerance and did what the little voice in the back of my mind had been telling me to do for days…to get the heck out of there and head for Connecticut.

At that point in time my attitude wasn't very good…yet, *again*! Other than IA and MN, the season had basically been swirling down the toilet ever since leaving Florida, with practically no gobbling heard after the typical morning flurry. Thus, I'd spent most of my days wandering around with no confidence of hearing or working birds. Furthermore, the string of bad breaks that I'd endured was alarmingly contributing to perpetuating an expectancy of failure. In other words, failure begets failure, and I had little hope of finding anything else. I was, in short, a mental mess and mad at the world.

One day in Connecticut changed all of that, but it happened in such a unique and interesting manner that I'll share the circumstances here. My old buddy Tracy Deckard raises show pigs in Owen County, Indiana, and over the years he'd sold some to a fellow in Connecticut named Joey. Joey had told Tracy to come on out and hunt turkeys at his place if he ever had the urge, but getting Deckard to leave his home county is a tough task. However, when I told him of my desire to take another bird in Connecticut, he called Joey and got permission for me. I then called Joey to formerly introduce myself and let him know that I would be rolling in at about midnight. Joey gave me directions to his farm and then told me to just pull on into the parking lot beside the barn, where he would meet me at 4 a.m. to show me around.

Now; I'd hunted Connecticut several times beforehand and I liked it. It was much more rural than I'd ever imagined, and I had actually found and killed my four turkeys to date on real pretty public lands. However, as I neared the address given to me over the phone by Joey, I became a bit concerned. This wasn't farm country, at all. In fact, it was very close to the town of Hartford, which is a bustling megalopolis, and the closer I got, I realized that the address was practically in *downtown* Hartford! When I pulled into the "farm," there was, indeed, a barn, but I saw no fields or wild lands... only a small chunk of overgrown land littered with school busses, old farm machinery, and a litany of other "junk." A "halo" of lights rising up in back of the barn illuminated the night sky in that direction, and the glow of city lights emanated from all around me. The interstate highway was only 400 yards from where I pulled in, and there were housing developments and bustling city sprawl on all sides of the barn lot. But, I was too tired to give it much thought or worry, so I crawled into the back of the van and went to sleep.

True to his word, at 4 o'clock a big pickup truck rolled up next to my van and this immense giant of a man said through his open driver's side window, "Hop on in and I'll show you where the turkeys roost." Well, at that point I was expecting us to leave the barnyard parking lot and head on over to an actual farm somewhere down the road, but instead, we simply circled behind the barn no more than 200 yards to the very back end of the lot where I'd glimpsed all of the junk. This flat chunk of ground beside the barn was no bigger than about 60 yards wide, and it was filled with all sorts of stuff: stacks of pallets, piles of barrels and railroad timbers, old broken down trucks, tractors, and old farm implements, a row of school busses, and a number of big 9-yard trash dumpsters. A portion of the lot had been divided into piles of different sized stone and gravel, such as you'd find at a landscaping business, and beside that was another section filled with what looked in the headlights to be produce. Joey informed me as we drove by that this was expired food and vegetables from grocery stores, and he claimed that this was where the turkeys and deer liked to hang out and feed. My overall impression of the whole place was that it looked like we were circling through a landfill, or a city dump.

Did I mention that Joey was a big fella? Well, I'd venture a guess that he tipped the scales at substantially upwards of 500 pounds, and his truck was large enough to accommodate his great bulk. I think it was a jacked-up F350 with duel rear wheels. But, he was jovial and friendly as could be in pointing out a small grove of perhaps a dozen medium-sized trees over beside the adjoining housing addition, and that's where he said the turkeys roosted. He then told me how this flock of birds liked to hang out all day in the gravel area of the barn lot or in a couple of small fields surrounding the roost trees, but now that those fields were mostly overgrown and so rank that a turkey would've had a hard time getting through them, they mostly just puttered around amongst the refuse and junk. Being as how it felt like we were right downtown, I asked if it was actually legal to hunt there, and he said, "Oh, sure; the local cops shoot their deer right here every fall and they've ok'd me hunting it for years." He went on to describe how this barn was the only remaining remnant of what was once a thriving farm, and that it now housed a butcher shop inside which slaughtered about 1200 goats per month. The busses were leased to the local school system, the dumpsters likewise rented out to the city's waste and recycling center, and the ring of lights that I'd mentioned earlier sat atop the highest mound of ground this side of Washington, DC. The government had purchased that knob a number of years earlier and then built it into a missile silo which protected our Capital!

Well, I didn't rightly know just how to react to all of this, or what to think, but the sky was already graying in the east as Joey dropped me back at my van. I most certainly didn't have time to leave and go anywhere else before gobbling time, so after gathering up my hunting gear I stepped back into the "landfill" as Joey headed for his office in the barn. He told me to be sure and let him know how things went, but to make myself at home and hunt wherever I wanted to.

No sooner had I leaned back against one of those big trash dumpsters to await developments, than a turkey gobbled. I could barely hear him over the din of traffic noise and city bustle, but he was soon enough letting 'em rip practically non-stop. As I scurried around looking for a decent place to set up, a loud-mouthed hen began yelping and cutting, too. The ground beside the dumpsters was real soft and mushy mud, so I ruled that out as a setup. It was the same for the brushy strip of soil where a pile of wooden pallets sat. Everywhere else just looked like I was too exposed and in the wide open, so I decided to simply lie down prone on the far side of a pile of crushed stone, and rest my gun in the "V" formed by two of the piles being dumped right beside one another. But, before I got settled in I went out and pounded a couple of decoy stakes into the underlying gravel of the muddy roadway with a broken cement block, and upon them I placed a Dave Smith strutter and a hen. It wasn't much, and certainly was like no other setup of my long and storied turkey hunting career, but it would have to do.

Well, the loudmouthed hen and one of her chatty girlfriends pitched out first, and they eagerly answered my calls and came rushing up to the decoys while practically screaming at me the whole way in. Another hen soon joined them, while the tom and another gobbler stayed treebound for a bit longer. Then, they too pitched out and landed at the far end of the barn lot. A jake raced in from who-knows-where to join the hens before the first tom could arrive, and when he was soon thereafter joined by the first adult tom practically kicking up gravel as he raced towards my strutter decoy, I didn't bother waiting for the second one to get there before dumping my CT gobbler in a heap. He was an interesting bird, physically. Half of his "Pope's nose" was completely missing, as if it had been chewed off by a junkyard dog, so he only had half of a tail, and what was there was very scraggly and misshapen. But, his spurs were impressive; in fact, they were so long and curled that they hooked back almost to his leg bone!

After stashing my tom and hunting gear in the van, I walked over to Joey's barn to tell him about the hunt and its quick culmination. As I opened the door of his office, I was shocked to find my host in his desk chair and sprawled out in a completely horizontal posture, with his feet on the desk, his head hanging backwards at an unnatural angle, and his mouth wide agape. It looked to me like he was dead as a mackerel, and I feared that he'd had a massive heart attack and I was now looking at a corpse! I called out Joey's name several times as I walked towards him, but he never even flinched. Then, as I was reaching for my phone to dial 911, Joey suddenly sputtered to life and raised his substantial girth up into a sitting position and groggily said, "Guess I dozed off there for a bit. Did you get that tom, already?" Relieved at not having to perform CPR on such a huge mountain of a man, I did indeed confirm that I had taken a gobbler, to which Joey

My "Junkyard" tom from Connecticut.

then replied, "Well, you're more than welcome to stick around and keep hunting here. I know that there are at least two toms in the flock." I thanked him for allowing me to hunt his place, but declined the offer. I think that I said I was supposed to meet up with a buddy elsewhere, or something like that, but in reality I was just ready to get the heck out of there and head out into the country! In only an hour or so of additional driving time I could be gone from the hustle and bustle of downtown Hartford and in amongst the peace and tranquility of a more "natural" setting. Jeesh…what a strange and weird trip to Connecticut it had been!

Up until that moment, my 2019 turkey season had been marked mostly by a series of personal blunders and bad decisions, only a few of which I've even bothered to mention here, but all of which were weighing heavily on my mind. I could point to numerous errors in judgement and silly mistakes that had cost me tom after tom, and only through pure hard-headedness, perseverance, and persistence had I managed to scratch out enough victories to make the season look decent on paper. But, I knew in my heart that I'd not performed up to my expectations, and I wasn't very happy about it.

Now, however, I made perhaps my best decision of the year by driving right on through the rest of Connecticut and up into Massachusetts. Once there, I headed straight over to Fred Solari's house in North Adams. I've written about Fred in previous books. He was one of those characters whom we sometimes are lucky enough to meet along life's crooked trail, and who add immeasurably to the quality of our own existence from that day forward. Fred was a pure joy to be around, with an obvious love of the wild turkey which served as the main rudder for our friendship. We met, and eventually hunted together often, at a farm that is perhaps the single most beautiful place where I've ever set foot, and which always holds a strong population of birds. However, try as I might, I'd never succeeded in helping Fred kill one. Oh; he'd pulled the trigger on plenty of them…missing four times the previous year alone! Now 88 years old, I wasn't sure how many more opportunities we might have together, so I was extremely eager to give it a go once again.

Fred Solari was ex-Navy and "tough as nails." He was also a bit hardheaded in his insistence that every time we hunted together I was always to shoot first. By his reasoning, I would only be there a short while and needed to get my bird(s), while he had all season to try for one on his own. If the opportunity presented itself after I had a tom down he would try to fill a tag, but that just wasn't important to him. I tried arguing with "My Friend Fred" time and again, but there just wasn't any changing his stance on the matter. Hence, the next morning I called in three toms at about 10 o'clock, and then I went ahead and laid one of them out in hopes that Fred might bat "cleanup" and shoot one of the two survivors. Despite them standing around for plenty of time if nearly anyone else had been the backup shooter, they eventually alerted and ran off before Fred could dial in and pull the trigger. Like I just said; he didn't care one lick and considered the day a tremendous and joyful success. Then, for the next two days the rain came in torrents and the wind howled unmercifully. We never even heard or saw a turkey, even though we hunted some each day.

Me and Fred Solari at Buzz's farm.

Massachusetts is another of those bassackward states which doesn't allow hunting on the Sabbath, so I drove the three hours over to New York that Saturday evening and hunted unsuccessfully with Trevor Bays till noon on Sunday. Then, I drove right back to MA immediately afterward. I arrived at Fred's about 4 o'clock, whereby he promptly asked me if I would help him flip his lawnmower back onto its wheels. Why? Because he'd rolled the danged thing over on himself an hour earlier and been pinned underneath it until he managed to squirm free! After making sure that Fred was physically ok, we righted the mower and made plans for the next morning's hunt, but by 3 a.m. the trauma suffered in the accident had taken its toll and he was too stiff and sore to go afield. I was thus forced to hunt at Buzz's farm alone, and although the weather was better and the birds gobbled fairly well, I failed to put one of them down. A number of Fred's extended family from Switzerland were due to arrive for a visit that afternoon, so I opted to go back to NY for a couple more days and return when they were gone and Fred was hopefully feeling better and fully recovered from his lawn mower incident.

The first morning back in New York, Trevor and I were invited to hunt with a couple of his buddies who had been keeping tabs on a flock of hens being tended by five longbeards. We were hoping to mess up the day for at least a couple of them (maybe more), so after putting the entire flock to bed in a small grove of trees, we came back after dark and erected a pair of blinds alongside each other and about a hundred yards from the roost. Then, we set out our rubberized flock of sixteen Dave Smith decoys, which included two strutters and two jakes. It was an impressive grouping, even in the moonlight, and then after a restless night of tossing and turning from nervous expectation, we snuck back in an hour before sunrise and got settled into our blinds.

Gobbling was fairly poor that morning, but I'll never forget the view of those five big strutters spinning in circles and silhouetted against the skyline as they worked down the ridge towards us. After two of the toms held up at about 60 yards, the remaining three gobblers and seven hens came on in and wandered around in our decoy spread for a long time. We were waiting for the reluctant pair to join the closer group in hopes of trying for a 4-kill slugfest, but eventually all of our birds in range began losing interest and

Trevor Bays, me, and Tom Erwin.

wandering back uphill to their two buddies, so I called the shot for Tom Erwin, Trevor, and myself. Trev's other pal Jay had elected to hold fire and merely play the part of witness to the massacre, but everything eventually worked out for him, too, when we headed over to another property soon thereafter and got him a tom within minutes of our arrival. Four toms by 9am....it was, indeed, a pretty good day!!!

That afternoon Trevor and I watched a big tom for the last hour of daylight, and then the next morning we set up quite a ways from him...just because we'd be sitting in a great spot that offered a breathtaking view of the farm where we were hunting. Well, it was also the place where this particular turkey liked to hang out anyway, so it was sort of a no-brainer, really. Once we were settled in, Trev asked me if he could yelp up my turkey for me, and I just grinned and said, "Of course you can, Weedhopper!" Trevor is like the son I never had, and we always have a great time hunting together, but up until that moment I had always done the calling. Now it was time to reverse roles and let the student begin flexing his own skills. I'm awfully proud of the boy, anyway, and seeing him blossom as a turkey hunter has been a pure joy for me. If I had ever been blessed with a blood son, I would be honored if he turned out just like Trevor, but there's truly only one Trevor Bays, and he's something special.

Anyhoo, the morning was starting out real quiet, with only a few distant gobbles, and I was a bit worried that our tom wasn't where we'd watched him fly to roost. But, he finally piped up and was soon on the ground with a hen, a jake, and another tom. It only took a few yelps from the Weedhopper's diaphragm call before all four turkeys turned and began their ascent to our position, and after a couple more pleading yelps from Trev, the two toms left their companions and hustled up towards us while totally ignoring the forlorn yelps of the hen trailing behind. It was a beautiful visual performance, all caught on video, as the toms pranced and danced their way towards destiny. Then, I laid one of them out good and proper to put a capstone on a great hunt with my little buddy.

Being as it was still early and there were other turkeys now bellowing out regularly, we then called Trev's good friend Salvatore Magro to see if he wanted to come up and go hunting. He did, but instead of returning to this farm, we went to join him at one of his properties. We immediately got onto a gobbling tom, but it was a bird already hung up with accompanying hens. Sal wanted to push the envelope, so while Trev and I kept the tom

Me and Trevor Bays in New York. The toms were roosted directly behind us.

gobbling to our steady litany of calls, he snuck in close. Then, Sal missed that turkey at about three steps distance with his Grandfather's old side-by-side 12 gauge. When the tom flew straight upwards at the shotgun's report, Sal punched a hole right through the middle of him with the second barrel, thus completing a rather unorthodox victory. Sal is quite the character and a fun guy to be around. We always have a good time.

Sal Magro took this tom with his Grandpa's old double barrel.

Returning to Massachusetts, I was hoping that Fred was feeling good enough to accompany me back to Buzz's, but he was still stoved up and stiff. I guess rolling a heavy lawnmower over on top of oneself at the age of 88 isn't such a good idea, after all! But, with his encouragement and well-wishes to enjoy my day afield solo, I set forth and climbed up the slopes above the farmhouse. Nearly all of my previous hunts over the years had taken place on the north side of the gravel road which bisects the farm. It's not that there were more turkeys on that side, but rather, it was just where I'd very first begun hunting on the property, and I simply enjoyed the view from that side. Besides, the turkeys regularly roosted along a deep slash near the top of the granite face of the mountain, and then they would pitch down into a field below and work along its grassy edge going in a westerly direction. Their behavior over the years was so regular as to be almost predictable, and I'd often found myself the beneficiary of their quirky behavior.

Not so in 2019. Three of the previous four trips to the farm had yielded zero gobbles heard from the traditional roost site high up on the mountainside north of the roadway, and after the first morning's success over there, no other toms had even been seen on that side of the farm. Hence, I'd decided to move my base of operations to the south side, up near a small fenced-in pasture where Buzz was keeping 28 cows and 8 calves. The view from up on that slope was no less spectacular than the other side, and of even more importance was the fact that it was where I'd seen and heard nearly all of the turkeys encountered so far. One thing is for certain in turkey hunting: you've got to hunt where the birds want to be. I'd watched a pair of toms strutting in the vicinity of the metal gate of the cow pen on a couple of different days.

Today, however, they (and no other toms, either) never said a word as dawn broke, and I was left pondering whether I'd made a wise decision to move into unknown territory; especially so when I eventually spied three hens across the valley coming down out of the traditional slash roost area and walking right by where Fred and I liked to sit. I figured that it was only a matter of time before their boyfriends would be seen following behind, but no toms ever materialized over there. However, a bird did eventually gobble at about 6:30, and that beautiful sound came from *my* side of the farm and within the tree line closest to me, which was only about 300 yards due south.

With just a little calling on my part for encouragement, the tom soon left the woods behind and made a B-line straight to me. Not long after that he was dying a glorious warrior's death after strutting almost defiantly next to the green metal gate of the pasture fence.

A gorgeous tom from the south side of Buzz's farm.

With Fred still not fully recovered from his spill, I decided that it was time to make tracks for a season-ending week of camaraderie and good times spent with some buddies in western Pennsylvania. But, I left Massachusetts a bit torn. My only real reason for going there in 2019 was to help Fred kill a turkey, and although I'd shot two of them myself, I felt like I had failed my friend. I knew that he didn't care in the least about actually killing a bird, and I was also aware that he took away a huge amount of satisfaction in my own successes while in his company, but even still, I'd wanted desperately to help him out. Fred had recently been diagnosed with bladder cancer, and I think that we both knew our opportunities to hunt together were slipping away by the day. I vowed that if there were any way possible to do it, I would be making a return to Massachusetts in 2020.

Besides Bill George, his daughter Belinda, and their fellow Floridian friend George Snyder showing up at Bill's Pennsylvania hunting camp for the final week of the season, there was also the Palehorse Production crew of Stephen Spurlock, Ty Eubanks, and Gabe Cuomo. They wanted to film even more footage for the movie. My old friend Gary Shepherd from Indiana also came in for a couple of days, and Doug Pickle from Virginia graced us with his presence. Local friends Craig Morton and Dickie Clark stopped in regularly too, and they even brought their wives over one evening when Dickie cooked up a bunch of delicious turkey nuggets and walleye fillets. It was a great week, even though it rained every night and during most days. Despite the inclement weather, Gary and I managed to shoot birds together during a heavy and persistent downpour, albeit a couple of hours apart.

Me and Gary Shepherd at The Farm in Pennsylvania.

Thanks to my old Double Bull blind, we were dry and warm as toast the whole time.

While driving back home and thinking about the 2019 season now complete, I realized that it had not been a very good year. Yes; there were lots of turkeys killed and memorable hunts shared and enjoyed along the way, but statistically speaking, my journal had recorded the vast majority of days as poor weather events with minimal turkey encounters. Number of toms heard at daylight was way down from the norm, and late morning gobbling had been practically non-existent throughout the entire season. And, when I had happened to encounter the occasional gobbling bird, they'd been very reluctant to respond to calling. An even worse statistic was that my totals for birds called "into camp" had hit a historical low. It had only been by way of a few "normal" hunts in FL, MN, IA, CT, and NY that the statistics had been pushed upwards to raise the grading curve for the entire season.

However, as mentioned earlier, there had been lots of positives to counteract any negative aspects. For instance, I had either hunted or guided other folks on 72 total mornings. Anyone who has read any of my previous four books knows that it's the number of days afield which is most crucial to my own personal view of whether the season could be deemed a "success." I truly feel like any day spent out in the turkey woods is time which should be added on to our allotted lifespan here on earth, so in that regard alone it had been a great spring and a resounding victory.

Chapter 3

2020

H<small>AWAII!</small>

This was to be my third trip to the islands for turkeys, and I was very much looking forward to it. I'm asked often about which states are my favorites, and although I have a difficult time picking even a top 30, Hawaii is definitely in the running for any number of reasons not necessarily involving its hunting. The people, the scenery, the food, the uniqueness of the opportunities, and the sense of "home" I feel every time I return…these, and so many more are just some of the reasons why it's one of my "go-to" destinations.

However, a little earlier in the year an unforeseen and foreboding factor had reared its ugly head…the Covid 19 pandemic which had begun raging across the land. As time for my airline flight approached, this heinous disease was threatening to completely shut down all travel by plane and we (me, Doug Pickle, and Ken Greene) had to jump through a few hoops in order to be able to take our flights. But, eventually we all arrived on the Big Island and settled into a great Airbnb house that Doug's wife had arranged for our living quarters for the entire 9-day stay.

As a veteran of two previous Hawaiian turkey hunting adventures, I was sort of the unofficial guide for my fellow travelers, so after procuring carrying permits for our firearms and buying hunting licenses, we ventured up onto the Mauna Kea volcano the day before the opener to do some scouting.

While driving around and looking things over, we ran into a Conservation Officer who gave us a few tips for productive areas where I'd never before hunted, and then later on we encountered yet another CO who not only confirmed those areas as being good, but offered additional spots, as well. Then, we embarked on a little adventure...

There's a "road" which completely encircles the volcano at about the 9-10,000 foot elevation contour. It's called R1. I'd hunted along it many times, and had always wanted to drive the entire circuit, but knowledgeable people had warned me of how incredibly rough that path was. Ordinary 4-wheel drive vehicles were forbidden from using it, but our rental was a bad-ass Jeep Gladiator that was tricked out to the 9's, and when that second CO said he thought our rented ride could make it, we headed out.

Well, the first few miles weren't too bad, but then things got much worse and it took us 6.5 hours in total to complete those 36 miles! I stated in the last paragraph that this road was rough, but let me be perfectly clear, here: it was *horrendous*!!! I've never seen anything like it. At several junctures I wasn't so sure that we would make it back to civilization in one piece. Ken, who was sitting in the back seat with Doug driving and me riding shotgun, was more than a little worried, and he expressed often his opinion that we were fools to embark on the trip. He was just sure that we would perish and never be found, or if so, all they would discover of us were the sun-bleached bones of three wayward tourists stupid enough to go where they had no damned business going! Doug and I (perhaps a wee bit worried, ourselves) got quite a kick out of Ken's hand-wringing and admonitions, but I will say this: I've now done that circuit once, and though I don't even own a t-shirt proclaiming the victory, I don't care. I ain't going back!

We did, however, see a few turkeys along the way, and that gave us hope of finding them again in the morning. The only problem with our plan was that when we reached the base of the volcano long before daylight, there was about an inch of snow on the ground. *Snow*, in HAWAII! The wind was howling too, at about 40 miles per hour. Worried about getting stuck or sliding off into a canyon along that rough-ass road in such conditions, Doug and Ken stayed closer to the main access highway while I began trudging on foot to reach one of the areas where we'd seen turkeys. It was a several mile hike to get there, but I had lots of time, as we'd arrived way too early due to our collective excitement about the first day of turkey season in this fascinating land. However, I was surprised and a bit concerned when I saw fresh tire tracks in the snow, and when daylight finally came those fears were realized when I spotted two hunters "sneaking" towards a pair of gobbling toms that I had already set up on. In that wide open terrain I was sure of their attempt's failure, and before long the turkeys quit gobbling and then flew away. I'd come halfway around the world to get boogered up by honyawks thinking that they could just walk right up to turkeys and shoot them out of the tree!

The rest of that morning was spent trudging around in the snow and wind, trying to find sign or see birds. I failed miserably, but when I returned to the Jeep at noon I learned that Ken had killed a tom and both he and Doug had heard lots of gobbling. As is so common in Hawaii, the weather fluctuated wildly all day, and by afternoon the sun was blazing, the snow had all melted, and the winds were totally abated. Then, it clouded up and rained. Then, it cleared out again. Hawaii...the land of ever-changing weather! If you don't like what it's doing outside, just wait a few minutes and conditions will be completely different.

I killed a tom on Day 2, another on Day 3, and fulfilled my annual bag limit of three birds on Day 4. Ken also shot his second bird on Day 5 and then passed on a couple more opportunities on Days 7 and 8. Doug? He struggled mightily throughout the trip. That is highly unusual for Doug Pickle, because he's a very good turkey hunter, but those finicky toms covered up with willing and interfering hens absolutely put the screws to him. Hawaii's public lands are not an easy place to hunt, anyway, and there's a definite learning curve to figuring out how to get things done on that jagged and craggy lava. Doug did finally come close to doing so and killing a bird on our 9th and final day of the trip, but close only counts in horse shoes and hand grenades, and that was the last chance he got before we had to catch our plane flights bound for the mainland. A return trip was already in the planning stages before we left…

As mentioned earlier, the Covid 19 pandemic of 2020 was just beginning when we arrived in Hawaii, and by the time I got to Florida it was raging in full force. People were dying of that disease at a rate of over 8,000 per day, and the country was in the midst of shutting down in trying to curb the impact. This had a devastating effect on my guiding business when 9 of my hunters canceled their trips during the 48 hours prior to opening day. But, there were a few brave souls who came anyway. We used every precaution possible to minimize anyone's exposure to each other, and things worked out as good as could be hoped for.

Ken got on the board first.

First up to bat were longtime friend/client Charlie Southworth and his buddy David Stallings. David was only 2-1/2 years past surviving being struck by a vehicle doing 70 mph as he was standing alongside his truck; the impact of which broke many bones, nearly severed his leg, and threw him all the way across the 4-lane highway and into oncoming traffic. It was only by herculean medical efforts and a miracle or two that he lived to tell the tale, and to say that this man now appreciated every little thing would be a huge understatement! David is a super-nice fella, and very inspirational in his approach to life, and I vowed to give him and Charlie a hunt to remember.

My third tom came on a classic and utterly fantastic hunt.

Doug never could scratch one down.

That's why we started out with a "Loveboat Cruise," but for one of the only times that I've ever hunted there, things didn't pan out. Oh, we probably would've eventually killed a tom or two if we'd stayed put, but I was eager to get these guys into birds and decided by about noon to abandon our spot and go hunt elsewhere.

My next-closest property is a doozy of a turkey killing place and I had every confidence in something good happening. Almost immediately after getting set up in the blind we had birds within view. For the next four hours we were nearly continually in contact with hens, and even heard a distant gobble or two, but it wasn't until about 4:30 in the afternoon that David said he could see a couple of big birds out in the pasture. When I glanced that way with binoculars, I noted that the big birds he was referring to were a pair of Sandhill Cranes, but what the Swarovski's picked up far beyond them were two blood-red heads just then arising up over the land's contour. Once they got close enough to see my DSD strutter decoy, they abandoned the lone hen in front of them and assumed that telltale posture of head down and shoulders up as they began a deliberate march towards eternity. At 27 yards David let the first tom have it, and when his buddy came back to flog his death-flopping friend, Charlie smoked him, too.

The FWC (Florida Wildlife Commission) had closed down all of the WMA campgrounds for 2020, which meant that our traditional turkey camp had also fallen victim to the Covid-19 pandemic. That was terrible news for all of us who so enjoy the good times we have in that camp every year, but in

Charlie Southworth and David Stallings doubled up in Florida.

looking on the bright side, the high number of guiding cancellations freed me up to actually carry a gun for myself a little bit. Prior to the season, things weren't looking good that I would even have an opportunity to do any of that. And so, with no other clients due to arrive for a few days, I accompanied Bill George to Green Swamp West, where he'd drawn one of their limited-access "Special Opportunity" quota permit. These kinds of quota hunts can be pretty good sometimes, and our first day certainly turned out that way when we managed to call in a big flock of birds at 9:17 a.m. There were several longbeards in the bunch, and Bill made good on his shot at one of them. I simply had no quality shot opening, so I held fire.

For the next couple of days I hunted across Highway 471 from there, on the Green Swamp East WMA which is accessed through a daily quota system of being one of the first 200 people through the gate. This place can get crowded, with frequent run-ins and hunter interference incidences being fairly common, but it's a place where I've hunted since 1989 and I've learned a thing or two about avoiding other folks. I even find a turkey there every once in a while who is willing to play the game. On my first morning of flying solo I heard one tom gobbling far in the distance, and yet, I was able to get fairly close to him before flydown time.

Well, hearing a tom gobble on the crowded grounds of "The Swamp" is one thing, but killing him can sometimes be quite another. These birds tend towards being rather cantankerous and difficult. And quiet. Very often, very quiet, and this fella shut his pecking-hole before his gnarly feet ever touched sand. He never uttered so much as a peep afterwards, either. I gave him plenty of time to respond or come in to a few subtle calls, but when it looked like he wasn't going to cooperate, I changed my plans. Not wanting to risk bumping him, I simply snuck away with a vow to return at a later time, or day, when he might feel more like acting the part of an amorous tom in love and willing do the things that make turkey hunting so much fun. In other words, I didn't feel like sitting in silence all day long, so I opted to go try to find another bird with a better attitude.

Such a strategy often fails and you end up just wasting time, leg energy, and/or gas money for nothing, but on that day I was soon able to get within a half-mile or so of a tom that was certainly doing his best to boost my confidence by ripping the woods apart with gobbling. I hustled to close the distance between us, and before he could hush up I found myself on one edge of a huge burned area, with the tom all the way across it on the opposite side. Rather than sneaking my way around the edge of the burn to get closer, I decided to employ a rather risky tactic by slipping right out into the middle of all that scorched earth. While most of the underbrush out there was charred real good, there remained what looked to be just enough trees and vegetative skeletal remnants to give me cover to make the move, and I figured that calls emanating from out in the middle might instill confidence in the tom that they were being generated by a real hen.

Sitting down at the blackened base of an oak tree, I was encouraged when the tom answered my first yelps on a glass pot, and knowing that he was still safely far enough away to risk the movement, I quickly hustled 30 yards to the base of a big pine. When the bird answered another call from there, I once again made a quick move to a new locale, and did likewise a fourth time just a soon as he expressed continued interest in my calls. I was trying to give that bird the impression of a hen moving about in the burn, or perhaps better yet, creating the illusion of multiple hens, and it seemed to be working as judged by his willingness to gobble and begin closing the distance between us. A final 10-yard switch to an even better setup tree was the last time I intended to move, other than to hitch my gun up onto a raised knee, and when the tom went silent soon thereafter, I felt confident that it was because he was working his way out into the burn to find me. Not long afterwards, I spotted the fanned tail confirming his buy-in of my ruse, and although neither one of us spoke another word, my Benelli soon thereafter had something to say about the whole affair.

Two days later I found myself battling with a bird for more than an hour, and it was finally looking like things were going to work out splendidly

Me kneeling beside an ancient Cypress stump in Florida.

for me. In fact, I had just spotted his fanned tail and flaming red head as he wormed his way through the thicket between us at about 35 yards. I was just about to flick off the safety of my gun when suddenly a loud explosion startled both me and the turkey. I flinched, and the tom ducked low into the brush as a quick second blast rattled through the leaves of the trees. Then, as birds completely unknown to me before the shooting started came flying through the treetops overhead, I heard the unmistakable sound of a pump-gun slide being worked from less than a hundred yards away.

It was at that very moment when I spotted the tom which I'd previously been focused on killing, but who was now fleeing from the unseen hunter by running away. Unfortunately for him, the path that he'd chosen to use as his escape route passed directly between my feet, and so, at 14 yards I stopped his departure rather abruptly, and permanently! It wasn't exactly the calm, cool, and collected killing shot that I'd been planning in my head for the past several minutes, but it was a highly lethal execution, directed about 90 degrees away from where the heretofore unseen hunter had just wreaked havoc upon the morning's peace and tranquility. I spoke with that guy a little while after exiting the woods with a fine old tom in my turkey vest, and found out that he'd been driving down one of the Swamp's main sandy roads when he spotted four jakes crossing in front of his vehicle. Slamming on the brakes, he'd tried to kill one of them by shooting out of the truck's window (a perfectly legal practice in Florida!), which certainly brings up no less than a hundred questions and grave concerns about both safety and ethics, but that's for another time and place.

Repeat-client Stephen Riddle arrived around noon the next day, and although we only saw a single hen during an afternoon hunt, I felt pretty good about our prospects for the next morning. Why? Because before Stephen had arrived, I'd watched three toms, three jakes, and a whole plethora of hens filling up the pasture field where I intended to take him. One of the hens had even run circles around the boss tom about 25 times before laying down in front of him to be bred, which was a cool thing to witness.

The next morning we only heard a far-off distant gobble or two, but I remained confident of staying the course and awaiting developments. And, sure enough, about 8 o'clock we spotted a tom up close to our farm's far distant property fence. He didn't exactly rush towards my setup of four DSD hens, a jake, and a strutter, but he certainly didn't run away, either. Rather, he simply maintained his position and gobbled occasionally at my calling, all the while strutting around by himself. It wasn't until a jake came on the scene and ran right up to us that the longbeard showed any interest in coming closer, but only by incremental advancements. At about a hundred yards distance he hung up again and refused to budge another inch.

Hoping to instill a little bit of jealousy in his brain, I then began purring aggressively on a pot call. At first I thought this tactic was going to work out, as the tom quickly closed to around 60 yards, but that's where he once again put on the brakes and drew a line in the sand. Obviously, he wasn't ready to totally commit to the charade of my decoy pack, so I picked up the calling a good bit and really worked over both my Cane Creek glass and a Bear Hollow Ghost-cut diaphragm. I also began drumming with my voice. The Jake in the decoys loved everything I had to say and strutted around gobbling like crazy, and his growing excitement seemed to do the trick on his elder brother or cousin to a degree, as the tom began a slow and steady approach…quite different than the typical response I get to a DSD strutter setup. Instead of rushing in to fight, this guy approached more like he was scared, and after Stephen put him down for the count at 33 yards and we had a chance to give him an up-close "in-hand" examination, it became quite obvious why he'd been so reluctant to approach: his spurs were short for an Osceola, and he was cut, bruised, battered, and missing quite a few feathers. Obviously, some bigger and badder tom(s) in the area had been keeping him in line, and no matter how good those fake hens of mine looked, he just hadn't been overly eager to get another butt-whooping.

Stephen Riddle with another Osceola on a fog-shrouded morning.

The following morning also started out slow on another favorite property, but as had happened the day before, turkeys began showing up at a little after 8 a.m. This time, the four jakes and a tom gave me exactly what I'd expected on our previous hunt in terms of their attitude in charging my DSD's, and in short order Stephen's little 20 gauge spitting TSS 9's had taken out the longbeard of the group. That tungsten matrix shot is mighty lethal stuff, and its effectiveness on turkeys impresses me every single time I see an old gobbler take a load of it upside his head.

Fellow Hoosier Mike Piqune was up to bat the next day, and we hunted one of my favorite places. It's not a big farm, but turkeys seem to always hang out there and it seldom fails to produce. The toms are usually roosted quite a ways north of the property fence, however, so patience is oftentimes both needed, and rewarded. Hence, I wasn't at all worried when the only roost talk I heard at dawn (about 6 a.m.) was by a couple of hens, and even they weren't very close. Nor was I concerned when the first gobble at 7:17 was also far, far away. I knew in my heart that we would eventually be into turkeys.

The vast pasture north of our property fence has just enough roll in it that turkeys approaching from that direction aren't visible until they're within a couple hundred yards, but I knew from past experience that they were undoubtedly out there…somewhere…and it was only a matter of time until we might spot a red head or fanned tail rising up over the contour. A half an hour later, that's exactly what happened when one, and then another tom eased into view, accompanied by several hens. However, they totally ignored my calls for the most part until about 9 o'clock, when I got into a rather spirited conversation with some unseen turkeys to the northwest. Their insistent-sounding 3-4 note yelps descending in tone made me think "jakes," and once they came into view, I could see that it was three teenage boys headed our way. The good part is that two longbeards also accompanied them!

The bad part is that the flock weren't totally sold on my decoy spread and got a little "hanky" at about 50 yards out. I'd been watching the group through binoculars the whole way in, and could easily see that both toms sported real nice daggers on their legs, so I was a bit disheartened when they eased away in the direction of some hens further out in the pasture. I knew the range was "iffy," though, so I was totally fine with Mike not taking the shot. However, in jest, I asked him if he'd declined pulling the trigger because he was holding out in quest of a particularly-good Osceola, or if he was just on a picture-taking safari? Never missing a beat, my old friend and repeat client replied that after driving 18 hours to get here, he just wasn't ready to pull the trigger and end the hunt so soon. I then immediately called our mutual buddy Jon Bronnenberg and asked him to explain to Mike that we were on a hunting expedition; the goal of which was to actually *kill* a turkey. We all shared some good laughs as I also pointed out that the day was getting hotter by the minute, and we could've already been sitting in the "high-cool" of an air-conditioned restaurant just up the road.

As all the turkeys in the pasture faded back to the north and out of sight, I did, indeed (at least a little bit) wonder if we'd perhaps blown our best opportunity. But, like I pointed out earlier, patience pays in this sport, and particularly at this spot, so we continued to wait things out. As the sun rose higher and the day grew hotter (especially-so in my popup blind, which was becoming more and more exposed to the sunlight), I figured that the only good option was to lay down upon the cool ground and take a nap. I always claim that I'm "mind-melding" with the turkeys when I'm doing this, and explained such to Mike, who looked at me skeptically but promised to keep a vigil out over the pasture while I caught up on a few winks.

I don't know how long I slept, but I was definitely deep into dreamland when Mike gently shook me by the shoulder and said that he could see turkeys out in front of us. It was two toms and several hens, which were then joined by another gobbler who was noticeably larger than the others. When I yelped, they all turned and came towards us, but the big fella was still lagging behind by a hundred yards or so when the rest of the group came into my decoy spread like they were looking for a rumble. Mike didn't wait for Gobbzilla to arrive; instead, pole-axing a fine tom on the second shot after whiffing completely on the first attempt. Surely you'll believe me if I claim that I didn't give him a hard time about his accuracy, or lack thereof! Mike is big fun and a helluva good guy.

Five days at Green Swamp WMA with alternately Mike (1 day), Bill George (3 days), and Belinda George (1 day) resulted in only three birds heard gobbling a grand total of about a dozen times, and we never even came close to killing any of them. Heck; the only turkey I laid eyes on during that spell was a single, inquisitive hen, but in truth, those are the kind of results which tend towards being "typical" of that place, so our lack of any good luck came as no great surprise.

Mike Piqune didn't let this one walk away.

My final scheduled hunter of the Covid year 2020 was a little nervous about driving 18 hours from Oklahoma and then being turned away at the Florida state line due to the raging pandemic, but he mustered up his courage and came on anyway. After Justin's arrival we went out to pattern his 10 gauge, and it was a good thing that we did because that gun was shooting about a foot high and 10 inches to the left at 30 yards! Luckily, he'd also brought with him a real pretty Remington 870 12 gauge done up in Mossy Oak camo, and it shot a great pattern right where aimed. I felt like we were now ready to make something good happen, so the next morning we went back to the same property where Mike had killed his bird six days earlier; on a hunt where we'd seen at least two other toms, but more than likely, four. However, at dawn I only heard two gobbles far to the west, and one single gobble a similar distance to the northeast. That was it for gobbling, but I did hear some jake "yawks" to the northwest and a few hen yelps in the direction of the northeastern gobble. Despite the limited amount of audio encouragement, I remained totally unworried because as I've said again and again about this particular property, it's just a matter of time before turkeys start showing up.

That is exactly why we'd set up overlooking a mega-flock of Dave Smith decoys consisting of two strutters, a jake, and seven hens, and when I spotted the western tom entering our pasture at about 7:30, he was already fuzzed up and advancing towards us in a rather menacing manner. Rapidly approaching the first strutter deke on the west side of my spread and only 22 yards from our blind, he began posturing for a fight, and when he then paused the battle with his head thrust upwards to eye his adversary, Justin took the shot...and missed! For some reason the tom didn't panic and exit the scene, but rather, merely flew upwards and then came right back down only ten yards further away. While he was beginning a slow retreat to the west and looking quite non-plussed in doing so, Justin jumped up out of his chair and thrust his gun's barrel out another window of the blind, and this time when he pulled the trigger, a great tom with long, hooked spurs began flopping in the sand.

We'd already discussed his desire to kill a second gobbler, so once I'd hustled out to retrieve Justin's very first Osceola, we settled back to await developments...and they weren't long in coming. A tom to the northwest answered my first strident yelps on a Cane Creek glass pot call, and then a second bird fired back from the northeast. The vast pasture north of us has a lot of tall thistle growing in it, and when you couple that with the gentle roll of its contour, spotting turkeys coming from that direction can sometimes be a little problematic. As I said before, oftentimes the first thing you'll see is a red head or the tip of a fanned tail easing up into view or coming out from behind a big thistle plant. Now, the first thing I saw after the most recent answering gobbles were two rounded fan tips of strutting toms headed our way from the northeast. When I then glanced to the northwest, I could see two more!

All it took was for the closest set of toms to catch a glimpse of my flock and here they came with heads down, shoulders up, and on a determined march to confront the strange strutters who dared to invade "their" territory. After stomping up to my decoys, they began aggressively posturing, chest bumping, and purring loudly in the typical intimidation tactics of a fight just fixing to get underway. When the left-hand tom then stood tall and glowered down at his rubber opponent, Justin pulled the trigger on him… and once again, he missed. Shockingly as it might sound, that gobbler had nearly the exact same reaction to a column of shot whizzing past his head as the dead tom in the blind with us: he merely jumped/flushed upward, came right back down, and walked away as if nothing happened. When Justin yet again cranked off another round, I fully expected this tom too, to fold up, but it was another clean miss. At that point I cutt hard on a mouth call and made both toms gobble, but my gunner then turned to me and said sheepishly that he was out of bullets.

Now, the way I conduct my hunts is by guaranteeing the client an opportunity to make a kill. However, there's no possible way that I can guarantee their ability to actually *hit* what they shoot at! And that's especially true if they happen to cripple a tom, at which point the hunt is abruptly ended with my obligations to the hunter having been fulfilled. But, these latest two shots so obviously hit nothing other than the air somewhere in the vicinity of the tom's head (although not close enough to do him any harm), that I decided to go against my usual practice and give Justin another chance. Grabbing his gun, I slipped out the backside of my blind, snuck through the swamp between us and my van, exchanged Justin's gun for my own while grabbing a fistful of fresh shells, repeated my wet trek through the swamp, and crept back into the blind…all while there were four longbeards and who knows how many hens still within sight in the pasture before us!

My pocket watch showed that the first kill occurred at 7:30. The latest misses came at 8:30. From then onward, we had turkeys either within sight or we could hear them talking for the rest of the morning hours, although only hens approached our decoys. Then, at about 11 a.m. two nice toms accompanied by a noticeably larger gobbler (the same one seen by Mike?) came close enough to warrant our intensified interest, and when I yelped hard at them on a diaphragm, they immediately took note and approached us in a typical fighting stance. But, once again, the big guy held back and that undoubtedly saved his life, because *my* gun (even in the hands of someone else) does NOT miss!

Justin with a fine pair of Osceolas.

Justin wanted to shoot a wild hog while he was in Florida, so I then took him to a place that sold hog hunts, where he (what else could be expected!) missed one. Despite the accuracy of this fella's trigger pulls, he had a great time and headed for home with quite a few stories to tell. Of course, I'm quite certain that my versions told here might differ substantially from what he claims to his friends.

As mentioned earlier, Covid really hit the country hard in 2020 and I'd had a total of 15 clients cancel their hunts. Justin was supposed to be my last scheduled hunter for the year, but then Stephen Spurlock's cameraman for "The Doc" film (Ty Eubanks) contacted me about wanting to kill his first Osceola gobbler. I was stoked about that, as he's a good dude and we'd formed a tight bond during the filming of the movie. Ty and Stephen had just spent the last 10 days trying to get him a bird with Mike Tussey's outfit south of my own, but they'd failed miserably, so I assured them that I still had turkeys aplenty and we would get it done. In anticipation of their arrival, I spent a couple days scouting my properties and found three absolute stud toms on my all-time favorite farm...a place that looks in appearance like the most proverbial "perfect" Osceola-producing cattle farm that a turkey hunter could ever imagine. I'd been guiding on it since 2005, with an outstanding success rate.

The day started out rather slowly, but very pretty, with a bit of typical Florida ground fog blanketing the cow pasture and hiding the surrounding pinelands and swamps. In anticipation of encountering the three toms and numerous hens which I knew to be hanging out there, I'd driven in the night before after dark and set out a full entourage of Dave Smith decoys: two strutters, a jake, and seven hens. Then, a half-hour before gobbling time the next morning, the three of us slipped into a pair of Barronett blinds (Ty and me in one, while Stephen and his cameras occupied the other) guarding over a natural "pinch point" dividing the north end of the property from its southern portion. This was where an old east-west running barbed-wire fence had once stood, but the only remaining remnants of its existence were a couple of ancient cypress fence posts and an open cattle gate in front of a deep gouge in the sand where the cows had walked through for many, many generations. The barbed wire itself was long-gone, but critters large and small (cows, deer, hogs, and turkeys) still walked "through" that gate in their normal movements around the farm. This was a place which I often referred to as a "money pit" due to how many turkeys we'd killed there over the years, and from my blinds beside it I could see most of the half a section which comprised this property...the farm being a half-mile wide by one mile long going from north to south.

Normally, there are three or four "traditional" roosting spots along the pasture's edge, from which I can almost always count on hearing toms gobbling or hens yelping fairly close to the pinch-point. Not today. The dawn drifted in silent as a graveyard. Perhaps that was due to the fog and sticky feeling in the humid air, but for whatever reason, I didn't hear the first peep from a turkey until straight-up 7 o'clock (a full hour or more later than expected), when a nearby hen softly yelped from somewhere back behind us. I answered her in the same gentle, inquisitive manner, and she did likewise back to me a couple of more times over the next few minutes before then uttering the sweetest, prettiest kee-kee's you could imagine at 7:06 a.m. Those melodious notes were simply too much for a hot blooded tom to stand, and a loud gobble blurted out in answer from the wood's edge further northeast of us.

My blinds were facing due west and backed up against the western edge of a small, wet cypress pond of perhaps 50 yards in diameter. On the opposite side of that pond behind us was a thin strip of our pasture about 20 yards wide, which in turn curved around the southern tip of a long, thick swamp forming the eastern half of the northern section of the farm. The hen was still roosted in some tall pines along that main swamp edge behind us, and her boyfriend was in another copse of pines towering above the swamp proper 200 yards north of her.

When the hen pitched out, she landed in that thin strip of grass visible from the back window of my blind. At first I thought she was going to go north towards the bird which had gobbled only once in the tree, but then she reversed direction and began pecking her way south and out into the expanse of pasture in that direction. The gobbler then hit the ground and ripped out four or five more thundering calls as he followed along behind her, and only when he stepped into the grass strip where she'd previously landed could I see that he was actually a jake. A jake with a great gobble, but a jake, nonetheless. That surprised me. At this point I became a bit worried, because I hadn't heard or seen anything of the three adult toms which I'd spent the last two days watching. Then, I heard a gobble much further off to the north, and after that bird answered two or three of my calls, I anticipated his arrival.

Instead, looming out of the fog in that direction, I began seeing large, lumbering shapes, which then materialize into about 50 cows. They very much wanted to go to the south side of the farm, but my decoy spread caused them undo concern, and even though they could've easily and simply walked around my faux flock and continued on, they seemed bound and determined to go precisely through the old gate area. However, they were afraid to do so, and before long we had the whole herd standing around mooing annoyingly and hung up by fear.

Meanwhile, the jake which had followed the hen south had spotted my fakes and come around the pond to join them and begin causing quite a ruckus: alternately flogging my jake decoy, breeding a couple of the hens, and strutting nearly continuously for THREE HOURS straight, all while those damned bovines stood there looking stupid as cows do! During that interminably long timeframe, several hens also showed up and hung out with us too, either aggressively intimidating my lady dekes or simply lounging around and at peace with both the flock and herd. Oftentimes, they would even lie down and/or stand around preening, seemingly with not a care in the world.

It wasn't until 10 o'clock before the first "brave" bovine gathered up enough courage to pass the decoys and make her way through the imagined gate and on into all of that beautiful southern grass. Others took encouragement from her incredible survival and imitated the dash, and soon thereafter we had a whole stampede of dumb-ass bovines fleeing for freedom. The jake merely stepped aside of the dust cloud made by their pounding hooves, then went right back to trying his best to impress my immovable flock of beauties, which continued to show no emotions one way or another.

After that goofy, lovelorn jake finally wandered off at 11 a.m. and we'd shared a few laughs at the comedic hopelessness of our situation, I suggested that we walk back to my van for snacks and cold drinks. By now the sun was up high and it had become one of those miserable-hot Florida days. I hadn't initially anticipated us being in the blinds for so long, simply because I'd convinced myself that we were in for a short, classic, "shoot-'em-right-after-flydown" type of hunt. But now, in need of nourishment and after what we'd just endured, I told Stephen and Ty that we needed to hustle back ASAP, as I'd been seeing the three toms in this pasture for the previous two days from 2 p.m. onward. I didn't have any idea where they'd been so far, or why they hadn't shown up yet, but I was still confident of their eventual arrival.

Chips and granola bars, coupled with ham and cheese and cold water from the cooler gave us all a renewed sense of purpose and an attitude adjustment. We were soon back at our stations for the afternoon hunt. First, I had to reset a couple of hen decoys and the fake jake, who had all been vigorously assaulted during the morning's happenings. A breeze had picked up and that helped to keep us moderately comfortable in the stuffy blinds, but only because our setup was under a couple of massive old live oaks and well shaded from direct sunlight. It was certainly tolerable for Ty, who was soon sprawled out on the ground inside our blind and sound asleep. Nobody goes harder as an outdoor videographer than Ty Eubanks, so now that he had a chance to catch up on a few winks, he took full advantage of the situation while Stephen and I kept vigil.

At 1:30 p.m. I heard Stephen whistle lightly, and when I glanced around to see what had alerted him, I spotted a most beautiful sight...my three long-spurred longbeards walking purposefully towards us from the south! I gently rousted The Beast (Ty's nickname, as given for his relentless attack on whatever task is at hand), and told him to get ready for action. Partly because he'd been so sound asleep, partly because he never gets to be the gunner, and partly because this was going to be his first Osceola, Ty went practically wiggy with excitement. He nervously wanted to call Stephen on the phone to make sure the cameras were running, but I calmed him down by telling him that we were all ready and good things were about to go down.

At 100 yards the toms began jogging towards us in that ancient dinosaur, velociraptor-type of movement signaling imminent confrontation, and after slowing to a walk once in the spread, they went right on past my first strutter decoy with only a bit of posturing, stalked on by the jake with hardly a nod, and then proceeded to begin flogging the second strutter without any hesitation whatsoever. All three toms were beating up on my deke at once, and it was a vicious, violent thrashing, too! At one point they even knocked off the real-feather turkey fan that I'd attached to the strutter, and then they jumped up and struck the poor tailless rubber tom so hard that it was left spinning around on its metal stake like a top.

By now Ty was dialed-in and ready to rock, and when one tom separated from the onslaught and stood tall, he got smote down like a bolt of lightning had struck him. His buddies then left the fracas reluctantly; making haste only when the hunter, the cameraman, and the guide all exited their blinds laughing, high-fiving, and whooping it up. The video footage which Stephen acquired that day is simply amazing to see, and Ty was one happy, happy guy. I couldn't have been more thrilled for my good friends, too.

Carlos Lopez is a local Floridian friend of me and Bill George who occasionally graces our camp with his enjoyable presence. He's a good dude, but had been trying unsuccessfully to get his son a turkey for six

Ty "Beast" Eubanks with his first Osceola.

long years, so I took them to the property where we'd already shot several birds and seen several other survivors. It was a tough day overall, with *zero* turkeys heard at dawn...neither gobblers, nor hens. This was a practically unheard-of occurrence on that farm, but as I've said time and time again here, it's a place where turkeys just like to hang out. At some point of the day they're going to show up, and sometimes you've just got to be patient to succeed. We were, they did, and finally, at 1:33 in the afternoon, Eric was able to take his first wild turkey. I like it when a plan comes together!

Well, Covid 19 had tried its best to wreck my Florida hunting and guiding experience in 2020, and in some ways it had succeeded. For instance, Bill George and I had not been able to set up our traditional turkey camp at Green Swamp WMA, where so many of our friends have enjoyed good times and camaraderie throughout the years. The only folks from camp who showed up to hunt that year were Doug Pickle, Allan Stanley, and his son Bonce, and as mentioned earlier, I'd had 15 people in total cancel their guided hunts. At least the state had kept the WMA's open and we'd been able to keep hunting, as that had been a huge question mark going into the season. I might also add that the actual turkey hunting action of 2020 was nothing less than stellar! Having so few people to guide freed me up to hunt quite a bit by myself, and I'd shot both of my toms during the four day stretch between Monday and Thursday of opening week. I couldn't even recall the last time that I'd had such good luck in Florida. However, I

Me, Ty Eubanks, and Stephen Spurlock at my favorite Florida farm. The van is parked where the blinds were located.

counted any of us so privileged to participate as the lucky ones. So many of my friends from all across the country weren't, and they'd lost loved ones, or their own lives, to the cursed Covid 19 virus.

After dropping off my trailer at home (as well as a whole cooler full of alligator meat that Bill had given me), it was time to head out west. But, I did so with a deep, hollow feeling inside my heart. I missed the way Florida had always been such a positive experience for me in terms of good times shared with a bunch of people whom I love and admire, and I could only hope that things might somehow return to a semblance of normal the following year. But, for now I had in my possession a public land tag for Nevada, although it wasn't valid until April 18. Rather than drive the whole way out there in one long pull, I opted to break the journey up by stopping for a few days in Arkansas, where I met up with Jim Spencer and his lovely bride Jil Easton. They had stayed for a few days in my Indiana home during the 2019 turkey season and hunted the surrounding State Forest Lands while I was off elsewhere on my annual travels, and yet we didn't really know each other all that well. This certainly changed over the course of the next two days when they put me up at their humble abode and showed me some public grounds where wild turkeys supposedly existed. I say "supposedly," because I failed to find or kill any of them, although I do feel quite confident that it was merely an unfortunate happenstance and not because of some malicious intent on the part of my hosts. I'm just joking around here, because I couldn't have dreamed up more cordial, hospitable, and sincere folks. We became lasting friends forevermore.

I noticed on my journey that all of the highways were much less congested; due, I'm sure, in no small part to the entire population hunkering down in fear of the raging pandemic. And, while I saw hardly a soul on the few public lands sampled in Arkansas, word on the street was that license sales around the country were exploding as people self-isolated by staying out in the woods all day and hunting turkeys. That was certainly my own plan to ride out the pandemic, even though this wasn't really any different than what I normally do every year!

Well, after leaving Jim & Jil's place I ventured up north into some National Forest lands where I'd hunted back in 2018, and for the next three days I had a fine time of it flying solo. On Day 1 I heard two toms gobbling early and slipped in to set up less than a hundred yards from their roost. I don't normally call to birds still in the tree, but on that morning I did so and was thence greeted by one of the toms hammering back a reply. A few minutes later I yelped into the back end of that bird's next gobble, and both toms ripped hard into my call. Their subsequent gobbles sounded like they were now facing me on the limb, so I never uttered another peep, and when the first tom flew down I watched him sail towards me and land less than 50 yards away, although just out of sight over the crest of the ridge. I said nothing, and even before the second tom had time to pitch out, I heard the sound of footsteps in the leaves. A bright red head capped in white soon popped over the top of a fallen log only 27 yards in front of my gun's muzzle, and just like that, my opening day gobbler was flopping on the ground.

A thunderclap at 3 a.m. the next morning woke me up, and at 3 p.m. that afternoon another one signaled the end of the storm line. In between, it must've rained ten different times of varying durations and intensities, and while I didn't stay out there and hunt through all of it, I did make exploratory ventures time and again, getting soaking wet and cold every single time. I never saw or heard anything from a turkey all day, but the changing afternoon weather conditions bode well for hopes on the morrow, and the red hue of the western skyline at dusk ("red sky at night, sailor's delight") had me looking forward to a fresh start.

Sure enough, Day 3 of the Ozark NF portion of my Arkansas adventure dawned perfect, with clear skies, no wind, and 45 degrees. It just doesn't get any better than that! However, sometimes I find that it takes the turkey population some time to "recover" from a stormy day, and this was seemingly proven true once again when I only heard a single tom gobbling to greet the beautiful sunrise. The good news is that he was pretty close to me when he started up, and I was able to slip in tight because of the damp leaf litter on the ground. My set up spot was close enough that I was "in the game" from the very start.

I strongly suspected that this bird was the partner to the one I'd killed on Saturday, and now finding himself all alone, he was gobbling great to locate his missing buddy. In truth, I thought that he gobbled way too much for his own good, so I kept hoping that he'd shut the heck up before another hunter moved in on him. Eventually, I did hear yelping north of us, and while I judged that the notes could've been that other hunter I feared due to their "too-smooth" and repeating cadence, the tones themselves sounded very real and authentic. But, the tom ignored those yelps, and instead, answered my own right after he'd flown down towards me. Soon thereafter I heard a series of loud, inquisitive clucks from his direction, and when I clucked back in answer, a hen stepped out into the woods road that I was set up on about sixty yards away. I'd also been hearing drumming ever since the tom was roost-bound, and now I heard it even louder and practically non-stop.

Despite the increasing volume of the tom's vocalization, he didn't just follow the hen in blindly, and instead, maintained his position of perhaps a hundred yards away. I played him slow and gently, not wanting to force the issue, and after about 45 minutes I could tell by his booming gobbles and the incessant drumming that he'd finally bought into my ruse. Over the course of the last couple years I'd noticed that drumming was often actually emanating from the right of where my ears thought the sound was coming from, and that was true this time, too. I was thinking "left," but the tom was suddenly standing tall to the right of my focus. Fortunately for me, he stood there for too long while looking for the "hen" in my lap (a Cane Creek glass pot), and I was able to creep my gun barrel the needed few inches to be aligned with his neck.

Arkansas had graced me with two fine toms, each taken during classic and perfectly executed early morning hunts featuring all of the aesthetics and amenities a turkey hunter could want, and I left for Nevada feeling happy and satisfied.

Three times between the years 2004 and 2012 I had drawn turkey tags in Lincoln County, Nevada, and after working hard to do so each time, I'd found some isolated places that held birds. Heck; in that final year I'd pretty

Someone before me had left a plaque attesting that this was his favorite ridge, too.

much been surrounded by toms in a real pretty area and experienced a fantastic 3-day hunt that is one of my fondest memories. Then, for some reason unbeknownst to me, the state had closed that area completely. Thus, if my goal of eventually killing five toms in every state were to reach fruition, I needed to apply for a different zone in their lottery system, and in 2020 my luck came through once again. However, this new area was ground that I was totally unfamiliar with, and I found myself basically starting from scratch to find turkeys in the one state which offers the very most marginal options of doing so. In a word, finding success on public ground in Nevada is a *tough* proposition, and it takes some diligent work to get it done.

For the first five days I walked far and covered lots of unfamiliar ground, talked with many local folks who would know where to find what I was seeking, and generally put in the necessary effort. And, I did find turkeys... just not very many of them, and every single one was either the wrong age or sex. However, I looked at each failure as if it were putting me one step closer to finding a tom, and on the sixth day all of my hard work paid off when a beautiful Rio Grande gobbler strutted up to within 14 yards of me. When he piled up at the shot it felt both exhilarating, and like a pressure valve had been released in my brain, for while I generally like Nevada and all of her unique charms and panoramic vistas, I don't *love* her, and I now knew that only one more trip to the Silver State was called for before I might

My fourth public land tom from Nevada.

claim a fifth and final Nevada gobbler.

California was another state where I only needed one more kill to reach that ultimate 5-tom goal, and since it was close to Nevada and I was running ahead of schedule anyway, that became my next destination. Unfortunately, there were only five days left of their turkey season and I didn't really have any hard and fast options so far as a great place to hunt. In point of fact, California had beat me up pretty bad during the two previous times when I'd hunted there, and while she had given up four nice toms during those two trips, they'd only become cooler-bound following 23 days of grueling and often punishing hunts. Now, the need to get things done quickly became an unwanted and tangible factor affecting my personal serenity. I would've much rather allowed for plenty of extra time in case I ran into bad breaks, bad weather, and/or bad birds, but that wasn't an option, so if I wanted to keep from eating tag soup (the flavor of which I *detest*!), I would have to get busy.

Thus, while operating under those rather ridged time constraints, I probably put too much pressure on myself the first day and worked far too hard in covering too much ground in very poor weather conditions. I'm not sure how many miles of rugged country I hiked on that hot and rainy day, but

I do know for a fact that I physically hurt myself by rubbing huge blisters into the pads of both feet. Nightfall found me barely able to walk, and the next morning I was still too sore to even think about hunting. Oh, I tried for a while, but only succeeded in making the condition of my feet even worse. That left me with only three days until season's end, so I then did something that I'd never done before: I paid for a hunt on private ground.

In fairness, I was offered such a tremendous discount by a friend of a friend that I couldn't say no, and even though it felt internally like I was cheating, I went ahead and accepted his offer. Then, I used the eight hour drive down to southern California's foothills of the Sierra Nevada Mountains as additional time to help heal up my feet. When I finally reached the ranch, I found its rolling, grassy, oak studded hills to be just about the most beautiful country that I'd ever laid eyes upon, and that helped to lessen my guilt a bit. The ranch itself was also absolutely loaded with turkeys, so when I found that out it pretty much cured me of any more internal turmoil!

My host Ron Gayer and I formed an immediate bond from hello, and over the next couple of days he kept me entertained with tales of hunting quests and conquests far beyond my wildest imagination. Seems Ron had survived a bout of colon cancer at the tender age of 39 and subsequently reset his priorities to focus on the most important things in life: things like hunting, fishing, and the great outdoors. He began making his living through writing, photographing, and promoting his outdoor lifestyle, as well as by guiding hunters for elk, bear, deer, turkey, and other interesting game around the world. Now 71, he mostly focused on turkey and deer hunts conducted on a cattle farm which had been first settled by the Lavers family during the 1870's gold rush days. They had initially made their fortunes selling potatoes to the miners and then buying up land with the proceeds until an absolutely huge ranch had been amassed. Over the years the original ranch had been divided amongst family members into many smaller farms, but this remaining 800 acres where we were at was the cream of the crop. Just riding around with Ron on a four-wheeler, I could certainly see why he thought of it as such!

The ranch consisted of a high central ridge which basically divided it in two, with many smaller knobs, points, and side ridges jutting out from the main trunk. The ground itself was covered in wispy green grass, and there were huge, sprawling oak trees regularly spaced out. This ground was truly magnificent to gaze upon, and as we cruised around on our property tour, my mind worked overtime in conjuring up images of how the turkey flocks Ron spoke about would be using the land. Before too long we'd encountered our first birds, then more, and later on as dusk approached, we roosted two separate flocks. Ron assured me that there were many others, as well.

My feet were still hurting bad and the thought of hiking up and over those steep hillsides was something I didn't relish, so Ron suggested that we start things off on the "house flock" in the morning. These were a group of turkeys which roosted about 300 yards from the cabin where we were staying. And, the cabin? It was a virtual museum chocked-full of interesting outdoors stuff, including lots of Ron's photography. Enlarged pictures of bison, elk, bears, cougars, deer, and turkeys hung everywhere, as well as panoramic shots of California's amazingly beautiful scenery and other interesting photos from around the world. Ron gave me a real cool picture of a rattlesnake which still hangs on the wall of my house today, and after a great meal and many tales of his exploits and adventures told over coffee, we made ready for the morning's hunt. Ron already had a blind erected along the edge of a newly planted food plot fairly close to the roost, so well after dark I took a couple of chairs down there and put out some Dave Smith's in the bare dirt of the food plot so that all we had to do in the morning was slip into the blind and get comfortable.

The birds piped up right on schedule at dawn and they hit it pretty well. I called more often than I normally would to roosted turkeys (although, not a whole lot), and got answers enough that I felt like the flock would probably come our way after flydown. However, both Ron and I thought that the gobbles sounded rather "jakey," so we weren't the least bit surprised when the first two turkeys spotted working their way toward us were, indeed, jakes. I was watching them through binoculars and contemplating how soon we should get up and go find a longbeard elsewhere on the ranch, when suddenly a booming gobble erupted from deeper into the woods and three adult toms came rushing to overtake their teenage adversaries in the race for my dekes. Although they approached my fakes en masse, they completely ignored my strutter decoy, and instead, ganged up on the fake jake, which they began flogging unmercifully. Normally, I like to watch for a while and enjoy the show, but when one tom stepped off to the side and gave me plenty of separation from his buddies, I went ahead and put him down for the count.

The rest of that day was spent touring around with Ron and letting my poor, aching feet heal up. It was fun to actually take a break and share time with a real interesting character whose own soul was guided by a profound love of the outdoors and wildlife. I learned some things just listening to his many tales and observations, and had a real good time. Then, the next morning we went to one of his favorite spots on the ranch to start the day's hunt…it was the highest point on the property and offered a breathtaking view in every direction. As dawn approached, turkeys began gobbling from seemingly every point on the compass! Being me, I thought that we should make a move and close in on any one of them, but Ron assured me that the local turkeys really liked to hang out up here on top of the world, and I should just call loudly and see what might happen. I must admit that I was skeptical, since the nearest gobbling birds were at least 500 yards away, but after setting up against a big oak with lots of downed limbs offering us ideal cover, I broke out my Cane Creek glass.

When I called, I received immediate answers from five different directions! Again, I was ready to get up and go after any one of them, but Ron said that we were fine right where we were at and to be patient. Someone else telling me to be patient sounded funny to me, and I chuckled. Usually, it's the complete other way around as I urge my clients to settle down and give the turkeys time to do the right thing. I must admit that I'm not the least bit used to being the guided, rather than the guide, so I had to remind myself of the three rules which I've come up with for any guided hunt: 1) Never guide the guide; 2) The guide is always right; and 3) Relax, enjoy the show, and tip well.

It took a while, but Ron was right, and eventually we could hear two different toms working their way up towards us. From that point on things progressed beautifully, and the tom which "won" the race to our position strutted up and died a glorious warrior's death at 26 paces. The only negative to the whole ordeal (and it's just a minor one), was that he didn't have *any* spurs! Other than that, my first paid hunt ended up being a wonderful experience where I met another true friend and kindred soul. Unfortunately, I'm sad to report that Ron died in 2023 of a heart attack, but I take a lot of enlightenment and inspiration from how this man lived his life to the fullest. All I can say is that we never know when our time on earth will end, so act accordingly. Eat the cake; dance the dance.

My next stop was Utah. To that point in my life I'd already killed three toms there, so I knew that it would take at least two more trips to reach my

5-tom goal from this one bird per-year state. While I was out west and in the neighborhood anyway, I hoped to reduce that in half, and then when deciding on which part of the state to hunt, I realized that by killing a Merriam's I could inadvertently rack up another cool accomplishment... yet another single-season Double Grand Slam. That certainly hadn't been on my radar as a goal when planning the season out, but that's the way the chips had fallen after two Florida Osceolas, two Arkansas Easterns, two California Rio Grandes, and my Nevada Merriam's. Even though a trip to Wyoming was still on the schedule ahead and they have Merriam's there, too, rumors were spreading that due to the Covid 19 virus the state might require non-residents to self-quarantine for 14 days prior to acquiring a hunting license. I wasn't willing to take that chance, so Utah looked to be the best option for one more white-tipped tail fan.

In perusing Utah's regulations and internal data, I found out that there was only one area of the state where only true Merriam's had been stocked. All other zones were shared with Rio blood. Thus, I chose my hunting area to center around the Bryce Canyon region, with my first venture into the Dixie National Forest near there seeming to be quite promising when I heard five separate toms gobbling over the course of the first day. I could've shot one of them, but he was a tom which I practically stumbled upon while hustling towards another gobbling bird, and since I'd only had my feet on Utah dirt for 10 minutes at that point, I declined the shot in hopes of prolonging my hunt for a little while longer and calling in a bird good and proper.

When I heard zero gobbles the next day in that very same canyon, I began questioning my sanity and the choice I'd made of looking a gift horse in the mouth, and seven days later I was mentally kicking myself in the butt really hard for being so foolish! I mean, seriously; what kind of a dumbass passes up a chip shot at an adult tom in steep, rugged country which he's totally unfamiliar with, in hopes of finding another bird that might or might not offer up some unknown intangibles making him the "right" one? This sport can give us wonderful experiences and meaningful hunts, but it can also punish us profoundly and cruelly for foolish behavior or bad decisions.

Then, my van broke down.

Over the course of that first week I had jumped around into several different areas for various reasons (mostly due to getting run over by other hunters seemingly everywhere I went), but I'd finally settled into a place which gave me everything that I was looking for on a Merriam's hunt. It had picturesque mountains, stately ponderosa pines, fragrant aspens, clean air, patches of snow, and seclusion from other hunters. And, I knew for a fact that there was at least one tom turkey to be found, because I'd seen him while driving up the mountain. I dueled with that rascal for two and a half days, after which I thought that I had his pattern pretty well figured out... he would roost high on the mountain top, gobble good, hit the ground with several hens, and then they would all work their way silently downhill along a trickling mountain stream which followed a shallow ravine full of fresh green grass dotted with yellow dandelions. Turkeys really like to eat dandelion flowers! He would be gone all day, but would then work his way back up the mountain in late afternoon and gobble several times before flying up to roost. I knew his routine. I knew him. Now all I had to do was put it all together and shoot that tom in the face!

The only other hunter in that area was a fellow who I'd met and spent some time talking with in his camp on the next mountainside over from mine. We made plans to cook up some turkey nuggets for lunch the next day, but after my tom had ceased gobbling and wandered away on his daily walkabout and I'd climbed into my van to drive over to Byron's camp, the danged thing wouldn't run. Well, it would start, and I could put it into gear, but it would then only run in "limp" mode with very little power. My heretofore trusty Ford Transit had done this a couple of times after leaving Florida, but both times she'd snapped out of it after I let her sit for a bit and cool down. Now, she refused to cooperate further. I tried disconnecting the battery to reset the computer, but that was about all I could do out here in the middle of nowhere and it didn't work. At that point my only option was to basically point my van downhill and ease along at 2 mph for the 4 miles to the base of the mountain, then park and hike over to Byron's camp. Once there, he gave me a ride to the very peak of one particular mountaintop where he knew that we could both get phone reception, and then I called for Emergency Roadside Assistance from my insurance company. The act of getting the tow approved and the tow-truck lined up was grueling and pure mental torture, but eventually everything was worked out and promised. I didn't know when, or even if, I might be back up on the mountain to make a play for that tom, and that was bumming me out big time, but at least it looked promising that I would end up getting towed to a mechanic and get the danged van fixed.

More delays the following day really had my nerves frayed, but finally, the tow truck arrived in mid-afternoon and hauled me 130 miles to Richfield, which was the nearest town that had a Ford dealership. We pulled into their parking lot at about 6 p.m., and luckily for me, the service manager was just walking out the door to go home. When I told him of my troubles, he flipped me the keys to a car on the lot, told me to go get dinner or a motel or whatever I needed to do, and they'd get my van into the shop first thing in the morning. I found a great little diner, then came back and slept in my van and was already up and anxious when the mechanics arrived the next morning. Thinking that it might be hours or days before they might reasonably be expected to work on my van, I was delightfully shocked when they promptly opened the service doors and motioned me in.

By 8:30 the problem was diagnosed and a new throttle body ordered. It had to be flown in, but arrived at the shop by 1:30 p.m., and at 2:30 I was back on the road! Never in my life have I been so warmly and professionally treated at a car dealership, and I can't say enough nice things about them. If you're ever in need of mechanical help while in the middle of Utah, I *strongly* recommend Jorgensen Ford!! I will also vouch for having Emergency Roadside Assistance on your insurance policy. That $750 towing bill cost me nothing.

After stopping for groceries and making the return trip to the mountaintop, I pulled into my campsite at 6 p.m. I was hoping against all hope that someone else hadn't found "my" tom while I was gone and killed him. That fear was somewhat alieved when I spotted several turkeys in a nearby field while putting up my tent, but I wasn't able to get the binoculars on them in time to verify if the tom was among the group before they skedaddled out of there. Even still, the sighting gave me encouragement. Unfortunately, the next morning I heard no gobbling whatsoever, causing doubt and worry to once again slip in and cloud my brain. Was the tom dead and already in somebody else's freezer? Or, was he merely being "hush-mouthed" for no discernable reason? Had he simply not come back up the mountain as per what I thought to be his usual routine? I had no way to know any of this, but sticking to my plan, I stayed put and called in four separate hens throughout the day. All of them were alone, so that left me with even more questions than answers, but still, I really liked this area and felt that I had to give it another day before heading for parts unknown. There was just too much turkey sign here, along with too little human sign, to think that someone else had stumbled in and shot this tom.

The next day was a repeat of the previous one, including various lone hens called in. Some of them got real loud and mouthy without provoking any gobbles, which even further cast worries in my feeble brain that I was probably hunting the ghost of a gobbler done dead. But, if nothing else, I'm extremely hard-headed and persistent at times, so I held my ground. Despite my reluctant optimism, by 6 o'clock in the afternoon I'd convinced myself that this gobbler was history and I was beginning to contemplate where next to move operations. I decided to stay for one more morning, since it was too late in the day to make a major move, and then I would pack up and head out.

At that point my attitude sucked. Here I was, already 10 days into a fruitless hunt, with no strong idea of how to change my luck. Everything that could possibly go wrong had done exactly that, and my mind kept replaying over and over again the first 10 minutes of the trip, when I'd had a gobbler right in front of my gun barrel and consciously chose not to shoot. Added to all of those negative thoughts was the fact that the incessant wind had been blowing hard all day, which was *really* getting on my nerves; much like fingernails on a chalkboard. I *HATE* the wind when I'm turkey hunting!

Then, over the top of that maddening, relentless din, I was almost certain that I heard a gobble from further down the mountainside. A few moments later I heard the same sound again, and this time I was sure of its origin and source. YES! My wayward son had finally decided to return home, and as he steadily climbed higher up towards me, he increased his gobbling frequency without any encouragement on my part. Once he'd closed to a couple hundred yards of my hide, I finally called and without any hesitation whatsoever he gobbled right back. But, try as I might to lure him into gun range, that funky bird hung up and refused to budge an inch past the hundred yard mark. Oh, he gobbled great... at me, at nothing at all, or at a lonesome real hen who had snuck in beside me. But, he refused to move closer and eventually faded off to the west a bit, where he eventually flew up to roost at 8:55 p.m.

His first gobble the next morning was at 5:40 a.m. I know that because I'd already been sitting up against an Aspen tree about a hundred yards away from him for nearly an hour. The wind was still blowing hard, after almost threatening to roll my tent up into a wad all throughout the night, but that didn't stop the tom from gobbling very well. As the light improved I could actually see him in the roost fighting to hang onto the limb under his feet, and whenever he'd try to strut the gusting wind would nearly lift him up and blow him away.

I really thought that I was in the catbird's seat after the tom hit ground, but without any hesitation whatsoever, he moved rapidly on a course directly away from me. Following a couple of cursory gobbles, he grew silent. Then, before I could arise and pursue or make any sort of a countermove, a danged hen showed up and wouldn't leave my side for an hour and a quarter. I would've/could've/should've run her off, but she was lonely and her loud, persistent yelps sounded so good that I held my position in hopes of them luring the tom back to us. However, not even that raucous old biddy could reverse his course.

On the evening before this hunt, the tom had spent some time atop a high knob of ground just prior to going towards his roost. On three other times in our battles before the van broke down I'd also found him gobbling back behind that knob, so I knew that it was a spot favored by him. After the hen finally left me and I was free to pick up and move, I headed over there and was in the process of building a natural brush blind on the slope below its crest when the tom gobbled from perhaps 400 yards away. Abandoning my plan of sitting in that blind all day if needed, I immediately closed the distance to him by half and yelped, and when I did that, he blasted out a gobble right into the middle of my call. I then quickly moved another 40 yards closer to him and set up on the spine of the ridge that sloped down from the high knob.

By then the tom had begun gobbling good all on his own, while also moving closer, and after he answered another call from me, he continued on. I said nothing more as he gradually closed the distance, and when I thought that it sounded like he might be drifting too far to the left, I directed a diaphragm yelp over my right shoulder. Immediately, he straightened out his path and came on. At about a hundred yards out I saw him strutting beside a big ponderosa pine, but at that point he completely stopped his advance. Oh; he still strutted, or would stand tall and gaze for long minutes at a time, but the old rascal had definitely drawn a line in the pine needles which he refused to cross. I didn't care. I had all day to wait him out, and although I knew that he was also working on turkey time and things might take a while, I felt certain that he'd eventually get anxious and come on over to find the hen (me) that had promised him such sweet nothings in his ear. I'm a very patient man when the situation calls for it, and that was exactly what I interpreted the circumstances to be.

Then, I heard a nearby hen yelp very lightly. The tom heard her too, and he craned his neck tall to look for her. When I saw her, she was about halfway between me and the tom, and when I yelped ever-so softly, she answered likewise and began walking in my direction; soft two-note yelping as she came. That was very good news for me, and basically sealed the tom's fate, because after a couple of failed struts to try and influence the hen to turn back around in his direction, he folded down and followed behind like a lovesick puppy. I shot him full in the face at 18 yards, while the hen was standing beside me at less than ten.

It had taken me 11 days of tough hunting in rough terrain and while enduring brutal weather conditions, plus two mechanical breakdowns (the first being hardly worth mentioning in comparison to the second one), a 130-mile tow, and $450 in van repairs, but I finally had my fourth Utah gobbler and a Double Grand Slam to show for the efforts. All those problems incurred along the way? I didn't care about any of them one bit, because I'd held pat in my belief that it was the difficulties incurred along life's bumpy road that make sporadic victories taste all that much sweeter. And, they were! Even

Utah was an ordeal, but I toughed it out until the tides turned in my favor.

My camp up on the mountain with that glorious gobbler stretched out on the table.

still, I felt like my brain had been put through a meat grinder. I was ready for an "easy" one.

Stephen Spurlock's Palehorse Production Company had just released their short film titled, "The Doc" during the past week. It's an absolutely beautifully-done movie about yours truly, in which I'm somehow made to look much better than I am in reality. But, as I said, it's professionally done and considered by many to be a masterpiece. When I mentioned my recent Utah troubles to Stephen, he volunteered that I was welcome to visit a farm he leased in Colorado. He said that it held a good population of Rio Grande turkeys, which were generally pretty darned receptive to being hunted, and do believe me when I tell you this: he didn't have to ask me twice!

Slipping and sliding down a muddy gravel road to reach the farm gate after an intense storm with lots of rain and dime-sized hail, I pulled in at about 2 a.m. Expected gobbling time was 5:30-6:00, but I couldn't sleep, so by 4:30 I'd already carried a blind, a chair, and a decoy spread out 200 yards to where Stephen's shared "pin" on my OnX app suggested that I start. Daylight revealed a real pretty and open river bottom dotted with big, tall cottonwoods beside me, and the first gobble erupted promptly at 5:40 a.m.

It came from only about 60 yards away, and although I fully anticipated killing that tom soon after his feet touched mud, he had a much better idea concerning his own self-preservation and immediately faded into the timber towards one of the seven other turkeys that I could hear gobbling from both up and down the river.

I'd set my blind in between the iron wheels at the base of a large pivot watering system, with a few Dave Smith decoys scattered around me for good measure. The spread consisted of a strutter and four hens, and when all gobbling ceased very soon after flydown time had arrived, I made myself content to just relax and keep a vigil over my "flock." Yes; I even thought about taking a nap to catch up on my z's, but other than that, my intentions were to simply bide my time and see what the morning brought. I had nowhere to go and all day to get there, and over the next two hours, that's precisely what I did and where I went. I heard no turkeys, and I saw no turkeys. In fact, only a raccoon wandering through my setup served to break the monotony. I didn't care. It felt really good to be doing nothing.

Then, at 6:50 a.m. a flurry of gobbles echoed through the river bottom, and soon thereafter I spotted a hen and a tom about a quarter-mile away. Obviously, the litany of multiple birds gobbling hadn't originated from the single tom seen, but it wasn't long before the source of all the noise appeared in the shape of three big toms accompanied by about six more hens, which were all headed generally in my direction. Two of the toms sort of snuck off to the side of everyone else as they neared, and that maneuver's meaning became clear when they began a direct-line forced-march posture with heads down and shoulders up. In no time at all they were standing in my decoy spread and roughing up my strutter, so after resting my shotgun's forearm on the iron wheel outside the blind's window and taking careful, deliberate aim, I shot the bird with the biggest spurs at 11 yards, taking most of the top of his head clean off.

That fine Colorado bird gave me four toms in total from the state, so now I was looking at coming back only one more time to reach my ultimate goal. This pretty little ranch sure seemed like a good spot to make a play for Number Five, and when I called Stephen to tell him how things had gone, he told me that I was more than welcome to come back. Easy hunt now done and out of the way; it was time to move on to Minnesota.

Colorado was short and oh-so sweet.

I love Minnesota. There's just something about the terrain and its people which has always held a strong appeal for me. Heck, for some unknown reason I've been a Minnesota Vikings fan since I was a little kid. However, it wasn't until 2005 that I first hunted turkeys there, and then I'd made three additional trips since, including the last two consecutive seasons of 2018 and 2019. One more tom from there in 2020 would give me three in a row *and* a tally of five overall.

There is also a good amount of public land in the state, and I've usually had little difficulty in finding birds on it. That proved true once again in 2020, when it only took me two days before I killed a real nice tom on a classic hunt where he'd gobbled hard, strutted the whole way in, and drummed so loud that you would think the sound could be heard from a hundred yards away by my Mother, who is so deaf that she can't hear herself fart.

I arrived in New York on May 20th, the day after Jake Bays' (and mine, as well) beloved and great friend Charlie Luberger lost his 3-year battle with cancer. His death was tragic on so many levels, and it cast a pall over my entire stay. "Charlie Lu" was a wonderful human being with a brilliant mind and a personality which shone like the sun. We had shared many a laugh and interesting conversation over the years, and I valued his opinion

A much welcomed return to the lush green vegetation of the Midwest, complete with hard-gobbling toms and some morel mushrooms.

and outlook on life more than I was ever able to adequately express to him. I so regret that. Fly free, my brother from another!

The rest of my 5-day stay at Jake's deer camp that year is kind of a blur, but Trevor and I got after the turkeys pretty hard. I think that it was our best way of coping with the tragedy of Charlie's death, and it freed up our minds a little bit from all of the overpowering grief. Both of us shot a pair of real nice toms, and we also helped Cameron Yerton take another. Then, Trevor and Casey Doody took me fishing at the world famous Lake Oneida. I'd never caught a walleye in my life, and this place was supposedly THE body of water to change that. Well, the only fish hooked and landed that day was, indeed, at the end of my fishing line, but it was just a 9-inch white perch. That was it…skunked again! I can still say to this day that I've never caught a walleye, although many years ago I had one right up to the boat in the Boundary Waters of Minnesota before he shook free of the hook.

With the month of May winding down, I then headed over to Pennsylvania. Ending the season there had been an annual tradition for a good many years by then, when several great friends from our camp in Florida would get

Casey Doody, me, and Trevor Bays in New York.

together at Bill George's "cabin" for a few days of high jinx and fun. The George family encampment is in reality an old 3-story farmhouse with nine bedrooms and a full basement. Its official name is, "The Farm." I think the house has something like 13 beds in total, so we try to get a lot of buddies together there every year and these gatherings have taken on legendary status. In attendance that particular spring were myself and Bill, as well as George Snyder, Craig Morton, Dickie Clark, LT Pack, Steve Torman, Doug Pickle, and Ken Greene. Dave Owens even popped in for a couple of days. Everybody got along well, enjoyed each other's company, and shared many turkey hunting stories and tales told over good meals and warming flames in the fireplace. We also laughed our asses off. It's *always* a good time at The Farm, made especially so in 2020 because of how the Covid pandemic had so totally wiped out our Florida camp. Just being there felt real good, and smiles were the modus operandi for the entire time.

My final kill of the year came on the second day in Pennsylvania, with results that left me feeling like I'd experienced just about everything possible to be found on a day in the springtime turkey woods. I was happy and content with the hunt in every way, and in knowing that my success could be directly linked to the patience and knowledge garnered from 38 years of chasing after and studying these crazy birds.

The previous day this tom had gobbled good on the roost, but then slowed way down as it got closer to flydown time. I interpreted his actions as extreme wariness stemming from increased hunting pressure due to Covid 19-induced skyrocketing hunting license sales. People staying home from work and other obligations had suddenly found themselves with lots more free time on their hands, and they'd been flocking to the woods all spring long. That was especially true in Pennsylvania, and undoubtedly, by the time of my May 25th arrival, this bird had been messed with by other hunters. Thus, I knew that it was important to hunt smart instead of just hard. Rather than crowding him on the roost, I'd set up in a spot about 400 yards from there, where turkeys just like to eventually go and hang out. I know this, because I've hunted that farm bordered by public land a bunch of times over the years.

One final gobble from the roost, 20 minutes after the previous one, signaled his time to fly down, and then the old boy said not one more word. I didn't care. I knew that he would eventually show up in the corner of the corn stubble field. However, just about the time I expected his arrival, I saw a Jeep Wrangler driving up the woods edge towards me, and it then stopped about 15 yards away. I recognized the vehicle as belonging to the landowner, who knew that I would be hunting his farm, so I was a bit surprised when John and his wife Merete climbed out and immediately went to work lopping off tree branches overhanging the field. Before I could even react or say anything, John was standing practically beside me, where I'd been tucked deep into a natural blowdown to await the tom's arrival, and when I said, "Good morning, John," I think it nearly scared him to death! After recovering his composure, the three of us had a good laugh before I helped them clear brush for an hour or so. They planned to disk and plant the field in a couple of days; thus, the reason for their work to clear its edge. After finishing that task, we then stood around for a couple more hours jaw-jacking about the world situation and everything else under the sun before they headed to the house and I headed back to camp.

The next morning I was right back in there, having already slipped silently past the tom's roost site in the dark, and right on time he started gobbling. His behavior on that day was exactly like the one previous, including a long silent spell before a single last gobble just prior to flying down, and then total silence. Again, I didn't care. I was still quite sure of his eventual arrival, and this time I was equally certain that the landowner wouldn't be driving in and ruining my hunt.

For that morning I'd decided to go ahead and put out a Dave Smith strutter and three hens. I figured that this hard-pressed tom might be a little wary, but I wanted to give him an opportunity to throw caution to the wind in a mad fit of jealousy. There's no better way to do that than with a big old strutter decoy standing in the middle of some hens.

Not long after the tom's final gobble, a real hen walked into the field about a hundred yards away from me, and when I yelped at her, she periscoped up and then immediately came towards me in a trot as what sounded like a sick goose called out. No; wait….that wasn't a goose…it was the *hen*! She sounded absolutely pitiful, and much more like a goose than a turkey. Her "yelps" also had a weird, quavering quality to them, but she wasn't the least bit shy or conscientious about her vocal issues. She called often and came right into my decoy spread, where she then made herself at home and seemed quite content to finally be amongst friends. Pecking around, she continued to hang out; even as the tom gobbled a few more times from near the original roost.

Then, although he didn't gobble much, I could tell that he was getting closer, and when he was about 200 yards away, the tom actually answered one of my calls. The hen beside me answered too, in that same strange honking yelp of hers, and the tom thundered right back. Obviously, he was quite familiar with this particular hen, and he *liked* her! A couple of minutes later she honked again and the tom stepped all over her call with a thunderous gobble from just inside the woods edge.

Moments later he sidled into the field in full strut and went directly to his old girlfriend, who was about 50 yards away from me at the time. After doing a complete circle around her as if totally smitten in love, and yet getting totally ignored despite his glorious splendor, he rather reluctantly, I thought, took the hint and began heading my way, instead. Normally, a tom will go straight to the male decoy in a spread, but this guy was obviously a lover of girl turkeys, and that's where he headed. Even still, I could tell that his greatest interest remained true to the honking hen, and when he began slipping off towards her, I put an end to the season with an exclamation mark from my Benelli.

The next three days were spent hunting with Ken Greene, and while we didn't get him a bird, it wasn't because of lack of effort or failure to appreciate every single moment spent afield. We had a rocking good time and came close on numerous occasions before he had to head for home in Virginia. Then, on the final day of the season I took George Snyder to a place where Dave Owens had killed a bird the day before, while Dave took Steve Torman after a tom that Steve had roosted and Bill George accompanied Dickie Clark into an area holding at least five toms. Doug Pickle teamed up with LT Pack on a chunk of Collins Pine ground that was open to the public.

George and I had a fantastic hunt with wonderful results. So did Dave and Steve, as well. Doug and LT messed with birds all day long but failed to connect, while Bill George and Dickie Clark messed up opportunity after opportunity and came back to camp disgruntled and bitter. Well; Dickie was sour-pussed. Bill was just his old, regular jovial self and happy even though he'd spent an entire day with Dickie. In the end, we all shared lots of laughs and lived to tell the tales, so once again the season-ending escapades at The Farm were a rousing success.

The 2020 turkey season had now come to an end. It was a strange year altogether; feeling almost like a rollercoaster ride of highs and lows, twists and turns, bumps and hiccups, and with only the occasional smooth stretch when things were going right. The Covid 19 pandemic was responsible for a lot of that, having wreaked havoc on the country, and the world, by killing over 18.2 million people between 2020 and 2021! In 2020 alone it killed

Our 2020 gathering at Bill George's Pennsylvania camp called, "The Farm."

Dave Owens and me sharing a chuckle while hanging out with a couple of toms.

over 350,000 U.S. citizens and became the 3rd leading cause of death. As I mentioned earlier, many people stayed home from work, or school, or just about anything else, and a lot of those folks took to the fields and forests to find some respite and relief from the pressures and sense of hopelessness which was pervading the psyches of a large percentage of the population. Thus, we saw tremendous upticks in turkey hunter numbers in practically every state. Couple that fact with emerging technologies like OnX and other phone apps which keep people who are basically scared of the outdoors from getting lost, and I saw people and boot tracks far off the beaten path and in numbers like I'd never seen before. Low gas prices also contributed to that trend, as they allowed people to travel cheaply and afford to hunt in other states. Never mind that fact that those low gas prices were due to a tremendous drop in overall demand as people stayed home instead of driving places and mingling with other humans. Plummeting demand for gas was so bad that at one point oil prices were actually selling at *MINUS* 27 dollars a barrel, causing small oil companies to shut down and go out of business in droves. But, with the American public being as self-centered as they are, so long as they could buy gas at around $2 per gallon, other folk's suffering didn't even register in their minds. That's just the way most folks are wired. It's pretty disgusting, if you actually sit and think about it, but that's the current state of the "all about me" world.

Despite some real deep negatives, there were certain aspects of my 2020 season which were nothing short of phenomenal. Yes; I'd had a couple of mechanical breakdowns and a rough go of killing a bird in Utah, but I'd experienced great hunting and efficient success rates everywhere else I went. I'd hunted a total of 66 days in 10 states and called in 71 toms to under 40 yards; 29 of those went home in the coolers of either me or my clients and friends. It was pretty hard to find fault in those numbers, so 2020 went into the record books as a tremendous success, although with an asterisk beside it due to the Covid 19 pandemic. After everything else was said and done, I could hardly wait to see what 2021 might hold in store…

Trilliums are my favorite springtime wildflower.

Chapter 4

2021

The 2021 season began with a whirlwind of activity, and barely slowed down until June. That was ok with me, though. I thrive under pressure!

Of course, it all began in Florida as per usual, where I had lined up a rather ambitious itinerary starting with guiding a young man on Captain Billy's Love Boat Cruise during youth weekend. Will and his Dad Rick Grubbs arrived at the boat ramp ready for action, but the airboat didn't have enough room for all of us *and* Rick's girlfriend. Somebody had to stay behind for safety reasons, so Rick volunteered to take a nap in the truck while the rest of us crossed the big lake. We hated to not include him, but this wasn't even Will's first Florida hunt, and Rick had seen his son kill many other turkeys back home in South Carolina at their Waccamaw Hunting Services operation. It would be a first for Miss Tammy though, and she was excited.

Well, the hunt itself was over rather quickly. Although we only heard a single bird gobbling at dawn, a previously unannounced tom promptly drummed loudly as he snuck in from our backside and passed by the "shooting hut" that we sit in during these hunts so close that I could've spit on him! He was a good'un, too, with long, hooked spurs, and he lost his life to Will's potent little .410 loaded with #9 TSS shot. Although Will was only 14 at the time and already a seasoned old veteran in terms of turkey kills, this whole experience with the airboat ride to reach our little honey-hole prompted him to tell me that it was the best turkey hunt of his life.

Will Grubbs got to take an airboat ride, and so did his gobbler.

Next up was a trio of fun guys from West Virginia, and our hunt was truly epic with three absolute stud limbhangers on the ground by noon. All were killed from the same blind, but each separate encounter offered up its own unique and flavorful story. I'm quite sure none of those fellers will ever forget that day, and nor will I.

Things progressed splendidly from there on out and by the time I left for home on April 18, we'd amassed 17 kills, with only one client failing to pull the trigger. That man was non-other than the famous outdoor writer, Jim Spencer, but the reason he went home empty-handed wasn't because there hadn't been an opportunity: the old codger had let two perfectly fine longbeards walk right past us without firing a shot while he waited, instead, for three other gobblers then at 80 yards to come closer. I guess he was shopping for a special tom with 2-1/2" spurs, or something! Jim's wife Jil Easton, however, wasn't nearly so picky (read: foolish), and she was absolutely thrilled with her fine Osceola killed at about 12 steps and sporting spurs of 1- 1/4."

Jim Spencer relaxed when the action slowed.

While awaiting my last client to arrive, I had a chance to hunt one of my best farms alone, and that day will live in my memory banks for so long as I live. Turkeys were absolutely going bonkers on that morning, and hens were swarming into the pasture. One of the first boy turkeys to arrive was a brute of a tom that really caught my attention because of the hardware on his legs easily visible through my 10x40 Swarovski EL binoculars. I made the conscious decision to wait and make a play for him if possible, and although it took a while and I had to let a couple of other toms pass, the bird of my desires eventually worked in to 24 yards and I made the shot count. At the instant when I pulled the trigger, there were *eight* other adult toms visible from where I sat! And that "hardware" of which I mentioned? Matching 1-9/16 inch scimitars graced each of his legs…the longest spurs on any turkey which I'd seen die…EVER!! But, not for long, as the next day I brought my last client of the year right back to that very same farm, and the tom he shot had one spur which matched the length of my gobbler's set.

That was the day I received word that my old friend Fred Solari from Massachusetts had suffered a bad stroke, and he died a few days later. Florida had truly been an epic season in all regards, but this news really shook me up and took some of the shine off of it. I had been planning a return trip up there later in the spring to hunt with Fred, and I was bound and determined to *finally* get him to kill a tom in my presence. Now, that would never happen. In his memory I went out and had a scallop dinner (something we always did at a great restaurant near Fred's home), and then I dedicated the rest of the spring to trying to garner as much enjoyment out of each day as Fred always did. I'll miss the old coot and his obvious and enthusiastic love of the wild turkey.

I'm going to keep most of the 2021 Florida season's hunts untold or highly abbreviated for the sake of saving space, but here are a few pictures to whet your appetite:

My best tom to date had matching 1- 9/16 inch spurs!

Keith Ott and LT Pack talk box calls in camp while David Young and Joe Ross look on.

Kerry Speer in a beautiful swamp setting with his fine Osceola tom.

An early morning strategy session under the big tents.

Me and LT Pack yucking it up.

Scott "Wingbone" Manville with a dandy tom.

A group photo in camp before we head out into the woods.

I hunted more days in Florida during 2021 than in any year since I'd begun coming down there in 1988, but the truth of the matter is that I was having so much fun I would've stayed even longer if plans weren't already in motion for a bucket-list trip to Mexico with Stephen Spurlock and Keith Ott. And so, after hauling my trailer full of camping and guiding gear back home to Indiana, I forthwith found myself on a flight to Tucson, Arizona. After arriving there I met up with my traveling companions, and the next morning we rendezvoused with the Woodhaven crew of Billy Yargus, Darin Sims, and Mark Scroggins, plus our outfitter Jay Scott and his entourage of guides/interpreters/cooks/etc. Then, we all crossed the border at the little town of Douglass, Arizona. Once in Mexico, we drove another eight hours to Chihuahua, where we subsequently left some trailers and other extraneous gear in a conglomeration of a few houses called Willytown and began another long drive deep into the heart of a 75,000 acre ranch which hadn't seen a "gringo's" presence since 2005. Supposedly, this was where Lovett Williams had done his fieldwork on a book he wrote about the Gould's subspecies in the Sierra Madre Occidental mountain range, and to say that it was both remote and beautiful would be a major understatement.

Our "caravan" consisted of several trucks, a nice Razor side-by-side, a four wheeler, and about a dozen people. Stephen and I rode with our guide Phil Cramer in the last pickup truck in line, and as we slowly traversed the twenty-plus miles of rough dirt and gravel two-track, all of the vehicles eventually became strung out over a considerable distance…probably a couple of miles from one end to the other. Ever since we'd passed through the town of Agua Prieta (the Mexican side of Douglass) at dawn, any inquiry about how much further it was to our final destination had been answered by Phil with, "Oh, it's not far." Now, as we finally neared the cabin where we'd be staying, his response had changed to, "We're almost there." That was *great* news so far as I was concerned, because right before boarding my flight to Tucson I'd suffered a really bad hemorrhoidal blowout. It felt like I had an inflamed and excruciatingly painful portion of my intestines dangling outside of my body (mostly because that's exactly what was going on), and I'd been basically sitting on the danged thing ever since it occurred. That included riding around in planes and trucks the whole time, and spending the last eternity bouncing across that god-forsaken rough ranch road, so I was more than ready for the trip to come to an end!

Well, that's when I saw the woods ninja.

We hadn't witnessed the slightest sign of human habitation other than an occasional crushed Tecate beer can tossed out and laying alongside the road since leaving Willytown, and yet, here was this guy lurking back behind some brush, obviously trying not to be seen, while wearing black jeans, a long-sleeved black shirt, and a black do-rag atop his head. In one hand he carried an automatic rifle resembling an AK-47. To be honest, I hadn't agreed to this trip without some grave apprehensions, because I knew that Mexico had been in a state of revolt for some time following the capture of the drug kingpin "El Chapo." Violence was running rampant, and some of the towns we'd driven through had borne witness to bodies left hanging from the overpasses or dumped in the streets overnight on a regular basis. The thought of what this well-armed guy in black was doing creeping around in the woods in close proximity to where we would be staying was worrisome, to say the least!

Just as soon as we reached the cabin and disembarked from the vehicles, I grabbed Jay and Phil, along with our cook Pepe (who could only speak broken English) and ushered them off to the side for a little discussion concerning our safety and welfare. Describing what I'd seen, I asked the obvious question, "Do you think he was Cartel?" Pepe looked at me with what best can only be described as a bemused grin and said with a heavy Spanish accent, "Oh, si senor...he wa's Cartel."

My mind reeled as I thought about what that meant; instantly envisioning the Ninja and all of his henchmen buddies surrounding our cabin after dark and then rushing in with guns blazing. I could just imagine the headlines back home: "Murder, Mayhem, Rape and Pillage South of the Border Wipes Out U.S. Rednecks." That was NOT the way I wanted to exit this world, but, in looking on the bright side, at least I'd be going out while on a turkey hunting adventure...

The worry was surely telegraphed onto my face, because Pepe stepped over and clapped a big hand down upon my shoulder and said, "Don' wurry, amigo...hee's *our* Cartel!"

As just exactly what his words meant began to sink into my befuddled brain, I queried, "Do you mean, we're like, protected?"

"Si, si, senor. Relax an' haf a goo time!"

I learned a lot about Mexico on that trip, but I also learned a lot about folks north of the border, and how spoiled we are. And, I came to realize how much we take for granted. For instance: all of us Americans are guilty of arrogantly assuming that we are free to conduct our lives as we see fit. Nobody can tell us what to do. In Mexico, the people are most definitely *not* free, and the cartels make certain that the citizenry knows this in totality. Death as punishment for speaking out is always a very real possibility, and violence is just a way of life. Any freedoms that the people enjoy are only those which have been given to them by the cartel.

Pepe was able to communicate (despite the substantial language barrier between us) that it was by the local cartel's good graces that our huge presence in this rugged and remote country was not only tolerated, but protected from harm. It was simple economics, really. We were bringing in a lot of U.S. dollars to their economy, and they had no intentions of anyone else (i.e.: other cartels) disrupting that setup. We never did see any more "woods ninjas" during our stay, but I'm quite certain that they knew of, and were keeping track of, our whereabouts at all times.

From that moment on, I had a blast. We basically divided up into two groups: Phil guiding me and the Chasing 49 contingent, while the Woodhaven crew was off hunting elsewhere with Jay. Our own group's modus operandi was to kill only one tom per day while getting as much action video footage as possible before pulling the trigger. Then, Stephen would shoot loads of video and camera stills the remainder of the day, and we would repeat the process come the next morning. Although we never really heard an overabundance of gobbling due to the toms still being rather flocked up, we did find *plenty* of turkeys, and they all answered calls eagerly while approaching us in great big bunches. In fact, each flock called in during the first three days numbered upwards of 30 birds. On Day 1 I made the 26 male turkeys in front of us (22 jakes and four toms) all gobble in unison…twice…before I shot the main strutter of the bunch. On Day 2 it was Keith's turn behind the gun, and once again we called in a big flock of more than 30 hens and jakes being herded along by one lone stud of a tom. This old boy ended up being a legitimate limbhanger, too, with spurs of about 1- 1/4 inches. That's almost unheard of for a Gould's, and his NWTF score ranked easily in the top five of all time! Although a lot of the toms shot by our party had small spurs or none at all, they did have impressive beards. In fact, both of my birds sported whiskers of 12- 1/16 inches long…the first and only legitimate beards of over a foot that I've ever been a party to taking! Then, as time was running out before our scheduled departure on the final day, Keith and I put forth a clinic of non-stop and loud calling to lure in his final tom from over a mile away.

While Stephen stayed behind to film more video for Mossy Oak and the NWTF, Keith and I were transported back across the border by Paco, a duel citizen of Mexico and the U.S., who had served as a Marine helicopter pilot in Afghanistan. The three of us all got along so well that he invited us to stay at his house in Tucson that night while awaiting our respective flights home the next morning. Paco was one of those folks whom you occasionally run into that become a lifetime friend from the very first instant, and even though we only got to spend about 24 hours in total with him, his wonderful wife, and their two small daughters, Keith and I felt like they would be a part of our lives for so long as we lived.

A couple of months after returning home, I received word that Paco had been killed in a helicopter crash.

Hold onto the precious ones in your life, folks, because you just never know what tomorrow might bring.

Here are a few pictures from my Mexico Adventure:

Guide Phil Cramer and Keith Ott with Keith's limbhanger.

Me, Keith "Young Bull" Ott, and Stephen Spurlock show off Keith's monster of a tom.

Keith Ott, Stephen Spurlock, me, and Phil Cramer celebrate a great and memorable trip.

My first Gould's was a brute, but he only had nubbin spurs.

The previous year I had visited Stephen's leased farm in Colorado and experienced a great (albeit: short) hunt, so after returning from Mexico I decided to go back there again. And, while it took me all day this time to finally coax a wad of toms into my setup, when they came rushing in I could plainly see the spurs on two of them even without binoculars. The one I shot was a bruiser sporting hooks of 1- 7/16 inches! After killing this bird, I just sat and admired the scenery and resplendent sunset while a tom with zero spurs approached my small flock of DSD's and tried to breed one of the hens that I'd set out 10 yards from my blind. He continued to snuggle,

I pose with an ancient molcajete, or grinding bowl, that I found.

caress, and mount that fake lady until it was too dark to see him through binoculars! The only way that I knew he was still there was by the sound of him drumming and jostling her about. The skies were pitch-black when he finally slipped off and I heard him fly up to roost about a hundred yards away. Never in my life had I seen a gobbler so love-struck, or who stayed on the ground so long after sunset, so out of curiosity I left the setup alone and returned to my blind the next morning. I wanted to see if that tom remembered the sweet hen of his dreams from the night before.

Well, long before any other turkeys had begun gobbling the next day, and in fact, while it was still quite dark out, I heard the spurless tom pitch out from his roost tree. Soon thereafter, I could hear his drumming as he approached, and moments later he was right back to his shenanigans of the night before with my decoy! This unprecedented and odd behavior put an end in my own brain to any arguments ever offered in the future that turkeys have a poor memory. They MOST DEFINITELY remember events in their past! I let the danged fool mess around with my Dave Smith feeding hen for a while after the sun finally came up, and then I ran him off and headed for Wyoming.

A dandy of a Rio Grande from Colorado.

In my early days of traveling all around the USA to hunt turkeys, I'd visited the Black Hills region of South Dakota a half dozen times. I always loved the beauty of that country, and killed a few of its Merriam's gobblers, as well. I even ventured over into the Wyoming side of "The Hills" a couple of times. But, for unknown reasons I quit going there in 1996. I guess I was just too busy hunting elsewhere and one of my favorite areas got thusly overlooked and left behind. Now, it was time to remedy that situation.

Trevor Bays had hunted the Wyoming side of the Black Hills National Forest in 2020 and killed a tom there, so with that little bit of intel I showed up a step ahead of where I'd have been otherwise. Trev is a virtual turkey magnet, finding and killing birds anywhere that he hunts this side of a Walmart parking lot, so I wasn't the least bit surprised when I heard a tom or two real close to the "pin" that he'd dropped on my phone's OnX app. I'll talk more at a later point about these smart phone technologies which allow folks totally unfamiliar with an area to just waltz right in and hunt it like they've grown up there, but for now I'll just say that I love the app, while also hating it with a passion unbridled.

Merriam's are not my friends. In fact, I often times hate them. They make me do really stupid stuff and hike long miles, seemingly always going uphill, to try and stay within the sound of their funny little gobbles as they joyfully traipse about the countryside in wild abandon. The only redeeming qualities about hunting these goofy birds are their stunning beauty, and the gorgeous countryside in which they exist. I've always struggled in actually killing them, though. Despite what foolishness you might have read to the contrary, they are seldom easy, and they leave me frustrated nearly all the time. Only occasionally do they do the right thing and die good and proper.

The tom I put to bed on the second evening in Wyoming was the same one which had basically made a fool of me for the entire day, and after he'd picked out a satisfactory roost limb, he gobbled well over 200 times from there before finally shutting up and going to sleep. We've all heard the old adage that roosted ain't necessarily roasted, but man, I felt like I had this boy dead to rights and all that was left to do was come back in the morning and shoot him. Of course, being as how he was a Merriam's, things didn't go exactly as planned.

At dawn he picked right up where he'd left off the night before...gobbling at first to some sort of screeching, pterodactyl-sounding creature in the forest and then really turning up his frequency as the gray of day slipped in around us. In easily topping the number of gobbles that he'd issued barely eight hours earlier, this tom went absolutely berserk; gobbling at everything, or nothing at all. From my catbird's seat 75 yards distant and on the same shelf as his roost tree, I figured that I was in for a rare "gimme" Merriam's gobbler, and my hopes soared especially high when a hen yelped softly from only 40 yards to my right. I answered her demure tree yelps three times with similar calls from the diaphragm pressed up tight against the roof of my mouth, and every time I did so, the tom hammered back in response. Things were looking good!

Then, the danged fool tom pitched out and glided all the way out to the far end of our shared shelf and landed right in amongst a group of a half-dozen mule deer standing perhaps 175 yards away. Just as soon as he puffed into a full strut, the hen beside me exited her tree and floated down beside him, and after he chased her around in circles two or three times, she led him directly away and out of sight over the lip of the shelf. Just like that, the game was over.

Well; not completely, as he continued to answer calls from me, but yet, the parameters of the hunt had definitely taken a turn away from my previously expected results. As the tom rather rapidly descended towards my van parked at the base of the mountain, I remember thinking what a wasted effort I had put into awaking far earlier than need be, huffing and puffing to climb the steep ascent, and then sitting there in the freezing cold for nearly two hours. Rather, I could've just slept in and rolled out of bed after the tom had flown down, and then set up against my van's rear bumper. But, rather than being depressed about the turn of events, I was just mad. How dare that tom treat me like this! Didn't he know who I was? When I arose from my setup tree and stretched to loosen up and warm up, I had already set my mind to exacting revenge on him.

Dropping directly off the side of the shelf, I slipped and slid my way down to the old logging road in the bottom of the ravine and then walked it out towards the tom, who was occasionally still gobbling from what could only be mere yards of my campsite! When I then set up within eyesight of my van and he answered a call, I distinctly remember thanking him under my breath for saving me the trouble of carrying his sorry-assed carcass very far, because we'd just cut nearly a mile off the distance back to the roosting shelf and I was anticipating shortly thereafter slinging him over my shoulder.

But again, this old rascal had other plans which didn't entail sacrificing himself to me and my pride. Not yet, anyway. Instead, he began climbing up the ridgeline on the other side of my camp at a slow, meandering pace. I figured that he was just following along behind his girlfriend, so I could slip around and come up to him on a path that would intercept his travels and seriously disrupt his plans for the day. Again, this ridgeline was every bit as steep as the one we'd just come down, but I thought if I only hustled....

By the time I reached the top of the new ridgeline I was huffing and puffing like a grizzly bear had just chased me up a mountain (yeah, right....like my fat ass could outrun one of those!) and sweat was pouring from every hair follicle on my body like I'd sprung a leak. My chest was heaving, and I was sucking for air like a ShopVac. And, wouldn't you know it; that damned turkey had already beaten me to the top. He'd undoubtedly done so without ever even breaking a sweat. Yeah, I hate Merriam's.

One thing about this subspecies of turkey is that, while they do like to cover lots of ground, they are most often simply headed for a particular place, and once there, they sometimes will stay put for a bit. Such was the case with this tom. He wasn't content back on that beautiful shelf with all the deer where we had started, but rather, he'd simply sought out a very similar looking spot 3/4 of a mile away as the crow flies (more what felt like 15, or so, in Doc-miles). And, after getting there, he once again began gobbling in earnest and at nearly the same pace as that with which he'd ended the previous day and begun this new one. The woods here had been thinned to a "park-like" appearance by the Forest Service in an attempt to make it less susceptible to catastrophic wild fires (the openness of which also serves to increase the difficulty factor in calling up turkeys to the hunter's gun), but he was close enough to the "native vegetative" edge that I thought it might still be possible to work him.

A Merriam's chase up a mountain ended in my favor, for a change.

Sure enough, after I'd set up about 100 yards away and called, the tom turned to face me and immediately began strutting in my direction. Despite the protestations of the hen tagging along behind, he then proceeded to waste very little time in hustling down along that aforementioned "edge" and right up into shotgun range of where I sat behind the cover of a greenbrier tangle. My fourth Wyoming tom was soon thereafter flopping in the Ponderosa pine needles.

Montana has always intrigued me for a multitude of reasons. It's the one state which I most consider to epitomize "The West," and when I think of hunting big game, I think of Montana. When I picture in my mind grandiose vistas or majestic mountains, I think the same thing. Ditto for grizzly bears and wolves. However, if the wild turkey is the point of my daydreams, then Montana is far down the list of my most favored destinations in which to hunt them. Going into the 2021 season I'd previously killed three toms on public lands down in the southeastern corner of the state, so of course that's where I first turned my attention. However, I hadn't been there since 2009 and the first thing I noticed was that many of the forested places where I'd previously hunted were now skeletal remains left over from devastating wild fires in 2014. I put over 200 miles on the van's odometer during that first day in just driving around and trying to find habitat which looked promising.

Late in the afternoon I spoke with a forester who gave me some spots to try, and after slipping and sliding on muddy back-country roads as far as the van could go, I set up camp near one of his suggestions. There was still a little time to hunt before dark, but mostly I was just wandering around and looking for sign (I found two old hope-producing gobbler turds) when I yelped on a pot call and heard a gobble so far away that it couldn't have possibly been an answer, but when I yelped again, I got the same response. That was good enough for me, and I returned to the van with hopes for the morning and a direction to strike out.

Long before dawn I took a compass bearing and walked a straight line of over a mile out across open grasslands, then I sat down to await daylight. When the first gobble echoed out it was directed at a pack of coyotes and still really early, but also still a long ways off and on the same line of travel, so I hustled another half-mile or more and crept close to a wooded slope where I estimated the gobble's maker to be roosted. His next shout-out confirmed not only that I'd originally heard this bird gobbling from just under two miles distant the night before, but that it was actually three birds roosted close together, instead of just the one. From that point on and for the next couple hours after flydown this group of birds gobbled great to anything I had to say, and yet, they never came towards my calling and would eventually fade away. After this happened several times I began to suspect that they might be jakes. Their gobbles sounded good, but they always gobbled in tandem, and it wasn't until mid-morning before I caught a glimpse of the trio and confirmed that my suspicions were right. By then I'd wasted several hours on those teenage hooligans.

Being Merriam's, they'd also been covering ground all morning long and now I found myself out towards the tip of a long, thin ridgeline three miles from my van. The jakes at that point were down in the bottom of a fairly narrow valley below me when a new bird suddenly piped up from two hundred yards further downstream of them. When I threw out some calls in that direction I got gobbles back in answer, so I poured on the yelps and cutts in response. This bird's strident answering gobbles certainly sounded more tom-like to me, and we conversed in a fevered pitch for several minutes as he worked his way up the valley towards the jakes, which were still, as they had been all day, eager to answer anything that sounded anything even remotely like another turkey…whether that was me, or the new gobbler on the scene.

We all maintained our respective positions for nearly an hour with no real changes. For my part, I had no intentions whatsoever of dropping down into the valley, both because the slope was steep and long, and because I feared that the new bird might also be a jake and I didn't want to waste the effort if that were the case. No; I was content to maintain my upper hand and see how things worked out.

However, I eventually tired of the status quo and moved out further towards the tip of the ridgeline. This put me almost directly uphill of the newcomer, and once again, when I called he ripped out a gobble in answer. True to form, the jakes also gobbled, and I could tell that they had also advanced towards the solo bird's position. I soon spotted them far below me, and then I saw the other bird strutting in a little open "glade." He definitely sported a fully rounded tail fan and a beard dangling from his chest, and he was also headed in my direction!

The jakes closed in on him rapidly and looked to be primed for a fight, and when they all popped into the same opening, the elder statesman took immediate note of the numbers mismatch and ran away. Hurriedly! Emboldened by their bloodless coup, the young hooligans picked up their gobbling as they paced around what had just been their adversary's territory. As for me, I was left cursing under my breath for them ruining what had looked to be a very promising turn of events.

That's when I spotted the tom again. He had circled around and snuck back into view of me, yet hidden from the jakes, and was now at the base of my ridge and working straight up towards me! I never said a word, and neither did he while leaving those young fools behind and climbing towards a mid-morning tryst with the hen who'd been sweet-talking him (me).

I could've killed him at 35 yards as he picked his way up the rocky slope, but it was only a fleeting opportunity and over in an instant. When he slipped back behind a huge boulder between us, I figured that I'd just wait and shoot him once he came out on the other side, but that never happened. I discovered later on that he'd dropped into an unknown creek bed, and the next thing I knew, he'd topped out onto the ridgeline and gobbled from above and behind me at about 50 yards! Obviously searching for the hen, he then began easing away and gobbling good all on his own, so I waited until he'd put a hundred yards between us before repositioning up onto the flat, cedar tree covered ridgetop. After going only 30 yards, I then found the perfect brushy cedar that afforded me ideal cover as I stood in the middle of it with my shotgun resting on a limb, and when I called from there…once… the tom gobbled hard. I cut into the back end of his gobble with a three-note cutt from a diaphragm, and when I subsequently heard drumming, I flipped off my safety. It wasn't any more than a minute later before his big beautiful presence came strutting out from behind some scrub brush directly in line with my shotgun's rifle-type sights at 26 yards. Game over.

Afterwards, I thought about how this hunt had turned out and I smiled thinking of how my friend Keith Ott (whom I affectionately call, "Young Bull") would've done it. His nickname stems from a joke that I'd told him in Mexico describing our respective turkey hunting styles. The joke goes something like this, minus a rather crude verb used twice in the original version but substituted for one more "less abrasive," here:

A young bull and an old bull are standing on a hilltop looking down on a valley full of cows. The young bull says, "Hey old-timer; let's run down there and screw us one of those cows!"

To which, the old bull says, "Let's walk down there and screw 'em *ALL!*"

Either mine or Keith's methodology could've worked to kill that tom, but the patient, "old-bull" style of hunting which I'd employed meant that neither a hike down, nor back up that steep-ass hillside had been needed. I'd simply let the turkey do all of the hard work, instead of me.

I spent a little time the next day hunting, but when blistering winds and torrential rain moved in shortly after dawn, I got out while the getting was good and hit the road for parts elsewhere. Trevor Bays and Matt Laymon were due to arrive in a couple days, so I headed into new terrain to begin scouting for them. I'm not even going to hint about where we hunted, because it ended up being really good and I have every intention of going back. Suffice to say that we found birds, killed birds, and had a great time over the course of several days. I will, however, recount one hunt just for the unique way in which it transpired.

After the boys and our host Cooper Davis had each taken toms, it was my turn behind the gun, so we were cruising around looking for turkeys when we spotted a tom and two hens standing beside a huge mechanized gate guarding a paved driveway winding gently downhill. The gate was open, so we drove on in to ask permission to hunt the property, although judging by the elaborate marble sculptures spaced along the 1/4-mile driveway, I was guessing that we were soon to be turned down by some filthy-rich anti-hunting landowner. Then, we drove up to a palatial mansion that was in a word *amazing*, and I was just sure of us failing. I'd bet that house was worth every bit in excess of five million dollars, with duel oak entry doors standing approximately ten feet tall. It looked like something you would see on "Lifestyles of the Rich and Famous."

It was Cooper's turn to ask, so he went up and timidly knocked while Matty, Trevor, and I sat in the car. As one of the massive doors swung open, a white-haired older gentleman stepped out and said in a gruff voice loud enough for all of us to hear, "Yeah? What the hell do YOU want?" Cooper, being rather soft-spoken and timid by nature, was obviously taken-aback and began stammering apologies about disturbing the guy. After a long, pregnant pause timed perfectly for effect, the homeowner quite suddenly laughed out loud and said, "I'm just messing with you, kid. Come on in." The boys and I just looked at one another in stunned silence.

Five minutes later Cooper came back out and slid into his driver's seat, and after his own eternally long pause, and with a straight face belaying zero excitement, he muttered, "We can park anywhere we want. He said to kill 'em all."

There was a long stone wall on the edge of the property line which stretched all the way up to the gate at the top of the hill, so Matty and I set up against a Ponderosa pine growing alongside it. That put us a hundred yards from the house and 300 from the turkeys. Trevor and Cooper drove back up to the gate to see if the tom was still around, and they soon texted us that all three birds were still there, although now laying down in the grass. The boys parked further up the road a bit to monitor the progress of the hunt as Matt and I began calling. Or, rather, I should say that my partner began calling. If you've never heard Matt Laymon run a mouthcall, then your life is the lesser for it. He's good. REAL good! But, not good enough to make that turkey gobble, so after I told him in jest that his calling sucked, I broke out my Cane Creek glass pot. When even that sweet sounding instrument of deception wouldn't elicit a response from the tom, I knew that we might be in for a tough time of it.

Trev and Cooper could hear our calling, so the tom obviously could too, but he was paying us absolutely no attention whatsoever and continued to just lie there in the tall grass like he was taking a siesta. These young guys I was hunting with are built a little different than me, and their tactics more resemble "Young Bull" Keith Ott in that if something isn't working, they will do whatever it takes to get results. Patience is not one of their strongest suits. And so, after perhaps 15 whole minutes of failure, a plan was hatched. It was time to "herd the bird."

Trev and Coop let us know that they intended to make that tom start moving one way or another, and a minute later, plain as day, we heard Cooper shout out, "GIT!" That was followed by a phone text which simply read, "He's on the way." Although they'd had to practically kick that bird to get him to stand up in the tall grass, the tom and his hens had rather reluctantly begun walking away, going right down alongside the stone wall.

Sure enough, in a minute or two I spotted all three birds ambling towards us. The tom never answered any calls from Matt or me, but to be honest, I can't recall if we even tried. This was a turkey drive plain and simple, even though the turkeys being driven could've opted to go in any other direction at any time and thereby thwarted our ill intentions. Still, I didn't even hesitate to pull the trigger when it was time. To do so would've cheapened a funny story, which the landowner loved upon hearing it. Coop now has exclusive rights to hunt that ground, and it's a doozy of a property with lots of turkeys and elk.

Trevor Bays, me, and Matty Laymon with the "GIT" tom.

The Umatilla National Forest of Washington is a large chunk of public ground where Trevor, Matt, and I next hunted, and on the first day there we experienced a truly epic adventure. None of us had ever been there before, but a buddy of a buddy had offered up a "pin" where he'd heard three toms gobbling a few days earlier. Not knowing the country or how rugged its roads were, we arrived just a little late at the designated spot, but sure as sunrise, we heard a tom gobbling just as soon as we exited the vehicle. He was close, too.

Matty was up first, so after moving only about 150 yards from our parking spot, we set up with Trev and me 25 yards behind the gun. Matt then motioned for what I thought at the time was Trevor to come join him (which he did), but in reality the signals were meant for us to start calling, which I did in Trevor's absence. The tom bellowed out an answer and I could immediately hear drumming as he waltzed right up to Matty, who killed his first Washington turkey about five minutes after our arrival! The tom was spectacular, too; sporting several solid black wing primaries and good hooks for spurs.

We could now hear other turkeys gobbling downhill from us, so off the steep-sided mountaintop we went, and soon enough we'd closed in on two separate groups of gobbling toms. I think there were five toms in total, and after getting in between both groups, the ones south of us faded away. The other group stayed put, though, and after another micro-move to get in better position, one of them came in to our calling. I could see him plain as day at 25 yards, but the heavy conifer underbrush had the boys' view blocked. When the tom then began drifting back towards his buddies, Trev couldn't stand it and decided to go get him. Trevor is one of the best, most efficient turkey killers I've ever been around, and if he decides a turkey is going to die, then that turkey's life expectancy takes a precipitous nosedive. Sure enough, after five minutes of slipping along and showing the bird a real fanned tail, a gunshot echoed out and Trev came back to us with the tom slung over his shoulder.

This was a really odd-looking bird…the complete opposite of Matty's beautiful specimen. Comparatively speaking, while Matt's tom was glorious to behold, Trevor's was a hot mess. He weighed less than 14 pounds, with a huge, semi-healed wound on his lower breast. Additionally, the feather patterns over his entire body were all screwed up. Some of them were also oddly shaped and/or of varying lengths, with one tail feather in the middle being freakishly long. Besides that, half of his tail fan was while-tipped, while the opposite side was buff colored. He was such an odd-looking feller that we theorized a rattlesnake might have bitten him (the scabbed-over chest wound) and the feather aberrations were due to that poison.

The other group of toms had gobbled at Trevor's shot, and they continued to gobble at our calls as we began a slow circling maneuver of their position. Crossing through a steep ravine, we climbed up the other side and intersected an old logging road that ran directly up above the turkey's location, and by slipping up a dirt embankment alongside it, I could carefully peer over the top of a fallen log and look steeply downhill towards where all the gobbling was coming from on a grassy slope. Immediately, I spotted turkeys 60 yards away, including one fuzzed-up tom, and after scooching up into a seated position against an old dead pine, I yelped on a mouth call. One of the hens craned her neck real tall, and then she wasted no time in walking directly towards me, clucking and purring the entire way. The tom followed dutifully behind, and when the hen was less than ten yards from me, he was at 35. At 8:43 we concluded that momentous morning of turkey hunting in which we'd taken three Washington Merriam's gobblers.

Matty, me, and Trev with the final tom of a fantastic morning.

The next day proved no less exciting, nor eventful, as we hunted with Trevor's old college friend Kyle Westover, who runs an all-around guiding business in Lewiston, Idaho: he offers great hunts for big game, fishing, and turkeys. But on that morning, we were just four friends out for an adventure. He took us to a fantastic piece of private ground, where I shot a dandy of a Rio to start things off. Matty and Trevor doubled up later on in the morning after moving on a pair of toms seen on a far-off ridgetop, and I concluded the day's events with my second tom a few minutes after hearing their shots echoing across the canyon between us. None of those turkeys roosted even close to the property where we hunted, and we'd had to await their eventual arrival as they slowly worked up the valley. This was yet another in a long line of examples where patience pays big dividends.

Kyle Westover, me, Matt Laymon, and Trevor Bays with an Idaho 4-pack of gobblers.

My second tom of the day in Idaho was a brute.

With Matt and Trevor heading to Oregon, I opted to stay and hunt in Washington for another day or two before joining them. I still had a tag in my pocket, and I was also looking forward to a relaxed morning of hunting alone and at my own pace. I truly do love those boys like they are my very own sons, but they're so good at this turkey hunting game that hunting with them can sometimes take on a lot of added pressure. They seldom fail to kill, and fully expect to do so on every outing and in the least amount of time. My personality is more low-key. I don't feel like the killing of a bird is the most important measure of success. In fact, I enjoy being beaten by these birds more often than when I beat them. Hunting alone is just different, and I've always enjoyed my solo time afield.

Returning to the spot where the three of us had hunted a couple days earlier, I heard nothing at dawn. I was sure that there were more turkeys around though, so I sat tight and eventually heard one gobbling far away. After hiking nearly a mile, I could tell that it was actually two toms gobbling together, and soon thereafter I realized that although I normally like to set up on the same level or higher than a targeted tom, it wasn't really an option in this case. Both of the birds were on top of a high knoll, with an open, grassy slope all the way between me and their position. Trapped as I was and unable to advance, I simply picked out a good setup spot beside a ponderosa pine offering some surrounding brush for cover, and when I called, both of those birds hammered my first yelp like they'd never been with a hen in their lives. They did the same thing on each of the other two occasions when I worked the old Cane Creek glass, and every subsequent gobble was closer in origin. In what amounted to very little elapsed time I saw them walking down the hill straight towards me. One of them broke into strut at 35 yards, so I shot him. Not much of a hunt, story-wise, but it was done in a relaxed, non-pressured manner and I garnered maximum enjoyment form every minute of it. Sometimes we're given turkeys that are quite simply too easy to be called "earned," but that doesn't mean they are any less honored or respected. I felt thankful the whole way back to my van.

Trevor had killed an Oregon tom the first morning the boys hunted there, and then Matty shot one in the afternoon. Once again, the cursed/beloved benefit of OnX came to bear fruit when they left me a "pin" on where to find a bird or ten as they headed elsewhere, so after I found their campsite, I hiked four miles deep into timber company land to see whether they had lied about the turkeys found there. They hadn't. That first morning I heard a half-dozen, but I was most interested in the one gobbling only a hundred yards from where I'd initially sat down on an old stump to await dawn.

*My second Washington tom entailed a long walk,
but the hunt itself was over in minutes.*

Within five minutes of his first gobble I was set up on a comfortable cluster of four Ponderosa pines growing close together and only 75 yards from the roost limb, and the tom gobbled almost viciously in defying the world to dare challenge him. I never uttered a peep before flydown time, and when he touched ground only 60 yards away and immediately popped into a full strut, I felt pretty darned good about my chances of ruining his day.

The tom could've headed out in any direction on the compass, but he just naturally chose to start walking towards me without my issuing any calls, whatsoever. Then, when he turned around and began heading away, I called very lightly and he turned right back around to face me once again. That's when the hen who'd been yelping in the tree beside his roost pitched out and glided right straight at me; landing only 30 yards away. Immediately, she continued on up my gun barrel while yelping forlornly. The tom never stood a chance. There was no way that he wasn't going to come towards her, and when she was only five yards from me, he was less than twenty. It was a long hike out to the van, so I appreciated the tom's light weight of 14.75 pounds.

Another easy one, but it took a four mile walk to get there.

The next day in the same spot proved fruitless as I spent my initial prime time hours chasing after echoing distant gobbles that I could never seem to pinpoint before a relentless, howling wind kicked up for the remainder of the day and ruined any further chances of hearing a tom. I HATE the wind when I'm turkey hunting! I feel the same way about high temperatures... which baked me all day long, too. After toughing it out in these tough conditions, I finally got back to camp at about 8 o'clock that night tired, beat up, and in a poor state of mind. I'd really wanted to get my second tom quickly and drive over to Utah so that I could meet up with Trev and Matt again, but when they both killed their birds quickly and I failed, those plans were squashed. Instead, they headed to yet another state and I drove to the nearest town, had a nice dinner at a great little Mom & Pop diner, and arose the next morning with a much better attitude. The weather had also improved exponentially, with clear skies and cool temps expected for the next few days. If it took me a week, I intended to just relax and enjoy my remaining time in Oregon.

Still, it was a long hike to reach the area where I was hunting (four miles), and the preceding two days of exertions back and forth and all around had my feet and knees aching. Generally, I felt like I'd been run over by a truck as I began the long trek back into "the promised land." But, there had been no fewer than five other gobbling turkeys in that vicinity on the first day, so my hopes and expectations buoyed me onward as I clicked off the miles.

I was thus stunned and disappointed when the only bird heard at dawn was so far away that his gobble seemed like only a whispered promise and nothing more. But, with no other good options, I continued on past my previous kill spot and trudged along the dusty gravel road which headed in the bird's general direction. I would cover perhaps 400 yards before stopping to listen, and just as soon as I heard another gobble (a wee bit louder), I would take off again. This went on for well-over another mile before the gobbles began to take on that ringing quality of a bird in workable range. Over the last 600 yards or so, I'd also begun to find quite a bit of fresh turkey sign (tracks and dropping), and the closer I got, I could also discern that there were actually three birds making all the ruckus. Two of them were fairly close together and in or near the valley floor, while the third was further along and up on top of a tall ridgeline.

The deeper I ventured into the valley serving as home base to the closest pair of gobbling toms, the prettier the countryside became. It was gorgeous! Ponderosa pines and aspen, with grassy pastures and a real pretty babbling brook. I knew that if my initial setup on the birds failed, I would be content to spend the entire day exploring this new country. And then, as I was really closing in on the closest tom, several elk all around me began barking. I'd been spotting their tracks all along the gravel road; together with those of deer, bears, and even a wolf. Like I said earlier: this was a really cool spot! Crossing over the creek, I snuck in a little closer and set up right down on the valley floor, which looked like a bed of green grass dotted with dandelions amongst sporadic aspen, fir, and ponderosa pines. Seldom have I hunted in a more beautiful place, and with the tom gobbling all on his own like crazy from slightly up the sloped hillside a hundred yards in front of me, I figured my chances had to be pretty good. Especially since I'd found several fresh gobbler turds in amongst the green grass near my setup spot.

The tom ripped into my first call on an old Cane Creek glass, and when I repeated the sequence 30 seconds later, he did too…already from much closer and down off the hillside! It wasn't long after that before I could hear him drumming, and when his next gobble sounded as if he was headed off course a little bit, I cutt into its tail end to redirect his attention. The drumming grew louder, and louder, and louder, but there was just enough brush between the two of us to keep him hidden from view; that is, until he popped out from behind a fallen pine tree at about 85 yards. After strutting briefly, he slicked down and began running towards me, but soon slammed on the brakes to stand tall and look around. That didn't last long though, before he once again jogged towards me in that funny, particularly dinosaur-like turkey gait, and this time when he stopped to survey his surroundings, he was only 29 steps away.

It was a pleasant, leisurely five-mile stroll back to the van, and I hardly noticed my aching feet and knees, or the extra 18 pounds of magnificence carried in my vest's game pouch.

I've not killed turkeys in any prettier place than this Oregon tom's home turf.

Trevor and Matt had once again dropped me a pin on a spot where they'd found gobbling turkeys "everywhere" in Utah and both tagged out quickly, but that wasn't exactly what I discovered in the same place three days later. In fact, I heard exactly two gobbles on the first morning that I hunted there. Not gobblers, but rather, gobbles! The cursed wind undoubtedly had something to do with my failure to hear anything else, but after what the boys had described, I figured that all I had to do upon arriving was to shoot randomly down through the woods and then go pick out a dead tom with the longest spurs. It was a mighty rosy picture that they'd painted, but all I'd found there were shades of gray.

Still, I'd definitely heard a tom, so I hunted hard all day and encountered enough turkeys to hold my interest. I learned a lot about the land, and I learned a good deal about how one particular tom and his girlfriends were using it. And at dusk, I watched him and those three hens fly to roost, separated by about a hundred yards. He even gobbled one time, which was half as many as I'd heard for the entire day, so that was encouraging. Then, as darkness crept in upon us I moved in tight and flushed the hens away. I didn't want them interfering with my plans for the following morning.

That night the temperature plummeted and it was downright frigid when I set up 75 yards from the roost tree an hour before daylight. First gobble was much later than anticipated, and it came from further up the mountainside, as well. I didn't care…ten minutes earlier I'd heard a turkey clucking close to me and then spotted it in the tree. Binoculars confirmed that it was my tom, so I knew there were at least two gobblers in the vicinity. One of the hens that I'd flushed away the night before finally yelped lower on the mountain, and my tom in front of me answered her with his first gobble of the day. Over the next seven minutes he ripped out a couple of additional ones before another turkey suddenly appeared gliding down through the pines from the direction of the initial gobble and then landed 30 yards from the tom's roost. A second bird followed behind, and once they were on the ground, I was able to confirm with that it was two jakes. Then, the tom pitched out and landed amongst them as yet another bird flew in and joined the fray. Yep; another jake. All of the birds appeared agitated and half fuzzed-up as they tried to intimidate one another, until finally the adult tom got the upper hand and chased his teenage adversaries around in circles.

At that point I yelped to gain their attention, and it worked. Every one of those birds immediately calmed down and began closing in on me, with one pair leading the other two in the procession. Once they had all closed ranks and were within shotgun range, I could see that the bird with the bright white pate practically glowing in the dim light was the tom, so I didn't bother waiting to pull the trigger for any longer than it took him to separate from the bunch. My fifth Utah tom was forthwith flopping amongst the same boulders in which I'd wrenched my knee real good as I was sneaking in an hour earlier. After gathering up my tom and leaving behind a small feather tribute, I hobbled out to my van with a knee that was throbbing in pain, but I knew that a long drive out east would give me some time to nurse it back to health.

Trevor lives in Independence, Kansas and runs a great waterfowl guiding

No pain, no gain is what "they" say, and this Utah bird hurt me.

operation owned by Joey Summer, called Summerduck Outfitters. When I called and told him of my interest in next hunting his ancestral home of New York, he expressed a strong interest in going along, so I made a three-hour detour to go pick him up. This not only allowed me to break up the grueling 40 hour drive between Utah and New York, but also to gain another driver who could share the load. The only thing which I don't much enjoy about my travels around the country every spring are the countless hours spent behind a steering wheel, so I welcomed the opportunity to have a traveling companion and kindred soul along for the ride.

We pulled into Smyrna, New York at 4:30 a.m. fully expecting to hop out of the van at Jake Bays' house and soon hear turkeys gobbling from the driveway as we broke out our hunting gear and traded road clothes for camo, but things didn't work out that way. When we still hadn't heard the first peep by 6:30, we hopped back into the van and traveled yet another hour to meet up with Preston Riley, who'd been having a tremendously successful month of May so far and was currently watching a tom with a couple of hens in anticipation of our arrival. By the time we got there, only the hens were still visible in the plowed field where they'd been hanging out all morning. Even still, I felt certain that the tom couldn't have been very far away and was more likely than not just standing in the woods edge and keeping tabs on his girls from the cover of shade.

When Trev hit his crow call the tom gobbled right back at him, so we then crept down through the woods and closed ranks with the hens, who had been slowly working their way toward an inside corner on the back side of the field and had just stepped into the woods and out of eyeshot. The tom was perhaps 200 yards further up the wood line in the direction they'd come from. He gobbled at my first yelp on the old Cane Creek, ignored my second, and once again gobbled at a third. Then, I said nothing more, confident that he would soon enough be coming towards his hens, and us. When he next gobbled, it was from *much* closer to where those hens had disappeared at the corner.

Trev, Preston, and I had initially set up about 20 yards into the woods and 50 yards from that corner, which was now hidden from us by a slight rise in the land's contour. However, there was enough cover between us and the field that I thought a slight move was both warranted and attainable. Since we had previously determined that it was my turn on the trigger, I left the boys behind and crawled in behind some tall ferns to reach a much better position from which I could see the whole field except for that actual corner where the hens had disappeared from view earlier. I thought the tom might simply walk out into the field and come right up its edge in plain sight, but there was also the possibility that he could cross out of his woodline at the corner unobserved by me and slip into our woods. Thus, I was watching in both directions as we played a coy cat–and–mouse game over the course of about a half an hour. I called very little and only very lightly with purrs and clucks, and the tom only gobbled a couple more times…both from apparently right in the field's corner, or just into the woods beside it.

Everything had been silent for ten minutes and my "turkey radar" was on full alert and buzzing silently in my head when I glanced to the left and saw the tom's big red head sticking up above the tall ferns in front of me. He had indeed come into the woods with us and was already in gun range, so when his head dropped below the ferns while he broke into a full strut, I swung my gun the needed few inches to align with where it had just been replaced with the tip of that big tail fan. Moments later, he periscoped back upwards right in line with the sight beads on the old Benelli. Checkmate.

That was an extremely satisfying hunt, made even more so when Preston told me that he never would have been as patient with that tom, and he was grateful to have learned so much from watching me in action. His admission once again drove home in my own mind the difference between

Some hunts are just real special and this one with Preston Reilly and Trevor Bays was one of those.

how he and Trevor's generation don't necessarily view the game of turkey hunting in the same light as us "old-timers." Whereas I grew up during a time of few turkeys, when we would almost always use our ears to find birds, these young cats are much more visual in their approach. While I am content to simply walk into a forest where I suspect turkeys might live and then sit to listen, using stealth, cunning, and patience to achieve success, these youngsters drive around until they see birds in a field, then figure out how to kill them; also using stealth and cunning, but not nearly so much patience. Hence, the development of their "reaping" mode so popular of late, whereby the hunter merely flashes a turkey tail fan to entice jealousy, lust, and/or rage from his targeted tom to invoke a quick charge into hand-to-hand range. I don't suppose that either approach is right or wrong, but the dependence on reaping and decoys during the last decade or so has clearly brought success to a whole bunch of participants in the sport who would not have gotten nearly so much of it using more traditional methods. Simply put, they've made turkey hunters out of some folks who aren't.

For the next three days Trevor and I couldn't have worked harder, nor achieved less. As good as we'd done out west earlier in the season with quick kills and efficient use of our time, it was now just the opposite, despite being back on familiar ground in New York; a place which had always been extremely good to us. A sense of mounting frustration began to pervade our thoughts and cloud our brains, and we began making unforced errors in both judgement and execution. It was a time of palpable trepidation and frustration. And then, with Trev wanting to knock off Pennsylvania from his "life list" before heading home to Kansas, we finally called it quits and admitted defeat. On May 26th we took off for Bill George's camp near Tionesta, with me still carrying a tag and Trevor having filled none.

Late-season Pennsylvania can be either really good, or really bad. A lot of that is dependent upon the weather and the advancement of the vegetation. If it's already hot and the ferns have grown tall, then turkey hunting can be very problematic. This was the case in 2021. Coupled with my favorite private-land spot being trampled on by folks who didn't have permission to hunt there, that made for a continuation of the poor luck suffered during the last part of the New York trip and I failed to kill a bird. Even Trevor struck out and limped on home to Kansas a broken soul. Pennsylvania had abused him just like New York had done, and he didn't much like it. Then, to make matters even worse, on the final morning of the season I allowed my own mounting frustrations to cloud better judgement and I took an "iffy" shot at a tom that was too danged far away. If I'd only been more patient and waited for things to change, I'm sure that the gobbler would've eventually come closer, but I let the pressure of "needing" to kill a bird make me do something which I knew was wrong even at the time that I did it. Thus, I dishonored myself, I dishonored the game, and I dishonored a fine old tom by giving him less than he deserved. In failing to kill a PA tom, I also ended a streak of 85 straight hunting trips where I'd shot at least one bird. That stung my ego quite a bit, but the worst part was how ashamed I felt for that lapse in judgement on the final day. At least I hadn't crippled the tom, so there was some consolation to be found in that.

Even ending the season on such a bad note (a moment that would leave a bitter taste in my mouth for the next nine months), as I drove back home and reflected along the way, I could without a doubt say that it had been one helluva good year, altogether! While my total days afield were the lowest (59) they had been in a decade, the total number (164) and efficiency with which I'd called birds into gun range had set personal records. I'd also shot my finest and highest scoring tom of all time (an Osceola sporting matching spurs of 1- 9/16 inches!), and another tom that I'd called in for someone else the very next day also wore a single spur which matched that length. I'd hunted in 11 states overall, and had added in Mexico, where my first two Gould's gobblers both wore beards of 12- 1/16 inches dangling from their chests. Those magnificent and beautiful white-tipped turkeys served as the capstone birds to my first two Royal Slams, and in addition to that, they helped me fulfill a Single Season Royal Slam; lacking only a second Eastern tom for a double. My guiding success in Florida had also resulted in a record number of toms taken, and when combined with my own kills, the season's total of 40 toms had set an all-time high. In addition, I was now only two states shy of my fourth U.S. Super Slam (needing just Arizona and Missouri), and another six states (LA, NV, NC, RI, TX, and WY) short of a fifth. At one point during the season, while sharing the woods with Trevor Bays and Matty Laymon, we'd been on a hot streak by killing 21 toms in 21 days. That was a mind-boggling stretch of good luck, but of course, I knew better than to let that cloud my judgement, for I knew hard times were sure to follow.

A tribute left to a worthy foe and an awesome season.
This one was also for Fred Solari.

Chapter 5

2022

Ahhhhh…back on the Island of Hawaii to start the year! I love Hawaii, and that has very little to do with the turkey hunting (although that can be very good). I feel more at ease and at home on that chunk of lava in the middle of the Pacific Ocean than I do in just about anywhere else that I've ever been. I can't explain it, but I feel so welcomed when I'm there. I love the scenery, I love the people, I love the food, and yes, I do love its Rio Grande turkeys, even though the physical aspects of hunting them can be brutally difficult.

In 2022 I traveled back there with Bill George from Florida and his wife Susie, along with her Mom and their daughter Belinda. We stayed in a couple of different Airbnb homes over the course of our 9-day stay on the north coast of the Big Island, and both of them were extremely nice. However, the only times when I actually saw the houses themselves were after dark, because myself and Bill, along with Belinda about half of the time, were in Hawaii for the hunting opportunities instead of being tourists, and that endeavor was an all-day proposition once you factored in the driving time both to and from the public hunting areas atop the volcano Mauna Kea.

Having been there three times previously, I confidently assumed the position of head guide for the trip, and my unofficial duties were topped in importance by getting a bird for Miss Belinda. She's been accompanying us afield since her youngest days of walking upright, and is a highly capable huntress in either the jungles of Florida where she lives, or in Pennsylvania at the George family camp, but I knew that this trip would be a whole 'nuther ballgame for her. That's because Hawaii is a *tough* place to hunt! There is no place in the world (well, at least in the parts of this globe with which I'm familiar) rougher than the slopes of Mauna Kea, where the least little misstep can result in a broken ankle, a twisted knee, or major cuts from a fall. In short, it's treacherous country not to be taken lightly. But, there are turkeys to be found there, and we heard multiple gobblers on the day of scouting prior to the March 1st opener. Well, I should probably point out that I heard no less than 20 toms absolutely ripping it, while Bill's deaf old ears honed in on exactly three *gobbles*!

The next morning's stillness was pierced with fewer toms sounding off, but there were still plenty enough, so the three of us gingerly picked our way towards the nearest gobbling pair. Once we'd set up at the lava-rock remnant foundation of some ancient-looking dwelling, both birds answered my calls willingly, and while one of them stayed just out of sight over the land's contour, the other came on in like it was his life's mission to sacrifice himself to Miss Belinda. In short order she'd pole-axed her first Hawaiian Rio Grande.

Belinda George started off our Hawaii trip with a bang.

A couple more hours of sitting in the same spot produced nothing of note, so we began easing back to our rented Jeep in quest of a snack. But, just before we got there, I spotted the fanned tail feathers of a strutter no more than a hundred yards from the parking area. We immediately went into sneak mode using the lush grass to hide our advancements, and after getting fairly close, I determined that there were actually two toms parading around for multiple hens. Lying prone in the grass, I called softly, and while neither tom answered, one of them immediately turned his spread tail fan to face us and then the whole flock began silently moving in our direction. Their position in a swale below our elevation meant that they disappeared from view once the flock reached the base of our hill, but then much sooner than I thought possible, I saw a fanned tail rising up in front of us at less than 25 yards!

We were waiting for the second bird to show himself, holding out as long as possible for a potential father/daughter double, when suddenly the tom within sight boogered at something and began retreating back downhill while alarm-putting with every step. It was now a now-or-never situation, but when Belinda couldn't get a bead drawn on the white-topped noggin stepping rapidly away, her Dad went ahead and did the dirty deed. Then, before we could even arise up on our knees to confirm that there was a dead tom in the grass, I saw the second bird advancing toward his fallen comrade intent on flogging him. Unfortunately, that desire to climb the pecking order was merely a fleeting decision, and when neither Bill nor Belinda was able to get a clear shot on him, the tom promptly thought better and departed the scene by hustling over to rejoin his hens.

Well, my most ardent hopes and dreams for this entire trip (getting birds for both Belinda and her Dad) had now materialized during the very first morning's hunt, and I could breathe a deep sigh of relief. All of the internal pressure that I'd been feeling was suddenly gone and I felt very relaxed. When Bill then drove Belinda out to meet her mother (the girls were scheduled to attend a Lu'au in Kona), I took a seat under a comfortable tree in case any other toms decided to do something stupid and approach my sporadic calling. They didn't, and when Bill arrived back at the parking area around 4 p.m., he joined me in the shade. Afternoon sun up on Mauna Kea can be quite brutal!

At 4:50 p.m. I saw a group of turkeys approaching our hide on a route which was going to bring them in close to us, whether I called or not, so I didn't. And sure enough, they did. The first half a dozen birds were all hens, and as they fed around within ten feet of me, a tom sauntered into view at their rear. Then, while bringing my gun up to bear on him, I discovered that some of the long, wispy grass blades where we were sitting had draped across the top of its barrel and were now totally obscuring the Tru-Glo rifle-type sights. When I raised my right hand to clear the grass away, several of the hens which were practically in my hip pocket saw me and alerted. Their alarm putts caused the tom to get all wiggy and hustle away too, and I, in turn, also panicked at the sudden and unexpected turn of events by firing too soon and without sufficiently taking a fine enough aim. My hurried and errant shot absolutely centered the 4-way intersection of a heavy duty hog-panel fence standing mere inches away from the gun's muzzle. This undoubtedly blew my pattern wide open, because I don't think the tom suffered even a single pellet wound. Stunned by what had just happened, my world was then rocked by the blast of Bill's shotgun very close to my right ear. I swear; that explosion was so loud that my brain was concussed!

I do believe the tom was struck by a pellet or two from Bill's 3- 1/2" 12 gauge cannon this time, because he wandered off going uphill and then promptly laid down about a hundred yards away and in the wide open, with his head held high. There was no way to advance on him in that unobstructed terrain without running him off, so we opted to stay put and watch, hoping that he might simply lay his head down and die. Then, a half-hour later and shortly before sunset, a heavy fog rolled quickly over-top of us and totally obliterated our ability to see anything further away than about twenty feet. That pea-soup made it even more impossible to find the tom before dark, so we decided to sneak away and come back in the morning. If he really had been mortally hit, he should be lying dead right where we'd last seem him. Hawaii has no predators like coyotes, which might carry him off.

Unfortunately, we never found a trace of that tom the next day, despite a diligent search right after it got light enough to see. We did, however, witness a very unique sight from our hide underneath that same setup tree a little while afterwards: it was a smoky-gray phase gobbler strutting at a range of about 500 yards. However, he never came closer than that before I shot a completely different tom which snuck in to my calling at 10:30.

For the next week the three of us chased turkeys around that magical island which I love so much but often times hate because of its brutal terrain, and we were even joined there by Trevor Bays and Matt Laymon. Of course, being the turkey killers that Trev and Matty are, they wasted very little time in filling their bag limit of three toms apiece. I also tagged out rather quickly,

My first tom of the Hawaii hunt.

Belinda George and her Dad Bill with their birds taken on Day 1.

Me and Trevor with my third Hawaiian tom of 2022.

A gorgeous tom and a beautiful view from up on the volcano.

while Bill and Belinda each ended up with two birds apiece taken during he first week. Then, we went "fishing."

I'd expressed an interest in hitting the world famous waters of Hawaii instead of spending all of our time hunting, so after my tags were filled Trevor booked us an afternoon fishing trip. While waiting for the boat to come back to the dock and pick us up, we got to talking with the wives of the two guys who'd chartered the morning hours, and they told us that their husbands had gotten one fish up to the boat, but then lost him. What? Only *one* fish? Up until that very moment I assumed we were going out for yellowfin tuna, or Mahi Mahi, or any of a bazillion other fishes found in abundance around the islands, but no.....we had inadvertently booked a danged blue marlin trip. Now, I've done a lot of fishing, so I know that if a boat catches one of those per week, fellow fishermen sit around their camp fires and sing songs about them! The LAST thing I wanted to do was waste time riding around on a boat for four hours with no hopes of catching any fish at all, but that's exactly what we did. Bill thought it was a great excursion, simply because he napped for the entire time and caught up on his sleep, but the rest of our party was bored to tears. I should have known what we were in for when our captain told us that he was originally from Illinois!

Before heading to the Big Island of Hawaii, I'd first driven my van and a cargo trailer full of guiding gear (tents, cots, bedding, blinds, decoys, chairs, etc., etc.) down to Bill's place in Zephyrhills and then caught a plane in Tampa. The flight was direct, taking eleven hours to reach Kona. *Eleven* hours! That's a long time to be in the air. And then, shortly after I'd taken my window seat, a lady and her toddler daughter sat down beside me. Almost immediately, that blessed child began screaming out in the most hideous, shrill, soul-shattering and ear-piercing notes imaginable. The weary-looking mother turned to me and said, "I'm so sorry. She just learned how to do that this morning." Well, that child born of Hades seed never stopped her ruckus for the entire duration of our trip, and while I have seldom actually hated children, I could've easily and willingly at any minute of that flight held that one down with a pillow until she stopped her infernal shrieking forever!

Lo and behold, as I boarded the plane bound back to Florida, I instantly recognized the same shrill sounds coming from further back in the plane. Perhaps the mother had learned how to quiet her daughter in the nine days since our arrival, or perhaps whoever was seated next to them decided to take matters into their own hands in much the same way that I'd only dreamed about on the inbound flight, because that was the last time I heard a peep from her. It was truly a blissfully quiet flight home, albeit still too danged long!

After making it back stateside I wasted no time in getting ready for youth season, where once again I was to guide Will Grubbs on a Love Boat Cruise. This time, however, we would be taking a skiff instead of the traditional airboat. Even though the passenger list included only Will, his Dad Rick, Captain Billy, and me, the wind was kicking up pretty good and the lake conditions weren't fit for an airboat ride. It really wasn't bad for anyone used to being on boats, but Rick wasn't, and he white-knuckled the gunwales the whole way across the lake. Once safely ashore, we then snuck into our honey hole and while Rick and Will got settled into the shooting hut, I put out a Dave Smith strutter, a jake, and two hens. Billy, as usual, stayed back at the boat and sipped coffee while watching dawn bloom over the lake.

We'd arrived a full hour before daylight because you can usually count on there being turkeys roosted real close to the hut, and sure enough, as the sky began turning gray I could see a hen almost directly overhead. She was hanging on tightly to her roost limb and swaying in the breeze, because by now the wind had kicked it up another notch. In fact, I was already kind of worried about the ride back to the ramp when Captain Billy texted me that he was headed home. That expansive lake is really shallow, so it can put out some very serious whitecaps during a storm and our skiff was not exactly what you'd want in those kinds of conditions. Billy was working on another way to get us out of there, but this was information I dared not share with my hunters. Rick would not have found any humor in our plight.

However, before I could waste any time worrying about our future, a gobble suddenly blasted out over that howling wind and I knew that the tom making it had to be really close! Then, I saw a second hen clinging to her roost limb beside us like she was hanging on for dear life. When both hens soon thereafter pitched out of their tree (undoubtedly feeling seasick from the wind rocking their roost so violently), they dropped almost straight down and landed right in amongst my decoys. The girls stayed with us for quite a while and I anticipated the tom coming to join them at any moment, but when he didn't show up or gobble any more they wandered away through the cabbage palms and I soon spotted them out in the cow pasture beyond our property line. Then, they suddenly started running…

straight towards a big strutting tom with several more hens in tow. The gobbler looked like a big one too, with a head glowing bright white in the pale, overcast early morning light.

At one point I thought that this tom was going to leave all of his girlfriends and come looking for the forlorn hen (me) that was yelping away in the oak hammock, but then he turned around and followed the entire group of vixens off to the west and out of our lives. That's when I heard yelping east of us, and when I yelped back, I got similar responses. We carried on quite a lively conversation as the yelping got closer and closer, until two hens finally stepped into our little clearing. Following close behind them was a silent tom, and when he saw my dekes, he immediately folded down into a typical aggressive posture and marched head down and shoulders up straight to my fake strutter. My calling at that point garnered only a slight lifting of the tom's head, but that's all Will needed and his little .410 barked a deadly charge of #9 TSS straight to its target.

Will's tom was a stud, too. Not many Osceolas can top the 20-pound mark, but this one sure did. He also had a thick beard of almost 11 inches, and wore daggers on his legs of 1- 7/16." The young man was pretty pleased, as were his Dad and me, but after a few pictures were taken it was time to think about getting back to the truck. To that point I hadn't shared the message received by Captain Billy a half-hour earlier, but now I told the guys that we were basically stranded until Billy could procure permission to drive in across private land to come get us. I think that news produced some more worry for Rick, who was still looking a little green around the gills from our initial boat ride, but twenty minutes later our ride back to safety pulled up to the gate. I breathed a sigh of relief, and I know that Rick was mighty grateful, too!

The next morning we returned with Mark Scroggins and his son Colton, and while the wind had abated by then, the temperature had also dropped precipitously. Osceolas don't like cold weather, and it was 36 degrees when we arrived at the boat ramp. We only heard two gobbles early, and another at 1 p.m., and failed to kill a bird for one of the only times I've ever hunted in that spot. I guess that's why we call what we do "hunting" instead of "killing," but I had a great time spending the day with those two guys and I think they had fun, too.

On opening morning of the regular season I took three guys out at the same time to a farm which I'd been watching carefully for a week. Thus,

Will Grubbs and his jumbo Osceola.

I was quite confident that the two fellers from my home state (Byron Ray and Steve Wynn), would get their birds, but I was also hopeful that the legendary Brent Rogers from Iowa might also score. I wasn't really worried though, because even if things didn't come together, we had several more days to make something good happen. As it turned out, no additional time was needed because shortly after dawn a single tom came in for Byron, and a half-hour later two more approached our setup. Steve and Brent promptly doubled up, and the high-5's commenced!

My next guest was Cantrell Lowe, who, along with her husband Jared are nearing what I'm quite certain will be the first husband and wife U.S. Super Slam duet. Besides being one of the nicest couples you could ever imagine,

Byron, Steve, and Brent tripled up on opening day.

Cantrell Lowe and husband Jared with her Osceola in as picturesque of a Florida setting as anyone could hope for.

husband Jared is also a top-tier caller on a diaphragm, so I acquiesced and let him do most of the calling during our hunt. It was a good outing, too; a hunt where we heard birds and saw birds, but couldn't actually kill one all morning long. Maybe if I'd been doing the bulk of the calling things would've turned out differently (ha ha!), but we didn't get Miss Cantrell's bird until mid-day. I think she'd agree that her magnificent tom was worth the wait and the thrilling hunt which he gave us.

I took my next two clients to a chunk of public land for which I'd drawn a coveted quota hunt permit. I don't normally take other people to this spot, but it's one of my favorites and I really enjoy the amount of acreage and the lack of other people hunting it. And, when both of my guys (Jerry Maness and Stephen Riddle) got their birds, I thereby saved myself the cost of having to pay out landowner fees, which is what I do for all of my private properties on a per bird basis. In fact, I did that very same thing on the following hunt with Brad Holmes, after Bill George gave me a permit for Green Swamp West. Brad and I experienced one of those epic hunts that had my knees quivering long before he finally pulled the trigger on a whopper of an Osceola. Fun times!

During the next two weeks I also shared wonderful days afield with a whole cadre of fine folks: guys like Wally Young, Lee Kellogg, Joel and Jay Harter, Justin Pfalzer, Tim Conley, and Aaron Cook. I think every one of them would tell you that hunting in Florida is an experience unlike anything else, and it's something that grabs ahold of your turkey hunting soul in a way which no other place can possibly do. The hunting aspect itself can be either good or bad, but those swamps always produce something exciting and you will see and hear things to spark your imagination and bring out the wanderlust in your heart. It captivated my soul a long, long time ago, and I cannot in my wildest nightmares ever imagine not spending a portion of any of my remaining springs in the Sunshine State.

The following pages feature a few more pictures from Florida's 2022 adventures:

Justin Pfalzer and Tim Conley with Tim's big gobbler.

Aaron Cook with the last Osceola of the season.

A typical afternoon camp gathering of fine folks and great friends.

Two of my favorite people...Earlow Costine and Charlie Parrish.

Another state which I like a lot in ways that have nothing to do with its turkey hunting is Louisiana. There's something about those folks who live in the Bayou State that really make me smile. They like good food and good times, and are always fun to be around. And did I mention the food? Cajun cooking is nothing short of awesome! One of their dishes, in particular, is amongst my favorite eats of all time, and that's a type of sausage called Boudin. If you've ever had it and didn't like it, then I quite simply don't know what's wrong with you, but you obviously ain't right in the head. 'Nuff said.

I like to keep my freezer stocked with Boudin, but I'd been out of it for quite some time when the 2022 season rolled around. This problem was something that I intended to remedy, but not until first taking a tom or two. One more from that difficult state would give me five in total, and when Charlie Rigdon offered to hunt with me on his leased ground, it was an opportunity that I quite simply could not turn down. Did I mention how difficult Louisiana's public lands can be for actually killing turkeys?

Well, for two days we gave it our best efforts but failed to get things finished with either one of a couple different toms that we heard gobbling. Then, Charlie had to leave town for a work training gig that he couldn't avoid, and being the true gentleman and good feller of which he is, he offered to let me keep hunting that same ground alone in his absence. The next morning those two toms were gobbling from about 300 yards apart, so I got right in between them before flydown time. I had a great setup position on both birds, and they obviously were without hens that morning, because each of them raced towards me after I called plaintively on the trusted old Cane Creek glass. I shot the "winner" of the race when he strutted almost violently up into close range.

With the weather being extremely hot and rain predicted to roll in overnight, I decided to do something crazy, even for a man known to do crazy stuff. First, I drove all the way diagonally across the state to buy 50 pounds of frozen Jamison's boudin near New Orleans. Then, I stuffed it all in a big cooler and partially retraced my route up to Scott, Louisiana, where I bought an additional 75 pounds of Don's boudin and another 75 pounds of my favorite boudin of all time; Billy's. Then, I pointed my van north and drove straight home to get all of this wonderful deliciousness put away in my deep freezer. The very next morning I retraced nearly my exact 16-hour route before veering off into Texas, where I met up with Rhett Hall, who is

A Texas public land Rio Grande gobbler. Don't even bother asking me where.

another fine feller who'd offered to help me find a bird in his home state. I arrived at 2 a.m., walked in to where Rhett had told me to go, and although I didn't hear any gobbling at dawn, I pulled the trigger at 8:49 on a bird that woke me up with one of those funny Rio gobbles uttered while coming to find the supposed hen (me) who'd initially promised solicitous nothings, but who had then begun snoring, instead. After that kill (my fifth total tom from Texas) I spent a couple more fruitless days trying to fill more of the three tags remaining in my wallet, but when that didn't happen I left for Arizona.

I arrived at the San Carlos Reservation as the clock struck high noon of the very first day when my permit became valid. Within an hour of driving around, I'd found fresh strut marks in a dusty back road and set up my camp nearby. Then, I walked back to where I'd earlier brushed out all of that previously found turkey sign with a cedar bough, and climbed directly uphill about a hundred yards. Finding a comfortable tree, I settled in to wait and listen. As the afternoon progressed silently, I was more or less just hoping to hear gobbling at dusk than I was actively "hunting," but I occasionally yelped on my pot call just in case.

At precisely 4:40 p.m. a nearby tom blasted out a gobble to one of my yelps, and in doing so, he just about scared the crap out of me! For some reason, I just wasn't expecting it. However, that bird never gobbled again and I heard no drumming to indicate his presence. Not even additional light calling from me could provoke an answer, and long, long minutes dragged by. In fact, an hour and a half passed with no hint whatsoever that there'd ever even been a turkey anywhere in the entire state. I almost questioned in my mind whether I'd really heard the gobble, or not.

I'd just about given up hope and come to terms with the reality that I'd somehow run the turkey off and thus blown a golden opportunity to kill an Arizona Merriam's on the first day, when suddenly, I heard the very distinct sound of wing tips dragging in rocky soil and the loud pulmonic huff of a drumming tom. Moments later there were suddenly two toms in front of my gun barrel, and seconds after that, I was standing on the neck of one of them. A couple of times in my life I've witnessed mortally hit turkeys shedding feathers in bulk, and this happened to be one of them. By the time that tom had stopped all of his flopping about, there were feathers *everywhere*! He'd released nearly all of his main tail feathers and coverts, as well as several of his wing primaries and secondary's. The ground was also littered by what looked to be hundreds of body feathers! It was really weird, but at least I had my tom and I was tickled pink. While driving back out of the reservation I passed a large group of locals camped in teepees and having some sort of a gathering complete with folks dancing around bonfires. A huge part of me wanted to ask for permission to sit in observance or even join in, but the cautious side of my brain won out and kept me driving. I just wasn't sure as a white man how much my presence would be tolerated.

Another quick trip to Stephen Spurlock's leased farm in Colorado followed, but I didn't find the high turkey numbers encountered during my previous two trips there. Oh, there were still turkeys around, but nothing like the first

I had to put a lot of his feathers back in place for his photo from the San Carlos Reservation, and you can see that he's still missing the tail coverts.

trip, when the whole river bottom had erupted in gobbling at first light. Then, when I finally did shoot a tom late in the day, I was somewhat disappointed to discover that he had no spurs, whatsoever. I know that you can't eat spurs, but there's just something that doesn't sit well with my psyche anytime this happens. I've killed spur-less toms of every subspecies, and while the hunts themselves which culminated in said birds suffer no dissolutions of quality in my memories, there is always just the hint of disappointment whenever I walk up to a fine, noble adversary and see slick legs. I almost feel sorry for the bird in how his contemporaries throughout life must have needled and made fun of him. Yeah, right....size doesn't matter, my ass!

Now needing only two birds (Wyoming and Missouri) to complete my fourth Super Slam, I headed on up to Wyoming once again. The previous year I'd found a new area in which I was really happy, so it was with a high degree of anxiousness and anticipation that I pulled back into the isolated valley and set up camp after dark. I was also a bit stressed though, because Trevor Bays was out on the east coast trying to finish up the last of his birds needed to complete his own Super Slam, and he'd called me that very day to let me know of his progress. He was now down to only one state: Rhode

Island. Trev was wanting badly for me to come out and be there with him when the final bird fell, so I'd told him to slow down long enough for me to get my Wyoming tom and then I would head eastward. Originally, I'd intended to hit Missouri after Wyoming and thus completely finish up my fourth Slam, but now it felt more important to forego meeting my own goals until the following year. Trev is the closest thing that I've got to having a son, and not only would it mean a lot to him that I was there to share in his moment of glory, but it would mean a lot to me, too. However, telling Trevor Bays to slow down is like telling a Jack Russell Terrier to not chase squirrels. The boy is downright *lethal* on turkeys!

Just as expected, I heard several toms gobbling at daybreak and closed in on the closest one before he flew to ground. I was so close that I could hear him drumming on the limb, but there were also numerous vocal hens all around him and when they all pitched down, the evil girl turkeys quite promptly took their boyfriend out over hill and yon and away from me, as Merriam's turkeys often do. Dangit; that subspecies of the wild turkey aggravates me to no end!

Of course I followed along, but then I bumped the whole flock once I'd caught up. Picking another gobbling tom in the distance, I headed in that direction and did the same thing. And then, I did it a third time before trudging back to the van and breaking for lunch. There's no doubt that my sense of anxiety to get a bird and get gone was making me press the issue, and I'd suffered for it. Yes; aggressive moves and countermoves are certainly a favored tactic of mine, but all morning long I had failed to read the situation properly and act accordingly. I needed to slow down and hunt like it wasn't my first time, and to use my brain instead of my feet to get things done. It was time to sit my sorry butt down while the chili was heating on the stove and give myself a good talking-to.

For the afternoon hours I picked a spot near the original roost, where there had seemed to be a good amount of morning gobbling being done on a regular basis, and I intended to stay right there until dark. At 2 o'clock I called in a single hen, and at 3:30 I had three other hens come to search me out. Then, at 5 p.m. a flock of six more hens approached, but there wasn't a tom accompanying any of those girls. I didn't hear a single gobble all afternoon until 5:30, when two separate birds piped up, but they were both so far away as to be entirely out of the picture and I didn't even bother heading in their direction. Besides, I felt certain that my original tom would roost in the general area where I was sitting. There were just too many hens around to expect anything less, and at dusk yet another hen approached me like she was late for a date before hurriedly flying up into a nearby ponderosa. No toms followed her, though. However, as I was walking out I made one gobble with an owl hoot. Several more gobbles followed, by at least two different toms, and after hustling to close the distance, I got their roost locale pinpointed quite well.

I hadn't heard any hens near those toms, but in the morning it was quite a different tale as *multiple* turkeys kee-kee'd, yelped, whined, clucked, and purred all around the two toms which were by then gobbling their brains out. My prior roosting session had afforded me the knowledge needed to get in tight long before any of that racket had begun, but despite numerous subsequent up-close encounters with hens as they passed by my position after flying down, I never even caught a glimpse of either tom. After everyone was on the ground it didn't take them long to group up a hundred yards away from me and promptly do as they had done the day before by departing for lands unknown, leaving me once again alone and in the lurch.

Just as I had done the day before, I followed dutifully along after the toms had given away their position with more gobbling, but this time I did it at a more conscientiously controlled pace and I spooked no turkeys in the process. In fact, I spent the morning in close proximity to that flock and none of them were ever the wiser about my presence. Despite much better patience and more thoroughly thought out maneuvers, I came up with the same frustrating results of nothing but close encounters and near misses to show for my efforts. The only good part was I hadn't screwed up and scared the bejesus out of any turkeys. Thus, the day's lunchtime pep talk contained far fewer harsh admonishments and mostly consisted of simply reminding myself to stay positive and bide my time. I knew I'd hunted well all morning, and it had only been by chance and circumstance time and time again that there wasn't a turkey already hanging in the tree beside my van with a validated tag wrapped around his scaly leg.

Returning to that same roost site for the afternoon hunt, I built a great pine-bough blind looking out over the gentle hillside where the flock had assembled after flydown, and then I settled in behind a couple of hen dekes alongside a strutter. I felt sure that the flock would spend the night nearby, or at least within earshot, so I occasionally called and kept alert for their approach. But, despite my vigilance, I never saw a single bird or heard the first turkey sound of any kind over the course of the entire afternoon. As the final hour of legal shooting time neared, my attention was averted for several minutes while I answered a few texts on the phone, and when I idly picked my head up and glanced back at my surroundings, there were seven hens and a tom already in amongst the decoys. I had no idea where they came from, but they were just suddenly *there*!

After taking out the short-spurred adult tom with a load of Winchester Supreme 1- 3/4 oz. 5's upside his head, I leisurely returned to my campsite and packed up for the long drive out east. A mile down the road I came upon a gobbler who wasn't the least bit concerned about my presence, even though he was feeding only 15 yards from my vehicle. In fact, I stopped and looked him over with binoculars for probably five full minutes, and then I drove further down the road, turned around, and came back to check him out again. The reason why I found that tom to be so intriguing? It was because that old rascal had a big, thick double beard and spurs of unbelievable length. He was a STUD! I would guess that the scimitars on his legs reached every bit of an inch and a half, but it wouldn't surprise me if they didn't stretch to 1- 5/8" or more. I didn't even know that Merriam's could grow such weaponry! He was glorious, but Wyoming has a one tom limit, so all I could do was admire him and hope to encounter his likes again with my next planned return in 2023.

The distance from Sundance, Wyoming to North Kingston, Rhode Island (where my friend John P Smith lives) is listed on the computer as 1,948 miles, and the time to drive there is estimated to be about 28 hours. That's if you're being refueled by a tanker truck running alongside, your body doesn't need any sleep whatsoever, and there's a Texas Catheter strapped to your leg so that you can simply pee into a bottle at your feet without needing to stop along the way. None of those things were true in my case, so it took me about 36 hours to get there. By then Trev had been waiting three days for my arrival, and believe me, that's a painful eternity for The Weedhopper to go without killing a turkey! But, he'd somehow resisted the urge to get things done before I could join him, and thus I was able to tag along with my little buddy on his quest to complete the final leg of his U.S. Super Slam. When (and I use that word instead of "if" for good reason) successful, it would make him the youngest (at the time) hunter to achieve that goal, being as how he was just 28 years old.

I've spent a lot of time hunting on Rhode Island's public lands, and I can

*The King of the Court was courting seven hens
shortly before this picture was taken.*

unequivocally say that they are some of the toughest places in the country to kill a turkey. Not only are there few actual birds, but the ones on those grounds get hunted hard. Additionally, there are a wide range of people using the properties for everything from bicycling to nature walks and about everything else in between that you could even imagine. Thus, unintentional hunter interference is almost a given. Heck; one time I was watching a couple of hens in a field when I heard car doors slam back at the parking area. A few moments later the turkeys alerted and ran off as two young women in long flowing dresses proceeded to walk out into the very middle of that 40 acre patch of grass and spread out blankets upon which to stand. Then, they began twirling around in free-form dance without any music while periodically raising their arms to the sky and chanting admonitions to the Mother Earth. It was bizarre, but only on a relative scale, for I've also had horse drawn wagons come creaking and groaning right through the middle of the woods with no discernable road or trail anywhere nearby; I've had entire groups of loud-talking birders come hiking through a setup in trying to find the elusive wild turkeys that they'd just heard calling (me); I've even had an entire troupe of boy scouts move in and set up a bivouac camp right under the very roost trees where they'd moments earlier unbeknownst run off a pair of hard-gobbling toms.

However, I've also had the occasional great hunt and I've shot some tremendous toms on a couple of different WMA's. It always feels really, really good when you can find success in that tough state, and that was exactly what Trevor Bays was hoping to do. We based our operation out of John's house trailer. JP, or The JP'er is one of the most interesting, good-hearted, caring and compassionate folks I've ever met, and I love him like a brother from another mother. He's also quite a character, and although he'd never met Trevor before I put them in touch, he'd unquestioningly taken the boy in and shown him around before I could join them. After a day of hanging out with JP, Trevor had jokingly texted me, "What have you gotten me into?"

Well, by the time I got there those two clowns were thick as thieves, and our time together was one continuous good time. I don't think there was ever a minute when we weren't all smiles and laughing at any one thing or a dozen. But, we also had a purpose for being there, so while Giovanni (his real name) was working at his job as a master carpenter, Trev and I planned to head out each day to a large WMA where I've killed the majority of my RI birds. Forgive me if I don't disclose its name, but tough noogies…some things are best left unsaid. Go find your own danged turkeys!

On the first day we actually heard several gobbling birds but only succeeded in calling in a group of jakes that really did it right and begged to be treated like adult toms. Luckily for them, their teenage status kept them safe from harm. However, a far distant gobbler which had ripped it really well early-on warranted further investigation, and even though he'd quieted down by the time we figured out how to access his home turf, we learned some valuable lessons about where and how to focus our attention the following day.

But, as turkeys often do, he wasn't exactly in that same spot come gobbling time of Day 2. He was definitely within earshot though, and hammered it nearly as much as the morning prior. The tough part was in getting to him. First, we had to fight through a huge tangle of mountain laurel, then cross a deep stream, climb up and down a couple hills, and fight through more laurel. After we got close enough to be considered "in the game," it looked like things might be easy for us because the tom gobbled at our first calls and headed in the right direction...walking casually down an old woods road alongside which we had set up in what I considered to be perfect position. We saw him coming at about a hundred yards out, and as the range between him and eternity shrank, I must admit that I was already feeling smug and anticipating the shot. In fact, I already had my fingers in my ears to muffle the gun blast when the tom abruptly turned on his heels and stepped off the road. He didn't appear in the least bit alerted, but for some unknown reason or sixth sense he just decided to change his course. I thought that he was close enough to kill, and told Trevor so, but my boy declined the shot out of concern that the range was too great and he might cripple such a fine gobbler. That was the last thing either of us wanted, so I didn't question his decision for even a second.

The tom continued in our general direction, but now he was circling us through heavy brush and never again presented a good shot opportunity. He also never got any closer than he'd been while standing on the woods road, but not much further away either, as he just eased along silently. Then, after his circling maneuver had brought him right back up onto the road but behind us at about 60 yards, he blasted out a gobble. Being as how we were now facing directly away from him, there was no need to call and risk him coming in from our backside, so we just watched him over our shoulders as he resumed his leisurely stroll right down the road and away from us. Occasionally he would gobble, but there was nothing to do but listen and silently curse this spate of bad luck as he faded away.

Trevor was heartbroken as he began second-guessing his decision to not shoot, but I consoled and assured him that this was only our *first* opportunity at this tom. If Trev had been uncomfortable with the shot presented, then he'd done the right thing. Simple as that. We certainly weren't done, by any means!

After pacing off the distance to where the tom had been standing (37 yards), we switched our setup location to the opposite side of the woods road and in a spot which offered even better cover and a more unobstructed view of the surrounding area. I just had a strong feeling that this bird wasn't done with us, and while we hadn't called since the tom first appeared, I couldn't rid myself of the premonition that the sneaky devil might be coming back to look for the elusive and sultry-sounding hen that had obviously piqued his interest.

Ten minutes later I spotted the tom down through the woods as he cut across the edge of a bright green food plot which was about a hundred yards away from us. He didn't answer my subsequent soft yelp, but he definitely turned in our direction and came easing along…this time through the woods and not up the roadway. He was also being very coy and looked extremely leery; stopping often to stand tall and use those powerful trouble-detectors on each side of his head to scan carefully for long minutes at a time before once again taking a few tentative steps. However, those steps continued to be in a favorable direction for the two nervous hunters tucked in tight against a form-obscuring deadfall, and every time I purred ever-so-quietly on the old Cane Creek glass call, his head would turn bright red. Finally, at 40 yards he gobbled once again and broke into a strut, and it was right at that moment when I knew in my heart that we had won the battle and Trevor was about to do what Trevor does so well. When the old patriarch stood tall at 25 yards, he forthwith died a glorious warrior's death worthy of his stature and elegance.

I cannot adequately describe the wave of emotions which nearly overwhelmed me at that moment. It was a mixture of giddy happiness, coupled with relief and about a million other feelings, and I knew the same was true for Trevor, times ten. We were both almost brought to tears by the whole flush of endorphins racing through our hearts and minds. In short, it was an incredible experience, and will remain one of my most enduring, endearing, and cherished memories of my entire turkey hunting life. I think only someone who has "been there/done that" can fully appreciate just how deeply the feelings well up in a feller upon taking that final tom of a U.S. Super Slam, and I'm so extremely glad that I was there for my buddy Trevor Bays at his very special moment.

Over the course of many, many, many proud instances in our time together on this earth, I don't believe that I've ever been more proud of Trevor Bays as I was right then. He had performed admirably and with honor once again and as usual. I've watched this man bloom during his entire lifetime, and

Trevor Bays joins "The Club."

Trev's very special bird had a monstrous tail fan.

one thing that stands out in my mind is how he reacted after the final trigger pull. No whooping and hollering or making a fool of himself. No false acts of overblown glee intended for the camera and his social media following, but rather, an honest admiration and respect for his fallen opponent, and some deep introspection. That other kinda stuff has always been a real turnoff for me on so many of the videos you see these days, and I guess that's because

I view every moment spent in the wilds of nature as if I was an invited guest to a sacred place. Thus, I tend to act accordingly and try to behave as if I've been there before. It's appropriate not only for the time and place, but out of respect for the glorious game animal or fish at your feet, who will no longer be free to live their life. Oh, Trevor and I hugged, laughed, and chitter-chatted for many long minutes afterward in telling and retelling each other's views and remembrances of the hunt's particulars, but we did so in hushed tones and whispers. It's all about respect and reverence. In other words, having grace.

Besides that, this hunt itself was a classic from start to finish. We'd initially worked hard to find birds and then worked even harder physically to reach them. Then, we'd come oh-so-agonizingly close to making the kill, only to suffer abject disheartenment and disappointment at losing out on the opportunity at the very last instant and thinking that the chance for glory was over and gone forever. But, we'd picked our heads back up and stayed positive, and were eventually rewarded with a second chance at an opponent who was much more than worthy to walk away the winner, and yet, who then provided us with a nerve-wracking battle that could have gone south at any moment. We had needed to summon up all of our inner strength, patience, and calling skills to convince him that we were the real thing, and then, without using any decoys, make him seek out a hen where there wasn't really one. Finally, we'd let him get in close enough for a 'sure thing" clean and humane kill. Trevor and I were lucky and blessed to win the battle, and I was humbled and proud to be there.

With the prime objective bird now down, we turned our attention to finding a turkey or two for me. In the days before my arrival, Trevor had been in contact with a couple of the top wildlife officers in the state, and they'd given him a few hints for private lands on which to look. One of them was a long narrow soybean stubble field where a strutting tom had been spotted frequently, and in driving the roads surrounding that property, we could find no posted signs which prohibited hunting. An attempt to contact the absentee landowner was unsuccessful, but the CO had explained in no uncertain terms that Rhode Island's laws stated they we could not be given a ticket for trespassing if the land wasn't conspicuously posted. Finding a neighbor lady who's house was close to the back corner of the field, she answered our query of whether she ever heard gobbling back in there with, "Oh sure. Right over *there*," while pointing with a finger.

"When was the last time you heard them," I asked?

"This morning...right *there*." Once again, she gestured in a way leaving no uncertainty as to where the birds liked to hang out at the very back corner of the stubble field. She said we were welcome to park in her driveway.

The next morning we snuck in real early and were sitting tucked up tight against a pile of logs felled and stacked long-ago but never utilized or hauled away when the first gobble blasted out from very close range. A second tom hammered out in answer to his buddy, and immediately Trevor motioned to me (we were separated by about 15 feet) that he could see both toms in their respective roost trees. From my position I couldn't see either of them. One tom was only 60 yards away, while the other was about a hundred, and after quite a few gobbles ripped out over a half an hour or so, they pitched down and landed even closer to us. Once on the ground, both toms answered my very first call in unison and came right on in like they'd read the script of how most of us would envision the perfect turkey hunt progressing. Then, I promptly missed the lead bird. I have absolutely no idea how, as I was resting my gun atop one of the logs and the tom was standing perfectly still and tall at about 25 yards, but I sure as hell did. Maybe the manufacturer forgot to put pellets in that particular shell?! I didn't even dare look at Trevor, because I knew that I would be able to plainly read the disappointment in me on his face.

Rather than fly or run away in panic, the tom merely walked back towards his buddy who'd been lagging behind, and then they drifted off in the direction of the roost. I kept catching glimpses of the duo down through the timber as they went, and while I was then taking a moment to hang my head in abject shame and total disgust with myself for having blown such a great opportunity, both birds suddenly gobbled at a real hen off to their side! Obviously these turkeys weren't too terribly alarmed by my errant marksmanship, because they then began gobbling regularly. Only then was I finally able to glance over at my partner and look him in the eye. Then, after he grinned back at me, I motioned that we should just sit tight and see how things developed. I had a good feeling about this spot, and about what might eventually happen if we would just bide our time.

An hour later I saw a hen *running* towards us through the timber, very shortly after I'd finally uttered my first light yelp on a Cane Creek glass. A second hen soon joined her, and then I spotted two big tail fans trailing behind. The hens commenced to pecking around on the ground right in front of us, and a few minutes later, one of the toms eased in close enough that I could consider killing him. However, I was a bit nervous after missing earlier. Blissfully, this time when I pulled the trigger a tom piled up in a heap. Of course, I expected all the other turkeys to flee, but none of them even acted very alarmed and almost immediately went right back to doing what they'd been doing…the hens contentedly feeding, while their boyfriend kept trying to impress them with how beautiful he was. I hadn't even considered the possibility of doing such a thing, but at that point I got to wondering if it was legal to fill both of my tags on the same day, and when I asked Trev, he pulled out his smart phone to look it up. At just about the time that the other tom was moving into gun range, Trev whistled lightly to get my attention and then gave me the thumbs up, so I promptly put the second tom to flopping in the leaves. Wow! What a turnaround! This was yet another hunt featuring a plentitude of emotions: excitement, dread, anxiety, suspense, elation, surprise, and finally, relief and joy.

After missing one of these toms an hour earlier, I doubled up on them.

The next morning we were joined by the infamous John P Smith in guiding the lovely Miss Maddie Prouix, who is President of the RI NWTF, as well as being head of the RI DNR Hunter Ed Department. JP had access to some private land that he swore held lots of birds, and sure enough, at dawn we heard several distant gobblers announcing the day. None were on the small piece of ground where we could hunt, but I didn't care; not after stepping into the woods and seeing that the leaves under the oak trees looked like street sweepers had driven through there the previous day!

Once we'd gotten set up in good hides (Trev sitting with The JP'er while I shared a tree with Miss Maddie), The Weedhopper and I got busy on our calls. We soon had turkeys fired up and gobbling well, but from far away, so Trev then walked out to the edge of our property line and began pouring lighter fluid to the embers. The boy is *good* on a mouthcall, and it wasn't long before we could tell that a whole group of gobblers was advancing rapidly toward his sharp cutts and yelps. I estimated that there were at least four toms thundering through the woods, but one of them was ahead of his buddies by a hundred yards or more when he practically ran into our small decoy spread in full strut. Maddie promptly missed him…twice!

For the second day in a row Trev and I then witnessed a tom just-missed walk calmly away to join back up with his fellow turkeys. Despite the two loud shotgun blasts, all those other birds were still coming towards us and ripping out gobbles almost ballistically, and when they got to about 75 yards away, I could count five longbeards in sight. They weren't the only ones, either: there were another two or three nearby which were gobbling hard, as well! Seldom in my life have I witnessed so many hot toms gobbling their brains out in a confined area, all while me, Trev, and John continued to work them into a gobbling frenzy with various calls, including JP with his natural voice. What a glorious way to start the day!

Maddie made good on her third shot of the morning, and then she did likewise on her fourth in taking a second tom. I think at that point she had only killed one other turkey in her lifetime (a jake the previous spring), but now she'd just doubled up on a pair of fantastic longbeards, and to say that she, as well as her three guides, were jacked-up beyond all reason would not do the joyous celebration justice! Upon leaving the woods, the first thing that we did was to head for an ice cream shop to celebrate and toast her successes.

My van was undergoing repairs by one of JP's mechanic buddies, so when Trev headed to NY I had no choice but to wait around until it was finished. That took three more days, during which I had no wheels to get around on and nothing to

Maddie Prouix outshines the turkeys, the flowers, and her guides JP and Trevor.

We got Giovanni to lower his mask just long enough to expose that pretty face with Trevor.

do but watch movies and twiddle my thumbs at Mark Plante's (another great friend who is also John's neighbor) home while he and JP were off at work each day. But, finally the repairs were done and I hit the road to meet up with Trevor in New York.

Jake Bays was due to undergo an aortal aneurism operation the week after my arrival, but before that occurred Trevor and I teamed up to call birds in for Wheeler Brunschmid (2), Cameron Yerton, Brandon Czepiel, and Preston (Hambone) Riley, as well as one each for ourselves. On the day of Jake's surgery, while Trev was at the hospital, I hunted with Preston again and we had a rather unique experience that I'll cover herewith.

As we had determined the previous spring, Hambone isn't real patient. He's a tremendous hunter though, and is successful on many, many turkeys for himself, friends, and family members every year. His springtime numbers are really quite impressive, and he's equally as adept at accounting for big stacks of waterfowl every fall and winter. But, I enjoy giving him a hard time because I'm not a real huge fan of the "reaping" method which he often-times utilizes on gobblers. In fairness, his home turf is primarily agricultural ground, so turkeys are usually visible as they strut around in open fields all day long. That makes them highly susceptible to flashing a tail fan from over a slight incline to invoke a jealousy-enraged charge.

Well, Preston took me to a spot where he'd been seeing two big toms hanging out on a disked hillside. We set up along the edge of the wood line above it, with a small flock of decoys spread out in the field, and the toms promptly gobbled directly uphill of us from their roost. However, on that day they decided to exit the scene soon after flydown by going further uphill and away from the field. A couple of hens did come towards my calling, but they eventually wandered off into some more fields down in the valley below us. Did I mention that Preston isn't the most patient of turkey hunters? It wasn't long before his feet were itching to go someplace else, so while he went out to begin gathering up decoys, I started packing gear into our vests and readying for the move.

Suddenly, I heard Hambone hiss out a warning that the hens below us were coming back. He immediately flattened himself out on the plowed earth right beside my strutter and began watching them advance from under the decoy's fanned tail. Meanwhile, I spotted the other turkeys which had been gobbling at us all morning, and forthwith whistled my own urgent warning. At the top of the tall ridge line south of the blind stood a tom and three jakes peering intently down at our decoys spread out in their favorite field. It didn't take them long to decide that my fake flock was something that needed a closer inspection, so they were soon picking their way down the very steep and cleared slope of a buried gas line.

Ignoring the hens coming from below, Preston scooched his prone body around on the ground so that he was now facing the descending gobblers head-on, and with the strutter deke shielding him from their view. When I texted him to "spin that decoy," he began slowing manipulating it by hand so that the fanned tail took on the appearance of what a real tom might be doing to show off his colors for a nearby hen. To be honest, the motion looked pretty darned good from my perspective, and it obviously did so to the approaching tom, because he quickened his pace a bit and put a little distance between himself and the jakes. The teenagers seemed a little intimidated by the strutter and shied away a bit (it couldn't have possibly been the camo'd human being lying in the decoy spread that worried them!), but the tom bought into the whole ruse heart and soul. I didn't dare let him get too close or even remotely in-line with my buddy before I put the tom to sleep in a permanent "dirt nap." I wonder what he'd have done to Hambone if I'd simply declined to take the shot...

This bird was the 12th tom taken or called in for others in the last seven days, but we weren't done. The next morning Trev, Hambone, and myself guided for Cody Baker and his girlfriend Nicole. Cody is wheelchair-bound from a motocross wreck, but that guy has about as much hunting passion as anyone I've ever met. His track-operated chair is really cool, and goes just about anywhere that it's called to go. And where we went on that day was to one of Preston's honey-holes of all honey-holes. At the morning's ultimate and amazing conclusion we had five big strutters in the decoy spread, along with numerous hens, when Cody and Nicole doubled up. Then, the following day Nicole shot a bird that didn't die outright, and Trevor had to chase the jake down for about 500 yards before tackling it. That made 15 birds in nine days, counting Rhode Island, but again, we weren't done!

After I called in a tom the next day for Trev with his brother Oria tagging along for the show, the sun glinting in his scope caused him to pass up the shot. That put an end to an "in a row" streak, but that mattered nothing to either one of us. The important thing was to get right back on track, and the following day we did exactly that with yet another amazing hunt where Trev, Zach Wyss, and Wade King all killed birds.

So ended the most successful New York season I've ever experienced and not even dared to dream about being dreamed about. In ten days there, we'd accounted for 31 toms called "into camp," with 14 kills. Absolutely nothing had gone wrong the whole time. The stars were aligned perfectly. Here are a few pics:

Wheeler Brunschmid got the New York onslaught off to a rousing start.

Trevor Bays, me, and Cameron Yerton had a very good morning!

Trevor, me, and Preston Riley experienced an incredible hunt with Nicole and Cody.

Trev, Zach Wyss, me, and Wade King on yet another 3-bird day.

2022

When Trevor left for Kansas I accompanied Hambone over to Massachusetts, where we stayed with Cody and Nicole. On the first day there I ventured out solo and took an excellent tom on a nerve-wracking, adrenalin-pumping hunt conducted on a WMA, and then the following morning Cody took us to a great farm where Preston and I doubled up. From there, Hambone and I took off separately and met back up at Bill George's camp in Pennsylvania, where I shot a tom on the second day there. This bird was number 23 for the month…and it was still only May 21st! Four days later Preston shot a bird that gobbled like an adult, came in to my calls like an adult, and died like an adult, too. But, we'd only been able to see the bird's head up over an old piece of rusted farm machinery in the woods as he approached our hide, and despite our thoughts and wishes to the contrary, he ended up being a jake. Now May 25th, that made 24 gobblers killed or called in or others during the month, while only hunting a total of 19 days. However, that's when I started accompanying Bill George afield every day.

Now, Bill and I have hunted a lot together, and we've killed a number of turkeys over the years. He is one of the most fun-loving, good-hearted folks that I've ever met. Besides that, there's always a silly smile on his face, and I'm proud to say that I love him like a brother. I would do anything for the man, because I know that he'd do absolutely anything for me (or anyone else). That being said, there's a reason why I once bought him a t-shirt that I'd ordered through the mail which was imprinted on the front side with the image of a washing machine's inner workings, underneath the words, "The Agitator." You see; Bill likes to pick at any issue of which he's become concerned; much like a 4-year-old would pick at a booger, or how you might relentlessly pick at an itchy scab. Friend or foe matters not; he'll dig to the very core. It's his nature. He's also deaf as a stone, and can't hear himself fart. That means when we're hunting together he doesn't hear what I hear, so most of the time he doesn't understand why I'm doing what I'm doing. I can't stop to explain every little move which needs to be made, so he constantly questions my motives and strategies. It drives me crazy. Couple all of that with him being about as stealthy as a rhino in a china shop. I guess it's because he can't hear sticks breaking underfoot that he's constantly breaking them with his feet. Heck; sometimes when he's following behind and I hear sticks popping, I would swear that he's carrying extras around in his pockets and breaking them just for fun! Because of his lack of stealth and general awareness in the woods, I sometimes reference my dear old friend as "Bumblefoot." Again, I love the man, but hunting with him can be a great challenge both to our success, and to my sanity.

Well, it took until the final day of the season before I was able to call in some jakes deep in the heart of National Forest lands for Bill, but he made the shot opportunity count. That bird was the 25th kill during the month of May alone, and although my own personal kills had been only average for the year, this last jake ended up being the record-smashing 50th turkey that I'd watched die in 2022! I'd hunted 70 days in total to get there, in 11 states, and called in at least 121 toms to under 40 yards. In short, it had been one phenomenal spring season, with long streaks of successful days where seemingly nothing could go wrong. Florida and New York had served up unheard-of-before numbers, but everywhere else had been good, too. Still, I think the highlight of the year was being able to watch and participate as Trevor Bays entered into "The Club" of successful U.S. Super Slammers. And, on a personal note, I was now only one single state (MO) shy of my own fourth Super Slam, and another four birds from acquiring a fifth. Those remaining states were AZ, NV, WY, and NC. As usual, by the time the 2022 season came to a close I'd already long been dreaming and scheming of finishing those goals up in 2023, and I could hardly contain my excitement as I began the preparations in earnest. But, you know what "they" say about counting your chickens before the eggs hatch…

Preston and me with our Massachusetts birds and Cody Baker.

Chapter 6

2023

In September of 2022 I had four big stones (each greater than 10 mm) removed from my left kidney. This was the second time in my life that I'd had to endure such a horrendous operation, and if you don't know much about it or have never suffered through it, I'll describe herewith the procedure: they take a jack-hammer, a ShopVac, and a 3-man wrecking crew in through the smallest orifice of your body and then the Doctor pulverizes the stone(s) into small(er) pieces. Then, he sucks up as many chunks of rock as possible with the vacuum before crawling on out of there, leaving behind a foot-long stent that runs down the urinary tract. It helps to keep the urine flowing while you heal up. A long string attached to the stent is left dangling from your pee hole.

For the next two weeks you're supposed to drink as much water as possible and pee as often as you can endure the pain to flush everything out. And I say "endure" because there's no other way to describe the act. Every single time you take a leak, it is *excruciatingly* painful! Blood and chunks of sharp crystals and sand come out of your body along with the pee, and the pain is so intense that it causes you to drop down and curl up on the bathroom floor in a fetal position with sweat pouring out of every pore on your body. It's absolutely horrific. And the string mentioned in the last paragraph? They use that to pull out the stent! When they do so, it feels like they're pulling your intestines out through your weiner.

Well, like I said, this was my second go-around at that carnival of fun, and it was bad. But, at least my urologist is a hunter, and a great guy, and he got the stones removed. Once I was past the pain and horror of the post-surgical mess, I went ahead with planning out my springtime schedule while at the same time working to acquire more land in Florida on which to conduct guided hunts. I was hoping to eventually bring in Trevor as a partner to my "Swamp Magic Osceolas" operation, so I needed to ramp up the number of clients.

Then, after an MRI and a follow-up visit to his office in January, Dr. Kitley told me that there was a tumor growing on my kidney. It was about the size of a racket-ball (approximately 2-1/4 inches in diameter), and it needed to come out. There was a high probability that it was cancerous.

My world crashed.

Up until then, I'd thought that I was invincible. I'd thought that cancer was something *other* people got. Death seemed no closer in my mind than when I was a child. I had things to do; things to see; loves to love; life to live. I didn't want to die! And yet, when I checked out the survival rates of kidney cancer patients online, it didn't look good. In fact, it was downright bleak. There was a very real possibility that this thing was going to kill me.

When I asked Dr. Kitley how soon I needed to get the operation done, he told me the sooner the better. But, he admitted that the tumor was probably of a fairly slow-growing nature, so we had a little time. He'd done hundreds of these operations and felt like he could get all of the cursed thing out of me with surgery, but this wasn't something to be ignored for very long. I told him that I was willing to do whatever he said was best, and if waiting to operate increased my chances substantially of dying then I would cancel the entire turkey season altogether, but I explained that spring was my time to shine and I had some very serious plans and goals which I wanted to accomplish. All things being equal, I wanted to wait as long possible without jeopardizing my health. He didn't want to prolong the operation until June, when turkey season would be over in entirety, but he did give me until mid-May.

Well, that meant I could get some birds killed in Florida and hopefully finish out my fourth Super Slam in Missouri. I might even be able to knock off the four other remaining states that were holding me back from that fifth Slam. Those locations were Arizona, Wyoming, Nevada, and North Carolina. I felt like I had a ticking time bomb in my guts, and I was a nervous wreck in the months leading up to the start of turkey season. I told very few people of my condition, as I didn't want my Mom to find out. She's a worry-wart, and at 87 years old, I thought she might worry herself to death. There was no way that I would let my cancer kill us both!

I had already set an ambitious itinerary in Florida with about 30 clients lined up, and once again Will Grubbs kicked things off with another Love Boat cruise. This would be the last year of his eligibility for the youth season, so he wanted to go out on a bang by shooting a pair of toms if the opportunity presented itself. It did, and he killed a fine pair of gobblers with a single shot from his little .410.

On opening day of the regular season I guided four guys while Trevor took out three. All of his fellas tagged out that first morning and one of them shot two birds, while two of my guys killed toms and another of them missed. Six toms and a miss in one day was a pretty darned good way to start things off, but the pace didn't slow down much afterwards and by April 9th we'd accounted for 30 Osceolas between us. Trevor and I had led our clients on lots of tremendous hunts, where they'd shot a metric shit-ton of awesome gobblers, and we'd made a whole bunch of new friends along the way (which is, in my opinion, one of the best by-products of guiding). We ended up with a 96.7% success rate; just missing out on the perfect mark because one fella could only hunt for two days. There's no doubt in my mind that given one more day, we'd have gotten him a bird, too!

The folks back at our Swarp Camp (so-named by West Virginians LT Pack and Joe Ross) were also experiencing a banner year, and there were lots of turkeys recorded on the tally board. This camp has continued to grow and flourish for many years, with Bill George adding new gadgets and accoutrements every spring to make the whole experience something special for everyone whom we welcome into the fold...which is, basically, anyone who walks up and starts talking turkey. Camp now features hot water on demand for the shower and the kitchen sink, two ovens, a gas grill and a Blackstone griddle, a long stainless steel table and multiple stainless steel storage cabinets holding all the cooking pots/pans/skillets we could ever need, etc., and all this housed under 1,000 square feet of circus-tent space to shelter us from sun or rain. Every night there are delicious communal meals served at our big tables, and at all hours of the day you're likely to pull in and find laughter and animated talk about everything under the sun except politics. That subject was strictly taboo. We're just a group of good friends enjoying our time out in the wilds of Florida and sharing a love of wild turkeys and everything about them, and we consider ourselves family; one and all.

I'd been so busy guiding that I never even had a chance to pick up a gun, but that didn't matter to me one iota. At 63 years of age and in my 34th Florida season, I'd already killed enough Osceolas that if I were to never shoot another, I was perfectly fine with it. However, the thought did cross my mind a time or ten that my pending kidney issue might make the "never killing another one" part a very real possibility in a manner unimagined previously and totally unwanted. That was a very sobering thought. Still, I'd watched a bunch of fine Osceola gobblers flopping in the sand, so it wouldn't have been fair of me to ask for anything more.

Here are a few photos of our Florida fun:

Ken Greene and Doug Pickle show off one of Doug's FL birds.

Hot brownies fresh out of the oven and ice cream, washed down with ice-cold Orange Crush...not a bad way to be "roughing it" at the Green Swamp!

Tim Conley and LT Pack on a foggy morning double.

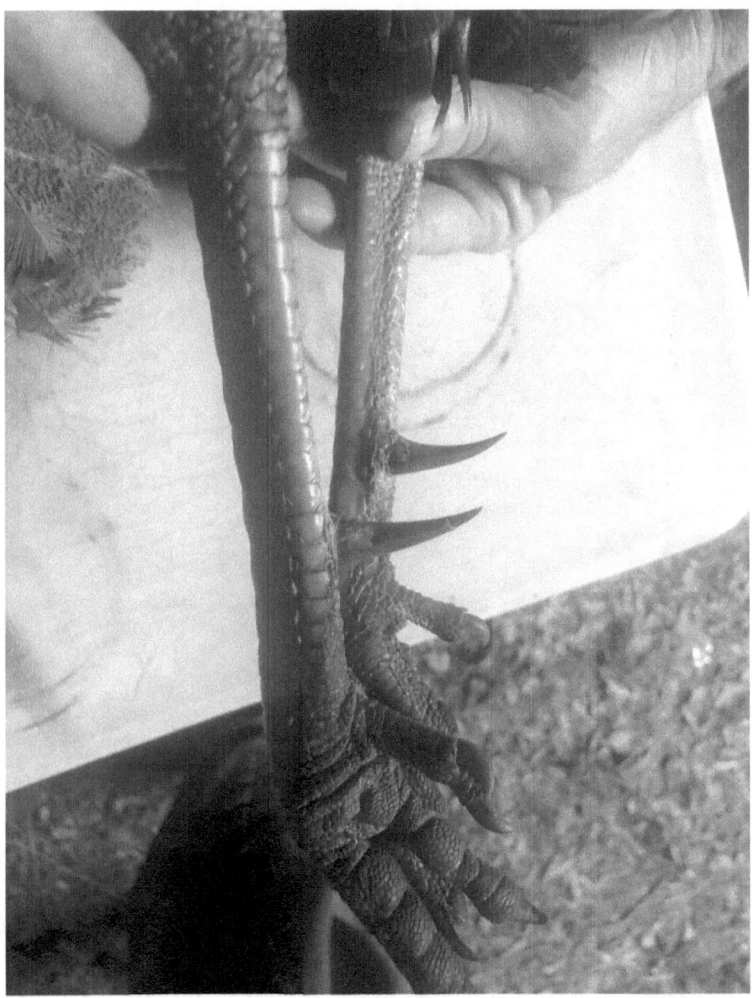

Trevor Bays killed a stud Osceola on public ground.

Every year we celebrate Willard Reedy's birthday. Wife Betty is ready for cake!

Tim Conley in a gorgeous oak hammock. Look closely and you might see Trevor's face peeking out from behind the tree.

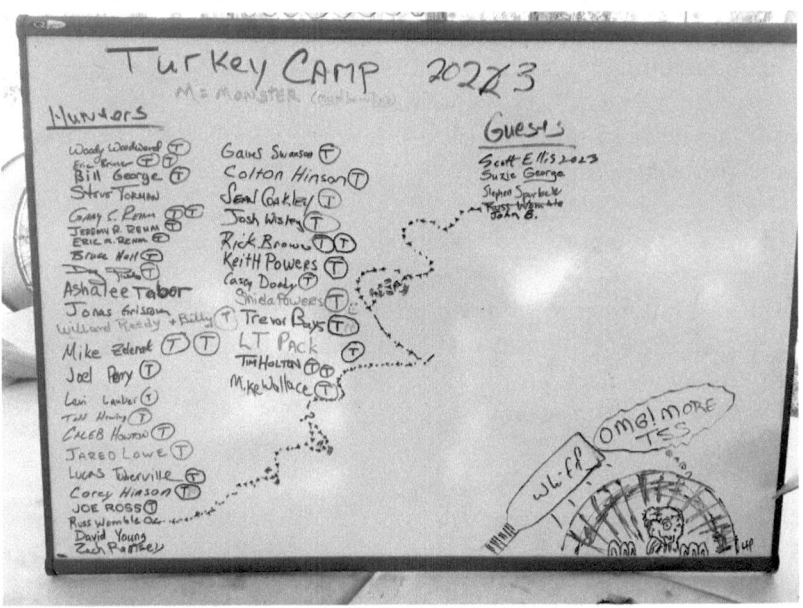

The Tally Board at Swarp Camp. Hunters and guests sign in, and if you miss a bird, you must also sign the "Whiff Bat." A circled "T" signifies a kill.

Earl Carpenter is a good friend of mine who lives in eastern North Carolina. I'd always wanted to hunt in that country anyway, so when Earl invited me out there I jumped at the chance. It would be an opportunity to knock off one of my targeted states, but I also looked at the trip as a chance to spend some time with one of the great "old-time" turkey hunters. Earl has hunted and fished with a virtual who's-who of luminaries in the outdoor world, and he has about a bazillion entertaining stories to tell...in fact, I'm surprised that we got any hunting done or turkeys killed at all, because the both of us were so busy yapping and laughing that we should've spooked off any toms goofy enough to come in to our calling.

He and I stayed for a couple days in a good turkey area near the coast with Earl's best friend Allen, who is just about the funniest guy that I've ever been around. That feller kept us entertained and fed us like kings, and I can honestly say that from the minute I arrived, I was dreading the time to leave these two fine characters simply because we were having so much fun! But, I was also there to kill a turkey, and they had a few prime spots to get that accomplished.

Several days before my arrival, that part of the state had received over six inches of rain. The rivers and bayous were flooded, and yet, they were still rising as the headwaters flowed down and backed up into the surrounding low country. Earl's favorite spot was practically underwater and getting wetter by the hour, but after hunting elsewhere in the morning and looking over a lot of other territory, he decided that we needed to give the honey-hole a looksee, so we paddled a boat over there in the afternoon.

The only ground still dry was a narrow strip between the river and a bayou, and when we got over there I was totally amazed by the number of turkey tracks in a long food plot that had been plowed just before the rains arrived. It looked like a bunch of turkeys had been conducting a square dance in the sandy soil! As we eased along deeper and deeper into the prime strip of habitat, Earl spotted a strutting tom up ahead of us and we were able to use the contour of the land and a strip of trees in the middle of the plowed dirt to move in a little closer. Then I yelped on my glass call and Earl worked his trumpet as the tom gobbled and came right in, drumming so loud that I could feel it. North Carolina tom number five was soon thereafter under foot, and his long curved spurs had me grinning like an Opossum chewing on briars. We went right back in there the next morning, even though the water had risen another foot overnight, and I shot my second long-spurred tom about a hundred yards from where the first one had died. Although it

Earl Carpenter and me with a fine North Carolina tom.

A little water can't stop turkey hunters like Earl and me.

was a rather short hunt, when we got back to the boat we could plainly see that the water had risen another six or eight inches since we got there!

Ever since I'd told Trevor about my tumor he'd been talking about how much he wanted to hunt with me that spring. I think he thought I was gonna die or something, and to be honest, I wasn't so sure he was wrong. Each of us had procured private land permits in Nevada over the winter, so that is where we rendezvoused after I'd first stopped by home to drop off my trailer full of guiding stuff prior to making another long, long drive out west. I was excited to be going there, though. My first four toms in the state had all been taken on public land, but with so many people now going for their Super Slams, I figured the odds were low of ever again drawing one of the states *four* permits allotted each year to non-residents. That's why I'd spent time writing letters to Paradise Valley landowners and then subsequently bought a permit from one of them. Back then, every ranch holding turkeys was allotted a certain number of permits to do with as they saw fit. The rancher who sold me mine asked in exchange for the turkey permit one bottle of good Irish whiskey, but I didn't think that was enough, so I'd brought him two. I hardly drink at all, so my knowledge about Irish whiskey was zero beforehand, but I'd done some research on the internet and then picked out two which caught my eye and received good reviews. One was a Redbreast 12 year-old Single Pot Still, and the other a Knappogue Castle 16 Year Old Twin Wood Single Malt. When I arrived at the ranch those bottles were very well received! Trevor had also brought him a couple bottles of some other brands, so we were quite welcomed to camp and hunt on the ranch.

Well, we heard turkeys at dawn all right, but they were about a mile away and on someone else's property. After realizing the futility of sitting on our ranch and hearing nothing close by, we decided to drive around and see what we could see. Those gobbler turds which littered the ground in the corral where we'd initially set up had caused us much excitement when spotted by flashlight beam when walking in, but after daylight arrived and we inspected them more carefully, it was plain to see that they were old and dried up. Turkeys had certainly been here at some point, but not in quite a while; probably not since the winter past. It was time to change the plan.

The funny thing about Paradise Valley permits is that while you had to have a landowner's signed form to apply for them, once that permit was in-hand, you were not limited to that particular property. Cruising around by vehicle, we not only easily located the original turkeys heard (a big flock now feeding along the road), but also their roost site of two large cottonwoods out in the middle of a large, brushy pasture. Then, we found several other smaller flocks scattered throughout the valley on other ranches. Once we'd gotten a feel for the territory, we started knocking on doors and asking permission, and by noon we'd not only learned that the ranch where the roost trees was located wouldn't allow anyone to hunt there, but that its neighboring landowners were friendly and willing to give us free reign. In fact, we acquired access on three sides of that forbidden property, with one of the fence lines strung only 75 yards away from the cottonwoods. Things definitely looked good for us at that point!

For the afternoon hunt we decided to set up about 180 yards from the cottonwoods, in a spot along a small creek bank that was littered with turkey tracks. The landowner had told us that he saw birds there all the time. It was a good spot, and at about 5:15 p.m. I called in a tom with two hens. Trev wanted me to kill my bird first so that I could scratch off another state, and that's exactly what I did. Then, we watched as a whole passel of birds began flying up into the cottonwoods an hour before what would be considered "typical" roost time. We counted at least 45 turkeys alternately flying up into the trees, flying back down, and climbing around on the limbs like a bunch of monkeys. Then, as we were plotting out our plans for the morning to set up even closer to those trees, a loud gunshot suddenly went off in the vicinity of the cottonwoods. I didn't actually see a turkey fall out of either tree, but there was no doubt that someone had snuck in and killed

Trevor Bays and me in Paradise Valley, Nevada.

a bird. All of the turkeys exploded out of there like a busted covey of quail, going in every direction, with two of them heading directly at us. Both of those birds were toms, and while the first one practically skimmed our blind to land about 20 yards behind us, the other gobbler hit the ground 10 yards in front. "What should I do," asked Trevor.

"Well, I think you should kill him," was my reply, and just like that, we had our two Nevada toms.

We both had tags for Arizona's San Carlos Indian Reservation in our pockets as well, but they weren't good for another week. Needing to fill that timeslot, we opted for California. On our first day there we hunted some public land down near where I'd hunted with Ron Gayer back in 2020. Several birds could be heard from our high ridgetop campsite, but they were all deep into private ground and had no interest in budging towards us. The rest of that day was spent cruising around and trying to locate turkeys on land where we could actually step foot, but the only birds found were on private holdings. We talked to several folks asking for permission and got turned down every single time. At one particularly good looking place there were no less than five toms within eyesight while I was speaking to the landowner, and while sympathetic to our cause and not an anti by any means, she told us that her grandchildren liked to see the turkeys so the answer was "no."

After several more hours of fruitless attempts to gain access, we decided to drive an hour south, to a spot where one of Trev's buddies had said we might do some good. I was following behind as we headed out, but at the last instant I turned back toward the property where the grandma had turned us down. There were just too many turkeys in that valley to not give it another shot, and sure enough, when I drove by her property there were still multiple toms strutting around in the yard. I did, however, notice a guy out trimming the hedges of a house diagonally across the road from there, so I stopped and walked up to his gate and we began chatting. He was real friendly, and when I inquired if he would mind if me and my buddy hunted his place, he thought for a moment and then said it wasn't something that he would ordinarily allow, but he liked me and it would be just fine if we took a few of "his" birds. According to him, there were too many of the danged things, anyway. When I told him about being turned down by the lady across the street, he said, "Oh, that's my father-in-law's wife. Don't worry about her. They don't own this side of the road." Just like that, we were "in!"

I then drove up the mountain a ways to get phone reception, where I called Trevor and told him to come right back. He couldn't believe that I'd pulled it off, but immediately turned around and headed my way. It would take 45 minutes before he could get there, so while I was waiting for his arrival I went back and chatted with the landowner, who showed me around his picturesque property. It was a magnificent farm of about a hundred acres, and they had about a bazillion chickens roaming around the yard and his small sawmill. I think they owned half a dozen dogs, too, along with some peacocks and a couple horses. And turkeys. Did I mention the turkeys? While they weren't tame birds, they weren't very wild in their behavior, either. A bunch of them roosted every night in a copse of trees right out by the gate. Then, they would spend a lot of time every day in close proximity to the house and the horse's feed lot out back. The landowner told me that we could hunt anywhere we wanted to go on his land, but to park out at the gate…right underneath the roost! He assured me that it wouldn't bother the birds in the least.

Well, most turkey hunts are tough. It's just the nature of the sport, and of the birds themselves. However, every once in a while you might luck into an easy one. I'm glad they aren't all like that, or else I would lose my interest in turkey hunting real quickly, but because the easy ones come around so infrequently, I think it's ok to simply enjoy them when they occur and appreciate them for what they are. Our days on that farm weren't exactly what one might call turkey "hunting," so much as it was a chance to study the nature of the birds,

Me and Trevor Bays with my first bird of the California excursion.

California certainly doesn't lack for beautiful scenery!

set up appropriately, take lots of great photos and video, and then gather some fine meat for the cooler.

Trev and I spent three days there. I shot three toms, but Trev only killed two; not because there wasn't an opportunity to fill his final tag, but because he got to feeling sorry for the birds and decided to ease up. That's not The Weedhopper's normal mindset, mind you, but I could certainly understand his thought processes. This was almost like shooting fish in a barrel, and there's no denying it. I could really see no need for his pity, though, since we were hearing upwards of a dozen gobbling toms each day, and like the landowner said, they needed thinned out a little bit because nobody else in the entire valley hunted them.

When we arrived at the San Carlos Reservation of Arizona my confidence was running pretty high. Trevor and I had been on a hot streak since the season started, and I felt like this would probably be another short hunt here, as well; just as it had been the previous season when I'd killed a bird only two hours after finding strut marks in a dusty road shortly after my arrival. Our permits were good for nine days, but I was hoping (and in truth, almost expecting) to be headed out for Wyoming and Missouri in a couple of days, at the most. Knocking off a tom in all three of those states would wrap up my fourth *and* fifth Super Slams before returning home for the kidney surgery scheduled on May 15th. If things went downhill after that, at least they could write of the accomplishments on my tombstone.

Due to how smoothly the season had progressed so far, I wasn't really in prime turkey hunting condition. Florida and coastal North Carolina, being flat as pancakes, offered little in the way of physical challenge, and in California we'd basically hunted from a blind less than a hundred yards from our vehicles. Oh, how times had changed from my early days of turkey hunting, when I would come into the season trim and toned from the exertions of my job as a tree planter. To put things bluntly, in 2023 I was fat and out of shape to a degree that I'd never been before. Now, those hills of the San Carlos Reservation looked pretty steep, and my aching old knees twitched in subconscious pain as I thought about having to climb them and chase after aggravating Meriam's. However, I knew that Wyoming would be even worse.

Thus, when we spotted a whole bunch of swirling and twirling strut marks while driving down a stretch of the very same road that had been so good to me the year prior, and they were located in a long flat section with gently sloping hillsides on either side, I felt pretty darned good about our chances of a quick kill with minimal pain and suffering. Boy; was I wrong!

I was much too timid initially, certain that we could just put out a flock of DSD's along the road and wait for our tom(s) to come to us, instead of chasing up and down hills in pursuit, which is what my zealous partner would've done if I hadn't been there. Hey; those tracks, droppings, and strut marks told the tale of a flock spending *lots* of time in that location, so I was really sure that my plan was a good one. And, it almost worked. We initially heard four toms gobbling at dawn, with two of them less than 200 yards behind the blind, and another pair a like distance on the opposite side of the road. At that point it seemed like we were in the catbird's seat and it was only a matter of calling a little and waiting for the inevitable turkey rendezvous to occur in front of our gun barrels.

Well, all I can say is that these birds were Meriam's. And like Meriam's anywhere that you find them, they did what they wanted to do instead of what we wanted them to do. In essence, we wasted most of the first day sitting in one spot and waiting for prospects that never panned out. We then came close to making things happen the next morning, after finally heading up into the hills like true turkey men instead of duck hunters sitting over a decoy spread. Once that flock flew down around us, I was a mere fraction away from getting a shot at one of the toms, but instead, they were visible only to Trevor. His desire for me to kill the first bird kept him from taking the shot, and after they left us, the rest of the day was a series of more close calls which all shared one common theme: Trev would be in position for the kill, while I wasn't. I could sense the hint of a growing feeling of anxiety in the Jack Russell terrier at my side named Trevor. You see, this man is a cold-blooded turkey killer. No if's, and's, or but's about it. He doesn't take very long to get it done, either. The only problem with that is his expectation of others around him needing to perform as he would, and the sense of pressure which that underlying current exudes upon anyone who doesn't. You can almost taste the disappointment and disdain if/when you screw things up. Sometimes, that pressure can be too much to handle.

Take, for instance, the morning of our fourth day. By then Trevor had been ready to get gone and headed home for about three and a half days, and I knew that. I could *feel* that! He'd already killed his tom (a whole 'nother story, in and of itself) and had only been sticking around to "help" me, but his patience of my recurring ineptitude was wearing thin and we were both getting frustrated. Nerves were on edge. Nothing I'd done to that point had been right, and every decision or tactical move which I'd made had turned out wrong. However, on the morning spoken of I really thought we had put all of those failures behind us and done good when we got in tight on a hard-gobbling tom and his small flock of talkative hens while they were still in the roost. I carried on a lively pre-flydown discussion with the girls, and the tom gobbled at all of us willingly and with great gusto. We were also in great position, albeit slightly downhill of the roost, because there was a steep ravine on the opposite side of the flock. The only logical place for them to fly down was right in front of us.

Logical? Merriam's? Yeah; right!

I have no idea why they chose to do so, but that entire flock promptly pitched out into the bottom of that deeply-cut ravine and then began climbing the mountain slope on the opposite side. I suppose the hens were probably just taking their boyfriend away from me, even though beforehand you would've thought that we were all the best of friends. Well, the only option as they drifted away was to follow behind, but do you remember how I said at the beginning of this chapter that I was fat and out of shape? The hillside which they'd climbed so effortlessly was danged-near vertical, and while Trevor didn't even break a sweat or breathe hard while climbing it, as we neared the top I was just about to die. My lungs were on fire, and my chest was heaving as I sucked in great gulps of air to keep from passing out. My vision was tunneling into the black void. I couldn't move another step.

That's when the tom gobbled from right up over the crest of the ridge in front of us. He was certainly less than 40 yards away, and probably more like 25. Trev looked at me bright-eyed and encouragingly whispered, "Just walk up that final 15 yards and kill him when you pop over the top."

I'm quite certain that such a scenario is exactly what this "Young Bull" turkey-killin' machine beside me would've done, with both great acumen and precision. I'm equally certain that if looks could kill (or, at least punch a guy in the throat), my glowering glare at him would've done exactly that as I wheezed out, "I……(huff)……(huff)……(huff)…...*CAN'T!*"

Things went spiraling downhill from there, and once the battle with that turkey had come to its inevitable and foregone failed conclusion, Trev and I regrouped for lunch back at camp before I told him to go ahead on home and leave me to the wolves. He had things to do and turkeys to kill back in Kansas, and I still had five days left on my permit to take an Arizona tom. If I couldn't get one killed in that amount of time, then I had earned exactly what I deserved. To be honest, at that point I truly thought that I stood a better chance by hunting alone, instead of trying to alter my methods and strategies to meld with the added pressure of Trevor's presence and critical eye. I might even get back to feeling like a turkey hunter, and performing like a turkey hunter, with him gone. I was wrong, of course, and five days later I licked my tail-end, ate my tag, and admitted to abject humiliation and a devastating defeat.

Sitting in Sparky's Burgers, BBQ, and Espresso restaurant in Hatch, New Mexico a few hours later, while eating just about the best Green Chile Cheeseburger on the planet and some spicy pinto beans on the side, all washed down with an authentic and delicious strawberry milkshake in an attempt to drown my sorrows, I reflected back on the previous nine days spent in the San Carlos Indian Reservation. Now, I've failed often in turkey hunting. I've gone for long stretches of time without killing a tom. But, NEVER before had I gone that many days in a row where I could positively say *every single decision* I'd made was wrong. Time after time I'd

Not even ice-cream could change my luck on the San Carlos Rez.

come close, but not close enough. And my failures certainly weren't due to a lack of birds. No; I'd heard and worked turkeys every single day, and yet, something always went wrong. Often times in turkey hunting it's only the fickle fate of chance and happenstance which defines whether you're a hero, or a heel, but I could unequivocally say without a doubt that all of my failures on that trip had been the direct result of a wrong choice or decision on my part. I felt like the greenest of newbies, or maybe just a fool.

Perhaps the most frustrating hunt of all during that timeframe had been the day when I'd heard three toms not far up a side canyon and left my van beside the road to climb up after them. After failing yet again, I'd dejectedly come back down to the road an hour later and about 300 yards from where

I'd started, and almost immediately stumbled upon strut marks in the dusty road. They were fresh, deeply etched into the gravel and dirt, and headed straight towards that big white van in the distance. I followed those tracks right up to, and then right on past my driver's side door, where if I'd been sitting inside when they were being made, I could've easily reached out through the open window and clubbed the tom with a baseball bat. In following the tracks another hundred yards down the road, I then spotted their maker up on a bluff too steep to even think about climbing, so instead, I tucked in beside a big cedar tree and yelped at him. At first I thought his answer to my call was a gobble, but in hindsight, I'm pretty sure that he was just laughing at me.

Well, in every life a little rain must fall. That's what "they" say, and I truly believe it. The failure to kill a bird in Arizona was certainly a damp spot in my pathway towards eternity, but not exactly a flash flood. If I lived through the upcoming surgery to remove part of a kidney and its heinous tumor, and if the cancer hadn't already spread to other organs and my life was about to end, then I might eventually come back to the San Carlos for redemption. That possibility was the great unknown and remained to be seen, of course, and I could cross that proverbial bridge when I came to it. What I couldn't do was spend too much more time on the road. My appointment with the Da Vinci surgical robot was looming, and those nine days wasted in Arizona had set me back so far that I dared not risk another long and drawn-out failure in Wyoming. Instead, I decided to head straight for Missouri, which was the final state needed to cap my fourth U.S. Super Slam. If successful in taking a bird there, at least I would have that proverbial feather in my cap as I faced the surgical unknown.

Trevor and I rendezvoused once more for that trip, and on the first morning at Joey Brock's leased farm we had a great and memorable hunt. The tom I ended up shooting had answered my yelps from a Cane Creek pot and covered a lot of ground to reach us, but then he'd flown up into a cottonwood tree 75 yards away and on the other side of a big creek. There, he sat gobbling for another half an hour to Trev's sweet "pillow talk" on a diaphragm before finally flying over to our side of the creek and coming on in. Trevor didn't even know beforehand that this tom finalized my Slam #4, so he was practically giddy with excitement when I told him the news while kneeling beside the tom. I am glad that my little buddy, Trevor "The Weedhopper" Bays, was there to share the glory and excitement of the moment!

The crowning bird for my fourth Super Slam was this Missouri tom.

We then traveled over to meet up with Ty Eubanks, who was the videographer for that short film, "The Doc" which Stephen Spurlock had done about me. Ty has led an amazing life for such a young man, and he's filmed/hunted/guided/fished all around the world. He currently runs an outfitting business specializing in big whitetail deer and turkeys, located right in the heart of western Missouri, and had graciously invited us to come spend a couple days with him and his partner Colby Clark. Man, did we have a large time of it, too! Those guys really know what they're doing, and they have access to lots of amazing ground. If you're looking to shoot trophy deer or a big old tom, then feel free to give Ty a call.

They took us to a farm where there had been several toms regularly hanging out in a big plowed field, but avoiding the overlooking roost site entailed a long, circling walk. Ordinarily, they said we would've heard a multitude of toms gobbling from our set up spot, but on that day the birds were being hush-mouthed at dawn and I only counted perhaps a half dozen distant gobbles in total, from two different directions. It took a while and some persistent calling from Trev and me before a pair of the birds approached us from behind, and after they'd circled out front and into our dekes placed amongst corn plants now standing three inches tall, I could see that one of the birds was dragging a broken wing. It didn't seem to bother him too awfully much though, because he was the one doing most of the strutting. I shot him as much out of pity as for any other reason, and Trevor promptly killed his partner.

Even before reaching the birds we could smell mine. Not only was his wing broken, but there was a ragged, maggot infested hole in the flesh about three inches across and the whole wing was rotted to the point where it should've already fallen off. It was a hideous wound, and he reeked like a dead cow, which made me even more grateful that I'd been given the opportunity to end his life in a quick and humane manner. Trev's tom was also broken up, bruised, and emaciated. We had killed two wounded warriors, for sure!

In riding around with Colby later that day, I inadvertently mentioned something about my pending surgery and the fear that I had cancer. That's when he told me of his own ordeal. Only one year earlier he'd been diagnosed with melanomas all over his body and in his brain, lungs, etc. He'd had multiple operations so far, and was undergoing Immunotherapy, radiation, and chemo to combat the dreaded disease. To look at him you would've thought he was the picture of health and happiness, and yet at the tender age of 25, Colby Clark was very sick and had been given a grim prognosis. At best, he was facing an uncertain future, with the very distinct possibility of death. And yet, he was somehow able to maintain a positive attitude and an optimistic outlook. The more we talked, the more I admired his heart and courage, and he instantly became sort of a hero to me, as well as an inspiration as I battled my own physical problems. I mean, here I was, a washed up old carpenter who had already led a full, lucky, and blessed life. If I was going to die it could safely be said of me that I'd had a damned-good run. In contrast, this young man had the whole world to conquer and everything to live for, but things didn't look good. Despite the dire probabilities, he'd made a choice; a choice to continue facing forward and fighting cancer head on. He was bound and determined to never give in, no matter the ultimate outcome.

As I write this chapter of the book in January of 2025, I just last week learned that Colby lost his battle. In reading through the obituary, I learned even more about an amazing young man who had lived a too-short, but truly incredible life filled with wonderful experiences and shared by an amazing group of friends and family. When he died, he was still engaged to be married and looking forward. It was easy to see why I'd found him to be such an inspiration to me, and it was heartwarming to read about all the lives he'd touched along his ill-fated journey. Although we only knew each other for a couple of days during that spring hunt of 2023, he and his friendship left a mark on me. I've written this before, but it's worth repeating a hundred more times: none of us know what lies ahead or when our time on earth will end, so get out there and enjoy every minute like it's your last. This ain't no trial run or rehearsal.

Life isn't the least bit fair, and cancer sucks!

Me, Colby Clark, and Trevor Bays. RIP, brother.

The time remaining of my 2023 turkey season was running out, but it wasn't over just yet. Trev and I thought that we could still squeeze in another hunt, so I followed him home to Kansas. The weather had grown hot and summer-like by then, and the winds were blowing at gale force for the first two days, but on Day 3 we found a fired-up tom on a piece of Matt Laymon's leased ground. However, just because the tom was gobbling good doesn't mean that he was a pushover. It took some patience, great calling, and a few slick maneuvers on our part to finally get the drop on that wary old rascal. He ended up being a gorgeous Rio-Eastern hybrid with good hooks, and after tagging him, we met up with Matty at a local diner for a victory breakfast before saying our "see ya later's." I tried to hide it, but that last meeting with two guys who I think of as both sons and brothers to me was pretty emotional. In fact, I ain't ashamed to admit that I had a lump in my throat and could barely swallow the food. I didn't know if we would ever again share time in the turkey woods, and that was a heavy weight to bear. We'd certainly stacked up a bunch of good times in the past, but now my own brush with eternity was looming and when I pulled out of the parking lot and saw them both waving in the rear view mirror, the tears started rolling down my cheeks. Certainly, that journey home started out as rather melancholy, but then I thought of how the boys would talk about me if I didn't survive, and the particularly funny stories which they might relate without me being there to defend myself, and that made me laugh and feel better.

When I got back to Bloomington I still had a few days to kill before the surgery. I seldom get the chance to hunt in Indiana anymore because I'm usually out on the road in some other state, but there's no doubt about how much I love my home turf. Indiana is a gorgeous blend of different types of habitat, depending upon where you're at, but I'm from the southern 1/3 and that is the prettiest part. North of us it's mostly ground flattened due to glaciation, but where I live it's primarily rolling hills covered in a mix of deciduous forests and croplands. That's where I learned to turkey hunt, and that's where I feel most at peace.

Me and Trevor Bays with my Kansas bird.

Trevor Bays, me, and Matt Laymon at our victory breakfast.

Initially, I considered going back to the very first place where I ever turkey hunted, but then I thought better of it. Coming "full circle" like that, after so many years of not returning, almost felt like I would be giving in and signaling that I'd already admitted defeat to the tumor growing inside me. At least, that's how I interpreted it. And so, I opted to hunt a farm where I've spent a lot of time recently. I'd never hunted there in the spring, but it was my fall turkey and deer spot and the ground always holds a lot of both critters.

I had a great and challenging hunt on that first day back home, and a little before 11 a.m. I finally convinced a pair of toms to come search me out. By then I hadn't uttered a peep in nearly an hour, but we'd been dueling for almost three. And when they did approach my hide, it wasn't in a glorious display of passion, but rather, they snuck in silently and very nervously, with long moments of standing tall and just looking. I'm not sure why they were so danged wiggy, as nobody else had hunted the farm all spring. I guess it was just the nature of the birds, or, maybe they were scared of encountering a bigger and badder tom that might whoop their butts. The one I shot had inch spurs, but he also sported some deep puncture wounds on his breast and legs.

My buddy Doug Pickle from Virginia was also in Indiana that spring trying to kill one of the final birds of his own Super Slam. For the last three days before my return he'd been staying at my house and hunting its surrounding State Forest lands, but so far without anything positive to show for it. With my tag filled I was now free to try and help him out, so the next day we went right back to the same farm where I'd shot my tom. Mr. Pickle promptly scared the holy bejesus out of a tom that snuck in and popped through the fence line behind our hide at about six *feet*, and then the next morning we had a tom pitch out of his roost tree and almost take my hat off as he glided by overhead before landing right out in front of Doug, who then missed him clean as a whistle.

My surgery was slated for Monday, and two more days of failing to get Doug a bird put us at the crucial point of needing to make things happen by the next day (Saturday) if I was going to be a part of his victory photos. We were running out of good options, so I called my young friend Brandon Ziegler, who has access to some fantastic properties in Brown and Bartholomew counties. Zieg took us to a couple of them on Saturday and tried to walk me into a coma in trying to find a bird for Doug, but we failed yet again. That was it for me…I simply couldn't spend any more time in the woods, so while I was prepping for surgery on Sunday, they went without me and Doug finally shot the tom that he'd been working so hard to get. Good for him!

On Monday, May 15 they took out about 1/6 of my kidney and its accompanying heinous tumor. I awoke from surgery and looked out of the hospital window beside my bed to see two Canada geese standing only five yards away on a limestone bench. One of them was banded, which I took to be a good sign. In hindsight, I'm pretty sure that vision was real, and not a figment of my pain-med induced imagination…

My final hunt before surgery and a fine Indiana gobbler.

Chapter 7

2024

Well, the fact that I'm writing this chapter means I survived the surgery, and the banded goose outside my window was almost certainly there and indeed a very good sign. After three painful days of shamelessly flirting with all the pretty nurses in the hospital they kicked me out and I headed home to finish recovering in my own bed. It was a couple months before I could resume light duties at work, but by then I'd already met with Dr. Kitley to review the pathology report. He explained that there are basically three types of kidney tumors. The most common is also the most malignant, and accounts for most of the deaths. Another type was almost as bad. The third version makes up only 5% of the cases, but it's by far the best kind to have. He then told me to go buy a lottery ticket, because my tumor was in that most-favorable category! Basically, it was benign and treatable with surgery only. And, while they'd taken out about 1/6 of my kidney, the rest of it was functioning just fine. The tumor was also totally contained (it hadn't spread to any other organs), and the margins looked good. Thus, it was unlikely that we'd need to do anything else like additional surgery, radiation, or chemo. We could keep an eye on my guts with yearly CT scans and hope there wasn't a recurrence, although the chances were good that it will eventually return. Dr. Kitley then assured me that there ought to be many more gobblers in my future, so I should go on about living my life.

Talk about feeling a sense of relief!!! A tremendous burden had just been lifted from my shoulders, and even though recovery from the surgery was painful and slow, I felt lighthearted and free. Instead of constantly thinking about the past and my own mortality, I began to actually look ahead. To be honest, over the last several months I hadn't expected this outcome, and I'd even put all of my affairs in order by making out a will, and a living will, "just in case." In truth, I'd really been expecting the worst.

Unburdened by those thoughts, I now did what the good Doctor ordered and began planning for the future. That included arranging a rather ambitious spring itinerary, starting of course with Florida. I even tried to get in better shape by losing some weight, and had been moderately successful at that going into my departure date from home, but once we were back at camp all those delicious meals and snacks began to take their toll and I was right back to where I'd started. Dangit; I love food too much for my own good.

The season began, as it usually does, with a youth season "Love Boat Cruise." This year, however, I had a new kid to guide, since Will Grubbs had matriculated after three seasons to the adult bracket. My new youth was Jack Parsons, from Indiana. Jack's Mom Tara had contacted me nearly a year earlier and told me that as each of her seven kids reached a certain age or level of maturity, she would take them on a special weekend of their choosing with just the two of them. It was a way to treat each child to something which held their greatest interest, and without any other siblings being around to share attention; a special time of just Mom and the child. Jack had chosen a turkey hunt.

In short, we had a blast! Jack was mature beyond his 15 years, a joy to hunt with, and obviously a crack shot, because he took both of his desired birds with one shot. He and his Mom had arranged for lodging at a real neat house built on stilts above the Kissimmee River Chain of Lakes at Camp Mack, and during their Mother/Son weekend they enjoyed several of the things that make Florida so special: fishing, taking an airboat ride to see alligators and other native wildlife, and of course, our phenomenal turkey hunt. At some point during the day I shared my kidney ordeal with Tara, and she in turn told me a spellbound tale of her own brush with eternity.

In 2020 she had been diagnosed with a rare type of leukemia that was more often than not fatal. In fact, after being admitted to the hospital her doctors predicted that she only had two weeks to live. Transferring down to the MD Anderson Cancer Center in Houston, TX and given bone marrow (stem cell) transplants over the course of four intense months of therapy, she defied all the odds and survived. Today, Tara Parsons is the walking personification of what great things science and medicine can achieve.

After surviving her traumatic ordeal, she was interviewed in 2023 for a short film that was subsequently picked up by ESPN. It covered the inspirational story of a little boy named Lachlan Tannery, who had died of the same cancer which had invaded Tara's world. Lachlan was from South Carolina and his Dad was a big Clemson Tigers football fan, so he and his twin brother were also Tigers fans by default. Word of this young boy fighting for his life had been picked up and circulated among the Clemson faithful, and as support spread they'd named a stuffed tiger found at their football stadium after him. "Lachlan the Tiger" was then used as a way in which to sort of keep the child's spirits up and bring an awareness of his plight to the Clemson faithful, and that stuffed toy soon became the figurehead of a huge groundswell of support for the young boy. Before long, the story had morphed into a viral social movement resulting in a tremendous outpouring of money and bone marrow donations given to help save the lives of people with this disease.

Lachlan died about a year after his diagnosis, but the support for his cause carried on with the creation of a foundation in his honor called, "Lachlan's Hope." It was designed to try and get people to sign up for the national bone marrow registry, which is called, "Be the Match." All it takes to sign up and register your vital blood markers is a quick cotton swab to the cheek and being between the ages of 18 and 40. And, since college aged students were the perfect candidates, the movement focused first on Clemson students, faculty, and staff. However, the "Lachlan the Tiger Campaign" exploded, and it brought national exposure to the cause. Donations swarmed in, resulting in thousands of registered donors and numerous matches which gave renewed hope to every family who had been impacted by that form of leukemia, as well as other blood disorders. The Parsons family became one of those beneficiaries when a member of the Clemson staff was notified that her cells were a perfect match for Tara.

By the time I finished watching that video my heart had swelled to bursting and my eyes were leaking. I'm telling you here and now that I was moved like I'd never been moved before, and went right out to register my bone marrow that very afternoon. Unfortunately, I was told that I'm too old. However, I encourage every one of you who reads this to watch the ESPN film, "No Greater Love." If it doesn't create similar emotions to what I felt, then there is something terribly wrong with you. Please give it a look-see, and do what your heart tells you to be the right course of action.

Trevor and I guided a total of 29 hunters that spring, and every one of them got their bird(s). Only a single fella needed to hunt into his third day before scoring, while the rest killed out on their first day of hunting with us. Having Trevor along for the ride was a tremendous help, and a hoot, as well. He's a phenomenal turkey hunter, and a really awesome caller on a diaphragm. The man knows turkeys, and he knows how to get them killed. I'm mighty proud of who Trevor Bays is and what he's become in only 31 years on this planet, and I'm proud to call him by several names of tremendous depth and importance to me...son, brother, and most of all; friend.

Because of our tremendous success rate I got the chance to hunt a bit for myself too, and I was able to take a great bird on a private farm, as well as a special tom from The Swamp. Looked at as a whole, the Florida season had been nothing short of phenomenal. Our Swarp Camp was once again a highlight and I was able to share good times and camaraderie with a whole bunch of people that I love and love to be around. There's little else in life that can compare to the joy of pulling into camp and finding a whole bunch of fellow turkey hunters and friends laughing, eating, and reveling in the moment. Then, too, there's little in life more depressing than pulling up the stakes of our "circus tents" after everyone has gone home, and packing everything away to be stored at Bill George's house for the next 11 months. Such are the highs and lows of Florida, but here are a few pictures that capture some of the good times:

After a 16-hour drive home to drop off my guiding trailer, and a couple of days to fix some stuff at my Mom's house, I took off on a grueling 31-

Jack Parsons and his double limbhangers.

Me, Jack Parsons, and his Mom Tara.

Mike Tippin and and Benett Malon got the regular season started off on a good note.

Dan Thompson and Justin Mettler with their two fine toms.

Jeff Fountain's bird sported real good hooks!

Gary, Robert, and Tony all scored on an amazing afternoon hunt.

I managed to slip out and kill a public land tom.

My second tom hanging in an old "spider" oak.

Trevor took this picture of a tiny tree frog resting inside a flower.

hour drive (broken up over two days) to California. I know that the place where I hunt there isn't everything I normally look for in terms of the "ideal" situation (I lean more towards tough public land toms and difficult conditions), but the scenery is phenomenal, the folks who allow me access to their land are great, and the turkeys are both numerous and vocal. I heard no less than a dozen gobbling birds each morning that I was there, and they continued to gobble all day long. I took my time, soaked it all in, and shot three great toms in as many days. After weeks of high-pressure guiding duties in Florida, it was a great way to relax and decompress while gearing my mind up for what the next stop along the turkey trails might entail.

In 2023 I had been given a total and brutally painful ass-whooping by the turkeys of the San Carlos Indian Reservation in Arizona. In planning my

A gorgeous California tom.

retribution tour, I'd purchased a pair of tags good for their third season, so I arrived a day early to scout it out. Although I fully intended to hunt in the same canyon which had abused me so badly the year before, I needed to make sure that there were still turkeys around. If so, I was bound and determined to make amends on those evil birds.

While driving in, I became immediately concerned because what had always been an incredibly rough road was now much different. They had used some sort of serious earth-moving equipment during the past year to dig up a lot of the huge stones and boulders that had made this road almost unnavigable, and then they'd graded the thing to nearly smooth. This development concerned me for the simple fact that I'd always counted on the rough access to keep riffraff (other hunters) out of "my" spot! Being as how my permit was good for the third season, I was also worried that this easier access might mean that there had been more hunters in here before me, and potentially fewer turkeys left alive in this canyon because of it.

However, I didn't have to go far until I once again began seeing turkey tracks in the dusty roadway, and after I'd driven back into my favorite core area, I found strut marks in the exact same place where the tom had waltzed past my van the previous year while I'd been out hunting elsewhere. Of course, it was highly unlikely that these current tracks had been made by the same turkey who'd subsequently laughed at me from up on the bluff above the road, but in my mind they were one and the same. I didn't need to look any further, for I had found what I needed to see. Rather than wandering around and potentially bumping birds, I just set up my camp nearby and sat there reading a book all afternoon. No other vehicles drove past me, which was encouraging, and then at 4 p.m. a tom came gliding all the way across the canyon and passed by nearly overhead before landing on that very same bluff as the "laughing" tom of '23. About a minute later, he gobbled. Oh; *yes*! Challenge accepted. Game on!

He wasn't the only tom gobbling that evening, either, as other distant birds began intermittently piping up. By dusk I'd heard at least five. In the morning that figure increased to a minimum of eight, but probably twice that many. There were, in fact, turkeys gobbling *everywhere*, and in every direction! Unable to sleep out of nervous anticipation, I'd already been sitting in the woods for an hour before that first gobble rang out at only 4:45 a.m., and from that point onward the entire canyon rang with the beautiful sound of tom turkeys in love. It was a really, really cool way to start my hunt!

I initially focused my attention on a trio of toms not far from camp, but they had a bunch of hens all around them and hushed up soon after flydown. When another bird started ripping it north of me a good ways, I got up and moved in his direction. Two others besides him then piped up closer and below my position, so I snuck over to the edge of the shelf that I was on and soon spotted them all the way down by the road. It was two jakes, who showed no real interest in anything other than walking down the dusty roadway and gobbling at every turkey sound that they heard, which was a bunch, because not only were gobbles echoing down the canyon, but I could also hear multiple hens. When that single bird that I'd originally come towards then gobbled directly uphill of me, I quickly repositioned on him and got set up. He wasted no time in responding eagerly and moving towards me like he was on rails. I really thought it was going to happen, but at 60 yards out he sort of lost interest and faded away. I guess another hen in the distance sounded more intriguing than me. At that point the thought did cross my mind that I might be in for another cursed season of near misses and disappointment at the San Carlos Reservation, but in my heart I knew better. After all, it was still early on Day 1 and there were *lots* of toms gobbling!

When two more birds gobbled north of me I angled towards them, and as I got closer they separated, with one tom staying on the opposite side of the main canyon, and the other crossing over to my side. Looking around with a newfound sense of urgency, I soon found the most perfect setup tree imaginable: it was a triple-trunked oak with a couple of smaller trees growing nearby that offered additional cover on that fairly sparse, pine dominated slope dotted with scrub oak and manzanita. There was even a sandy "bowl" of sorts at its base that fit my butt just right for comfort, and a low-growing limb which served as the perfect gun rest. I could've sat there all day.

Once settled in, I yelped on the old trusted Cane Creek glass and the nearby tom HAMMERED out an answering gobble. His next unprovoked pronouncement was closer, and then I could hear drumming. This tom came in quickly, strutting and drumming the whole way, and yet the thing I most remember was how vividly his bright white crown almost glowed as he was coming through the scrub brush. I shot him at 34 yards; perhaps a bit sooner than I like, but after failing so miserably in 2023, I was really, really ready to end the drought!

His buddy across the canyon gobbled at my shotgun's blast, so after gathering up my bird and laying him behind me, I sat back down and began calling again. At first I thought that I was going to fill my second tag from the very same tree, but the tom soon thought better of his options and left. Right about then is when a hen approached me, and she ended up staying nearby and in sight for over an hour; often within a dozen yards and continually yelping so forlornly that I was just sure she would eventually call in the departing tom, or some other one. However, it didn't work out that way and we remained just the two of us. Every time she started to leave I would call her back, but despite doing this multiple times, she eventually lost interest and wandered off alone.

Although still early, the once-cloudy skies (it had actually drizzled *very* lightly on me soon after sunrise) had begun to clear and it was getting hot, so I decided to drop down to the road and walk back to camp, where I could lose some layers of clothing and 20 pounds of fresh turkey. However, as I neared the spot where I'd started the day on that trio of roosted toms, I spotted a hen in the road up ahead. Easing into the scrub brush on the high side of the road, I soon spotted other hens with her, and then a rounded tail fan beyond them. As I watched from behind good cover, I could hear other birds of their flock in the woods ahead of me, and when I sat down and called, one of them gobbled.

Unfortunately, the six or seven hens and their tom along the road soon headed towards the bird that had gobbled, and then they all climbed further uphill. I decided to make a move. Circling around through the woods and then angling upwards, I came in on about their level; easily steered there by the light yelps of hens and the occasional gobble from one or two toms. I'd just gotten to where I wanted to be when I spotted a pair of big oak trees under which the ground had been scratched to pieces. That spot practically called out for me to sit there, so I did, and then I called a little bit and scratched in the leaves a *lot*. The flock was only 150 yards away, so I knew fully well that they could hear what I was doing. However, those oaks were growing on a little knob of ground fairly covered in scrub oak and cedar, and my view while seated was extremely limited. I thought standing up and leaning against the one oak that was already leaning might offer me a better view, so that's what I did.

The last gobble that I'd heard a few moments earlier was closer…only 100 yards…and soon afterwards I spotted one tom, then another, as they picked their way towards me. I continued to scratch in the leaves with my foot. They separated at one point and I thought the left-hand bird was going to come right up my gun barrel, but after dropping out of sight in a little creek between us, they both then emerged walking side by side and already in gun range, although off to my right a little bit. Unfortunately for them, they didn't notice me shift my gun barrel a few inches. The lead tom was noticeably bigger, so when he periscoped up at 30 yards to look around for the source of all that leaf racket, I put him down for the count.

Afterwards, the surviving tom commenced into some really strange behavior that I've never heard anyone speak of, or even read about. The old boy immediately came over to inspect his dead buddy, and then he began loudly clucking and uttering a sound almost like moaning, in addition to periodically gobbling. And, he wouldn't leave. He just wandered around almost aimlessly, yet never venturing very far away. I stayed put and even raised my binoculars to study him, and all I can say is that it was like he was broken-hearted over his lifelong pal getting killed and he refused to

This time the ice-cream worked to bring me good luck in Arizona.

Some trees just call out to be used as a set-up spot.

San Carlos revenge tour complete!

abandon him. Eventually, I walked out and retrieved my bird, but the mourning tom still wouldn't leave. I was in no hurry to go back to camp, so I set up my camera without making any effort to be stealthy or hide my movements, and then I took pictures for probably close to an hour as that goofy bird continued to cluck, moan, and gobble. He was still doing it when I finally walked away.

I fell in love with the Ponderosa-studded hills near Cloudcroft, New Mexico the very first time I hunted there in 1990. That hunt had taken place on the Mescalero Apache Indian Reservation, but I'd returned numerous times in subsequent years to chase turkeys around the Lincoln National Forest lands which lay both north and south of the Rez. It's gorgeous country, in a fascinating part of the world. New Mexico is a truly awesome place with many, many natural wonders.

Trevor and Stephen Spurlock were going to meet me in Wyoming to finish out the last state needed for my 5th Super Slam, but Stephen was tied up and couldn't get there until the second day of May. It was just now April 21, so I had some time to kill and I could think of no better way or place to do it than to make a return to Cloudcroft. It's a cool town. Back when I first started going there, I would occasionally turn off the engine of my 1968 Ford Econoline van and drift the 19 miles downhill to Alamogordo, where I would then fire "Petunia the Road Pig" back up and drive on over to Las Cruces to eat at a great Mexican restaurant called "La Posta." On one day of this trip I did the same thing, but without drifting powerless. I was younger then. The restaurant still has great food.

I am a believer in science. And science tells me that wind, rain, and erosion are forces that continually grind down and flatten out the mountains. Look at the Smokies: they are the oldest mountain range in North America, and yet, they used to tower far above their current height. However, my knees would beg to differ on that "flattening out" thing. Despite strong empirical evidence to the contrary, those "hills" of the Lincoln NF have definitely grown both steeper and taller since I was last there. I swear of it! I found a lot less air to breathe, too.

But, what haven't changed are those cursed Merriam's gobblers who inhabit that steep-assed terrain. They still hit the ground running after flydown and cruise up and over mountaintops like they're Kenyan marathoners. I hate them. And yet, I love them. Gawd; this turkey hunting thing is complicated!

In driving around and looking for a place that really "caught my eye," I discovered a long, rough as a cob, dead-end road that terminated in just about the prettiest series of canyons a Merriam's turkey could ever dream of calling "home." It figuratively called out for me to stop immediately, set up camp, and stay right there until I either killed my toms or it was time to meet up with the boys in Wyoming. As if to assure me that I'd made the right decision, a far distant bird then gobbled at dusk.

The next morning that rascal took me for a nice "walk-about" to show me around his home turf. I think we covered approximately 72 miles, and all of it was uphill. *Steeply* uphill! At least, it felt like that. And then, he quit gobbling and went away. Did I mention how much I hate Merriam's?

The following morning I limped in the 1.2 miles to where we'd begun our trek the previous day, and at dawn he was right there gobbling again. We messed with each other's melons for an hour or two while frolicking about the steep slopes before he once again resumed the silent treatment regimen designed, I'm sure, to inflict maximum mental distress on me, and it worked. By the time he'd shut his pie hole I was about three miles from camp, mad as hell, and ready to quit. And yet, I was too tired to even think about walking back to the van, so I blasted out what I can only describe as an attempt to insult his manhood in turkey'ese on a Cane Creek glass call, and then I laid down to take a nap.

I'm not sure what woke me up, but I was lying there on my back staring straight up through the limbs of the towering Ponderosas above me with my shotgun in hand, but at my side. Some remnant reasoning thought process then went through my feeble pea brain that told me I shouldn't make any sudden movements, so I just slowly raised my head until my chin was on my chest and I was staring at my feet. There, not 40 yards away and directly between my boots, stood a tom alongside three hens which were pecking around in the gravel of a forest service road. All I could do was continue to watch, while the hens gradually inched towards me and the tom simply stood tall; staring like a statue.

Eventually (as my cranked neck screamed for relief) the hens closed to 30 yards, and when they vanished from view in the shallow roadside ditch between us, I recognized that there was now only one set of eyes to contend with. After the tom finally took a few steps closer and bent down to pick

2024

Merriam's country simply can't look any better than this.

My first New Mexico tom of the year was sort of a gift from dreamland.

up a gizzard stone, I immediately sat up while simultaneously bringing the Benelli to shooting position. The tom alerted just enough to look really surprised, so I shot him in the face. Most of the time in this sport you earn your turkeys. Sometimes they're given to you. Every one of those victories feels real good!

After lugging 20 pounds of magnificence up over hill and yon, I finally hobbled back to camp. In route, I found a couple of fresh gobbler turds, which served primarily to keep me hunting in that place with a purpose for a few more days. However, the dropper of those deuces was every bit the equal of the tom in my cooler in terms of his evil intent to inflict maximum pain and mental duress on my soul, and I failed to kill him or any other of their wicked ilk.

By then I was beat up mentally and physically, and plumb worn out. I needed a break, so I headed back into Cloudcroft for a good meal. There was a restaurant in town that all the locals raved about. It's called Mad Jack's Mountaintop BBQ, and supposedly they were famous for really good brisket. My sister Lisa (Bug) Castillo is married to a Texan and they lived in Lockhart for a long time. That town is known as the BBQ capital of the whole state, with brisket being their specialty. Hence, she'd taken quite a liking to Texas BBQ while living there and now fancies herself as being a darned-good brisket chef.

When I told Bug about Mad Jack's, she excitedly replied that she knew all about the restaurant. It, and the town of Cloudcroft, had long been on her "bucket list" of places to visit. She was just looking for a good excuse and/or time off from work to come out and sample the fare at that restaurant. Then, she gave me a little of the backstory:

Seems her husband Jose's brother Rubin had grown up with Jack in Lockhart, and they'd even shared a house after graduating from high school. Jack had studied under all the famous brisket chefs in town and begun selling his own BBQ out of a food truck, until the bigger establishments in town succeeded in shutting him down out of jealousy. Jack's Father owned a used car dealership across from which was an empty lot where my sister and her eventual husband had often sat and eaten lunch while working at the nearby Motorola plant. When the old man was on his deathbed, he'd divulged to his family that his life's savings were hidden in the trunk of a 1971 Mercury Montego located at the dealership, and after he died, they found enough money in there so that Jack was able to buy the place in Cloudcroft and start up his BBQ joint. He still to this day travels down to Lockhart every six weeks or so to stock up on the post oak used in his smoker.

Well, after a story like that, I just *had* to give this place a try, and believe me; it was worth the long line to get in! They serve up some awesome food, and the crew working there makes the place hum with excitement and fun. Eating at Mad Jack's is sort of an event, but they're only open until the food runs out, and that doesn't take long. On my third visit I even met Jack himself (he'd been out of town on vacation for the previous two stops) and we talked about our shared family connections while he told me a few stories about growing up with Rubin: all funny stuff that can't be shared here...

By now I'd been hunting in the Lincoln for six days. I liked the area where I'd been camping, but I needed a change of scenery, so when Trevor's good buddy Wheeler Brunschmid got ahold of me to say that he was in the area, we made plans to hunt together. Unfortunately, he only had a single day left before needing to return to Fort Bliss, where he was stationed in the Army. We picked one of his spots close to town for the hunt, and the next morning we heard no less than four or five birds in that canyon. One of them had a deep, non-Merriam's-sounding gobble that just rumbled, but try as we might to kill him, and several close calls where I thought it was gonna happen, he eventually walked away unscathed and quit gobbling altogether.

With Wheeler's blessing I hunted in there solo the next morning and that same bird was roosted practically in the same tree. All of his nearby hens were talkative, but one of them was especially-so in yelping at one stretch a counted 35 notes in a row. Once again, I had multiple close encounters early-on before the birds simply vanished. This tom didn't like to gobble after his hens had gathered around him, and after shutting up, he was done for the day. I quit him at 10 o'clock, hiked the mile back to my van, and then drove to town for another delicious meal at Jack's. If you're not standing in line by 11 (doors open at noon), your odds of getting any food are slim to none.

With my belly full, I then trudged right back up the canyon and built a great pine-bough blind about a hundred yards from the roost. It overlooked a bare-dirt spot in the middle of a grassy patch where there was lots of fresh turkey poop, but I didn't see any turkey feathers attached to bird flesh until 6:30 p.m., when three hens and the tom suddenly appeared below me. They pecked fervently on that bare ground for a half-hour or more, always getting gradually closer, and the tom eventually was killable but shielded by some cedar scrub between us. I didn't want to risk crippling him, so I waited, and then all of a sudden the four turkeys turned and walked away with a purpose. I don't have any idea why they left or where they went, but an hour later I heard them pitch up to roost in the very same tall ponderosa pines back behind me a hundred yards or so: exactly where they'd spent the previous two nights.

Long before dawn I was already sitting nearby in another pine-bough blind built after darkness the night before, with my sights trained on a little open "glade" directly downhill of the roosted birds. I figured that it was the most natural place for them to land after flying down, and following some real good gobbling from the tom while treebound, one of his hens did exactly what the rest of the flock was supposed to do by landing directly in line with my gun barrel and at short range. The tom and three other ladies, however, flew directly *uphill* and landed on a shelf perhaps 75 yards beyond the extreme range of my shotgun. Nothing that either me or the hen at my feet subsequently said could convince the flock to come down and join us, and true to form, the tom soon thereafter shut up for the day's duration. Turkey hunting is hard, but when you can't pry a gobble out of one all day, it is also maddeningly frustrating!

My afternoon plan was to sit in the lower blind until 6 o'clock, and if nothing had shown up by then, I would hustle uphill to my newer blind situated closer to the roost. I even broke out a couple of decoys. It was time to get serious with this tom, and a strutter deke might be just the ticket for getting him into killing range. I was really curious about why they'd pecked in the dirt below that blind with such gusto the prior evening, and all I could figure was that they were gathering gizzard stones. To my naked eye, I couldn't see anything else of value in that strip of reddish soil, other than turkey turds old and new.

Well, at a little before 4 o'clock a hen yelped from about 200 yards away and the tom gobbled at her. A few minutes later she got even more talkative and her boyfriend answered three times, but then all turkey talk ended. Nothing I said made any difference, and nobody showed up at my patch of dirt. By 5 p.m. I'd heard nothing else, nor seen anything more. I was getting fearful that nobody was going to show up, so I left my dekes where they were at and moved to my upper blind. If this tom intended to roost in the same spot four nights in a row, then I fully intended to shoot him for being so predictable...so long as he got there before legal shooting time ended.

At 6:30 I spotted the tom, alright. He was leading a pack of five hens and *running* across the dirt patch a hundred yards below my position, headed straight towards the strutter deke. When he got there, the dangded'est one-sided fight you've ever seen commenced, with loud purring, flogging wings popping against rubber, and vicious kicks landing upon my poor, helpless strutter, who had to take all of the abuse because there was nobody around to defend him from the assault. I'd abandoned him. The hens soon joined in the fracas and did their best to bitch-slap the girl dekes, too. Then, after administering a thorough thrashing to the entire faux flock, the tom and his girlfriends did indeed come towards me as if headed for bed. I'm sure they were worn out from the rumble. But, when just about in gun range, the stud tom decided to go back down there and give the intruder one last piece of his mind. I thought that this last skirmish might mean the end of any opportunity to shoot the tom before legal shooting hours ran out, but just in the nick of time he suddenly sprinted back to catch up with his ladies, who were standing all around me. Then, the old boy stepped into the exact spot where I'd earlier visualized him flying up to roost. He stood there as if

My 2nd New Mexico gobbler was a real lady's man and a warrior.

waiting for his executioner to do the dirty deed, so after checking my clock for confirmation that it was still legal, I did it with only minutes to spare. This wasn't exactly a textbook turkey hunt, but it felt real good to finally get the drop on an evil, hush-mouthed and evasive opponent.

The time had come for finishing up my fifth and final U.S. Super Slam. One more bird was all that I needed and I could forevermore quit hunting in places where lofty goals dictated my presence. I'd been looking forward to this moment for quite a while, and could hardly wait for the day to arrive.

Trevor and his buddy Evan Walsh had arrived in Sundance, Wyoming a day earlier and listened for turkeys in the place where I'd hunted during my last two visits there. They heard a bunch. I was supposed to pick up Stephen at the airport and then we'd all meet up at a house owned by Walt Schroeder, who, along with his brother Randy were deer hunting clients of Trevor's in Kansas. However, at the last minute I received a text from Stephen saying that he couldn't make it. That was a shame, because I had a feeling that we were about to get ourselves into a situation which certainly warranted his vast and profound video skills. We did, too, but not on the first two days, when our only successes were in seeing lots of beautiful country and boogering up a couple of prime opportunities.

I will say this about Trevor Bays: he doesn't just ride out a bad streak. Instead, he does everything within his power to change the situation to his favor. That's one reason why he's such a good guide. Me being me, I would've just continued to work hard and slug it out on public land until we finally found a cooperative bird, but not my boy Trev. He couldn't stand the thought of potentially going three whole days in a row without making a kill, so he went out and found us a place to hunt where the odds were infinitely higher of finding success. It was a piece of private property that was absolutely loaded with turkeys, but which Walt had informed us as being ground where the landowner *never* granted hunting permission. Trevor stopped by the lady's workplace, introduced himself, and according to his story, he simply wouldn't take no for an answer. I don't know exactly what he said to her or what promises were made, but when he showed back up at Walt's he was grinning that big 'ole Trevor Bays smile and we had ourselves exclusive access to do whatever we wanted to do on her ground.

That little 89-acre chunk of river bottom ground was, in a word, amazing! Following dinner at a real good steakhouse in the middle of nowhere, we drove over there and watched about 80 birds milling around on the property for about an hour before they all flew up to roost in a grove of cottonwoods. Once it was good and dark, Trev, Evan and myself then walked out and set up two big Barronett blinds side by side about 75 yards from the nearest trees and 25 yards from where a raised tractor path cut across the shallow ditch which basically divided the property in two. Most of the flock (including at least four longbeards) had walked across that crossing on their way to the cottonwoods. Then, we put out a flock of DSD's: two strutters, two jakes, and eight hens. We were dealing with a huge flock of turkeys, on what was basically a big chunk of wide open pasture land. If we wanted to compete, we needed visual aids and a reason for the birds to come to us.

The longbeards we'd watched the evening before were all roosted on the north end of the 200 yard-long cottonwood grove and we were closer to its southern end. Long before daylight arrived, the five of us had already slipped into our blinds, with Randy and Evan accompanying Trevor in one of them, while Walt and I shared the other. The plan was for me to shoot the first tom, and Randy would then try to fill his tag. Walt initially said that he wasn't interested in killing a bird, so he didn't even bring a gun.

Gobbling commenced very early, and with much enthusiasm! In short, we were presented with a virtual cacophony of turkey talk for nearly an hour before any of the birds flew down. There were sounds and calls of all sorts coming from the roost, and it didn't take long to realize that we'd sadly underestimated the number of male turkeys in the flock. I was quite certain that there were at least a dozen separate birds gobbling, or perhaps more. After flydown commenced and the whole flock had loosely gathered together about 150 yards away from us, I counted at least 85 birds (it was hard to get an accurate tally) in total. Included in that figure were at least 15 jakes, as well as a group of seven toms which separated from the main flock and chased each other around for a few minutes as they re-established their pecking order. I could even hear other toms gobbling in the far distance... further substantiating Walt's claim that the birds along this shallow river would regularly trade back and forth between farms. These 85 birds here today might be 200 tomorrow, and he claimed that there were probably 400 turkeys in total within two miles of where we sat!

One bird in the group of toms was obviously the boss, as evidenced by his constant haranguing of every other male turkey in their little side-group; chasing all of them around and putting every member of their "boys club" in his proper place. Each of them eventually towed the line and acquiesced. Then, when I began calling loudly on the trusted Cane Creek glass so as to join in with all of the other talkative hens which were still carrying on, the boss tom suddenly turned on his heels, left the group of fellow toms behind, and marched straight towards us. Just as soon as I detected his interest in our flock of fakes, I whispered to Walt, "He just made a very bad decision."

However, this stud gobbler hadn't totally bought into our ruse, and when he sort of hedged about coming all the way in to short range, I presumed that it was because of the frost covering our decoys. They didn't really look convincing enough. The tom, however, was already plenty close enough to kill, so when it looked like he might leave and go back to the live conglomeration of turkeys gathered over by the roost, I put a load of TSS 9's upside his noggin. Mission complete! Slam Number 5 was now officially in the books.

No other turkey within sight so much as flinched at the gunshot, but when my tom started flopping around it really got their attention and I thought every one of them was going to race over for a looksee. They probably would've too, but the dying tom too-soon lay still and all of them went back to milling around and being turkeys. For the next two hours we (Trevor and me together now, since he'd wanted me to be the sole caller until I shot my tom) worked that flock over good. I switched up calls and callers often, trying to imitate different birds in the bunch, and it was fun listening to and watching how that many birds reacted to our calls and interacted amongst themselves. Several times we had birds approach us, but they'd get to about 70 yards and then fade back towards the flock. Again, I attributed their hesitancy to our frosty dekes, and I think that belief was confirmed later on in the morning, after it had warmed up a little.

By then the entire flock had crossed the ditch and were on the far side of the property. All of them had vanished behind the undulating contour of the land, except for three longbeards and another adult tom which had no beard. I'm not sure exactly what we said, or whether, as I claim, it was just because our decoys now looked more "real" after the frost had melted, but those four toms suddenly made a collective bad life choice and began marching towards us. Up until then Walt hadn't had much of an interest in killing one of them, but he then said to me, "Is your gun loaded? It would be kinda cool to double up with my brother." After sliding a couple shells into the magazine and another into the chamber, I handed it over.

When Randy killed his tom the others began exiting stage right and Walt wadded one up. After all the glad-handing and picture taking was over, we went to eat breakfast at a great little diner in Sundance called, "Uncle Louie's," and then Trev, Ev, and me drove over to Belle Fouche, South Dakota to try and fill the other tag in my pocket. We'd met a rancher from there the day before, and he told us we were welcome to come over and hunt his place, where he claimed that six longbeards regularly ate corn off of his porch.

Sure enough, as we got out of the van there were two toms gobbling on the far side of a deep canyon, and another bird forthwith stepped out from beside

A special feather tribute to the last bird of my 5th U.S. Super Slam.

Evan Walsh, me, and Trevor Bays with that final bird of Number 5.

Trevor Bays, Walt Schroeder, me, Randy Schroeder, and Evan Walsh pose with the morning's triple.

the house about 35 yards away while we were talking to the landowner about the lay of the land on his 250 acre ranch. Opting for the two hot toms in the distance rather than the "easy" one still standing around waiting for us to leave so he could get his free handouts, we dropped off into the canyon and spent the next couple of hours toiling in the broiling sun. It was a tough task, in the high-heat of a hot day, but eventually things worked out in my favor and culminated in a first for me: killing birds in two states during the course of the same day!

Remember how I said that the taking of the final tom of my 5th Super Slam was going to free me up to hunt in places where I just wanted to go? Well,

Trevor Bays and me with my South Dakota tom and a deer shed.

that meant a trip to Minnesota was now in order. Trev and Evan took off for that destination ahead of me to rendezvous with Matt Laymon, and when I stopped to rest for a few hours along the way, that Tasmanian Devil known to those of us who love him as Trevor Bays wasted no time in killing his bird during a flash afternoon hunt before I could even arrive to meet up with them. It was raining the next morning, but after it stopped we had an eventful day. Evan initially boogered up a bird with an errant shot, but then he made amends on a second one which Matty fanned in for him while Trev and I sat in the truck watching from 500 yards away.

Trevor and Evan then headed out for New York. Matt had arrangements to go hunt elsewhere, so that left me all alone. In truth, I welcomed the solitude and the chance to do things at my own pace, which is admittedly slower than how those young guns perform. Remember the "Young Bull" story? I was now at ease and feeling good about walking, rather than running.

The spot where Trev and I had watched Evan kill his bird was a private farm which still held a number of other toms. After the kill, we'd spent some time talking to the landowner and her husband about everything under the sun, but I never even considered asking them for permission to hunt there. Heck; I was perfectly content to go right back to the public lands where I've always found good success in years past. However, when the kind lady called me a little while later to ask if I wanted to hunt their land, what was I to say? It was definitely a honey-hole of a turkey spot, and I knew that I would likely have an enjoyable hunt and a memorably good time of it the next morning.

I was right.

After her much-appreciated phone call I went back and glassed the corn stubble field across the highway from their farmhouse while sitting in the same spot where Trevor and I had watched Evan kill his bird. There were another four toms strutting for numerous hens out there during that last hour of daylight, and while I didn't actually see which trees they roosted in because of how the field wrapped around a tall hill which the birds had ventured behind as the shadows grew long, I had a pretty good idea of what they'd be doing and where they'd be doing it come morning.

The hills on all sides of that narrow valley were really, really steep. The cornfield in the bottom was divided up by a grass waterway that went clear out to the highway where I was parked, and another one that intersected it coming out of a little side hollow. Not knowing exactly where the birds were roosted, I opted to bring in a blind and a couple of dekes and set up right in the green grass. I knew from watching them the previous day that these birds liked to spend a lot of their time in the corn stubble, so hunting up in the woods seemed like a low percentage option. It's kinda like selling real estate; success at the game is dependent on three things: location, location, and location.

When the first gobble erupted to a prototypically pure-sounding real barred owl hoot at 4:45 a.m., its maker was directly uphill on my right as I was facing downstream towards the highway and perhaps a hundred yards from the woods edge. Nothing else was heard for ten minutes, but then the morning's concert began in earnest as all four toms bellowed out practically non-stop from the same steep slope. I mean, they ripped it! However, I heard very little hen talk.

The first bird to fly down was a gobbler, and he sailed out across the valley to land perhaps 125 yards to my left in the corn stubble. Two others soon followed, and they both lit together in a different "quadrant" of crop field as defined by the waterways. Then, a fourth tom walked down out of the treeline and set up his own "lek" in another segment of stubble. All four toms immediately broke into strutting, and over the next several minutes a plethora of hens glided in from all directions, with each landing near the tom of their choosing. I counted six hanging out with the pair of toms, three with the gobbler closest to me (the first one that flew down), and four accompanying the stud who had walked in like an "Old Bull."

Of course, I was most-intrigued by the "walker," as I figured him to be the baddest of the bunch, but when those three hens beside the closest tom began drifting in towards my flock of dekes with their boyfriend following dutifully behind, I changed my focus. He had a nice thick beard and by far the loudest and most full-throated gobble of any bird in the field, so there was no need to hold out for anything better. Doing so would just be pure foolishness!

The hens were soon less than 50 yards away from me and their tom was at about 80 when a 5-pack of rowdy jakes came on the scene, running down out of the hills like they were on a mission looking for trouble. Their route obviously took them a little too close for comfort of "my" tom, who was having absolutely none of that nonsense and immediately broke into a hard charge amongst the hooligans. He first chased them around in circles, then ran them all ragged until the interlopers had been driven across the waterway and on into the territory of the strutting pair of gobblers. Only after the tom had settled his mind that they were gone for good did he turn around and retrace the route back to his girlfriends, who were by now pecking around in the corn stubble only 20 yards from my decoys. It didn't take long before their faithful lothario was right beside them again, and after waiting for enough separation to assure no collateral damage, I piled him up in the dirt.

Afterwards, I drove all the way to Kellogg and bought some pies at the Town and Country Café, of which I've written about before. I bought a Butterscotch-Walnut and a Custard-Rhubarb for my own family at home, and I also got a Custard-Rhubarb (my favorite) for the landowners who had just allowed me the extreme privilege and pleasure of hunting their gorgeous, turkey-loaded farm. Then, after delivering it, I grinned the whole way back to Indiana.

The next stop made on my 2024 turkey travels is always one of my favorites…Pennsylvania. I first hunted there in 2001, and have been staying

A fantastic hunt in Minnesota earned me this tom.

at Bill George's family "camp" since 2011. This past spring Doug Pickle was already there when I arrived, and my buddy Brandon Ziegler from back home showed up shortly thereafter. On the first day I guided Bill, but he ran off both gobblers I called in for him by fidgeting around when he should have been locked down on the gun. I noted his bobbing head movements on the first tom at about the same time as the gobbler did, and that skittish bird was not the least bit tolerant or amused. And, while I don't really think my host boogered the second one, that doesn't keep me from telling him different. My modus operandi is to always give Bill George a hard time, whether he deserves it or not. Either way, he just laughs that goofy Bill George laugh and goes on being Bill.

Two days after our host left camp for a brief return to Florida and work commitments, both Doug and Brandon shot toms. I should've made it a

Doug Pickle, me, and Brandon Ziegler get our good luck ice-cream at Haller's General Store.

triple kill day, but a series of blunders and miscues by other hunters around me ruined my chances. I hate running into other people in the woods. Then, I wasted far too many days on a tom with long spurs that we kept seeing near camp. I should've never even tried for that evil rascal. Sometimes I hate myself in the woods, too.

Bruce Hall from Georgia rolled in and promptly shot a tom, and then when he, Doug, and I were returning from our obligatory trip to Haller's General Store for ice-cream during the waning hours of daylight, we stopped near camp and I called on the glass. Two toms promptly gobbled back at me and then came walking out across the road right in front of our truck without ever alerting in the least. Bill was on schedule to arrive in time for gobbling the next morning, so just as soon as he slid to a stop in the camp's gravel driveway, Bruce and I took him back up the road to where those toms had walked off. They gobbled great and we had a thrilling hunt initially, but for the longest time the persnickety duo stayed out in a field and refused to approach our position in the woods. After an hour long standoff and a little bit of a rain squall, we made a move and circled in tight to the back corner of the field, hoping to break them free from whatever funk was holding them back from cooperating fully with our dastardly plans for their demise.

The toms had been quiet for a good long while as we got rearranged closer to where they'd been roosted, and I worried that they might've spotted us setting up the blind, but when the sun popped out I told Bill that its warming rays ought to start the birds gobbling again. Not five minutes later they proved me right all on their own, and they also began answering my calls. It wasn't long afterwards before we saw them prancing and dancing in the sun's rays and cutting the distance. Right about then is when a hen approached us from the woods behind our blind while raucously yelping the whole way in. The toms loved it, as did the three hens accompanying them, before all those field birds rapidly closed ranks with us and stepped into the woods already in gun range. I told Bill to kill the one on the right and I would clean up scraps, but as I was taking a bead on the left-hand bird, Bill suddenly killed him outright! His buddy ran away, but some aggressive purring from both Bruce and me, along with the dead tom's flapping wings, was just too much for the surviving bird's brain to handle and he came back for one last look-see. Forthwith, I killed him dead as a mackerel.

One tradition we've always done back at camp is to take pictures of our kills in front of the dinner bell. Bill's Mom loved to look at those photos so much, and she died in 2023. We still maintain the tradition, and now it has an even deeper meaning for all of us. Here's my shout-out to one heckuva fine woman: Miss Beryl George. Gone, but certainly never forgotten and much loved!

Me and Bill George pose with our birds for his Mom.

Trevor had decided to come join our fun at the PA camp, so I took him out to a great spot and called in a bird for him on a real exciting hunt. Then, later that afternoon I heard a tom answering my loud yelps on the glass call from a long, long ways off. Rather than trying to reach him by walking a direct line and having to cross a wide, deep creek, we plotted his position on a map and drove around to the other side of his mountain before hiking up there. Once we'd gained the elevation and homed in on his vicinity, he gobbled at Trev's calling but refused to leave the opposite downslope and come to our position atop the ridge. When it became clear that things weren't going to work out before dusk, we backed out of there and returned the next morning, where we found that rascal still in the same place. He gobbled great on the limb and rapidly approached my calls after flying down, but once again he hung up below the lip of the ridgetop. We had the upper hand and great position on him, so I don't know what his problem was, but he refused to cooperate. We tried subtle calling, we tried calling a lot, we tried long periods of silence, we tried leaving me in place while Trev backed away and called from different positions, we called with a variety of devices, both

Trevor shot this beautiful tom while hunting with me in Pennsylvania.

Porcupines in Pennsylvania eat the aluminum road signs!

of us called at the same time to give the illusion of multiple hens; basically, we tried everything in our entire bag of tricks, but for two hours straight he stayed right there, barely out of sight and unwilling to budge an inch. Finally, it was time to affix bayonets and make a frontal assault.

Trev kept the tom gobbling while I crawled towards him. As I moved in he was so close that I could feel the rumble of his gobbles in my chest. All I had to do was ease over the top and shoot him, but there are a plethora of very good reasons why this was a really stupid thing to do. I did it anyway, and the loud alarm putts should have been the end of it. Game over. Admit defeat, tuck your pride back in your pocket, and go home.

What did I do, instead? Almost out of pure instinct and certainly without a coherent or rational thought flowing through my addled and obviously deficient brain, I reacted to him flushing practically at my feet and flying up like a grouse by shooting him out of the air like a grouse. The only problem being that this fine gobbler was certainly not a grouse, and he didn't deserve to be bushwhacked in such a manner. I knew all of this beforehand and yet I did it anyway. I was instantly ashamed of myself, even before the worst case scenario materialized before my eyes when the tom bounced up far downslope (due to the steep angle of the hillside) and began zig-zagging away through the thousands of fallen treetops and brush piles. I tried to anchor him with two more shots, but that didn't work and the chase was on. He had all of the advantage from the get-go, due to the tremendous head start and complicated immensely by the rugged terrain and brushy ground chocked full of partially rotten tree tops and hidden, knee-busting logs. Not even Trevor's young legs could keep up, and the tom vanished from view. A thorough search turned up nothing, including my dignity. I felt like shit and a total loser.

Later in the morning Trevor headed to New York while I moped around for a day, depressed so terribly that I couldn't even look myself in the mirror, and then I followed behind and met up with him and Cameron Yerton to try and salvage my wounded pride. After the boys roosted three toms while I was sitting around drinking beer with Trevor's Dad Jake, they told me the planned morning's hunt might just be so good that it would make me forget all about being a lowdown crippler of turkeys. Ah; there's nothing like the support and encouragement of friends and family who really know you....

Our hide was up underneath a brushy crabapple tree providing great cover, and we set out a couple of DSD jakes with ten hens to lure the toms and their anticipated entourage of girlfriends into gun range. If all three toms came in, the plan was for me and Cam to shoot first and Trev would kill the third bird if the opportunity presented itself. If only one came in, I was to shoot it so as to buoy my spirits and pull me out of the deep funk where my brain was currently living.

First gobble came late, but from very close behind us, and not three minutes later its maker pitched out and flew right over top of us and landed 150 yards out into the cattle pasture. The second tom sailed in and touched down soon thereafter and only half as far beyond the dekes, but he immediately walked out to join his buddy. Once they were on the ground the pair gobbled at anything we said, or nothing at all, but they marched to the far side of the pasture and began parading along the tree line near a pond full of Canada geese. The third tom remained tree-bound behind us, along with some gently yelping hens. He only gobbled sporadically, and his pronouncements had a deep, resonating tone that made me think that he was older and undoubtedly the boss of the area. The mere fact that all of the hens were staying in the roost trees with him certainly pointed to that being the case, as well.

Suddenly, the geese all got up in unison, but they flew only about 50 yards before landing in the pasture. Then, they began walking towards us. There were probably 15 adults and a like number of goslings, and as they continued to advance on our decoy spread like they intended to join up with them, the two toms made their way over and fell in behind the geese like they were part of the flock. Then, they broke into full-on strutting mode. At that point I was wondering what the heck was going on, here: did those two goofy toms think that the geese were hens? Did the geese think that our turkey decoys were another flock of geese? It seemed pretty darned odd.

At about 60 yards the geese finally veered off a little, but the two toms had by then focused on the DSD's as the preferred species of their desires and they continued on towards us. I'd been hearing drumming all morning long, but it was right about then when I heard that beautiful sound with more of a clear, "booming" tone, and I knew that our tree-bound tom had finally flown to ground and was coming around our back side. Then, I spotted a hen already in our decoy spread out front, and her presence even further encouraged the two strutters to pick up their pace of advancement.

When those toms were at 30 yards, I heard the drumming so loud and distinctly that I knew its maker had to be no more than 10 yards away. I could actually "feel" the vibration of it! Our only openings from underneath the crabapple faced to the front, so it was a tension-filled few moments before I suddenly saw the big old stud tom come charging out of the wood line to our right and on a straight collision course for the closest of our two fake jakes. Once he'd muscled up against it, I told Cam that the time for action was upon us and I was going to shoot the newcomer right in his face, and then I did exactly that. Cam waited for the other two toms to separate a bit, and then he killed the one on the right. Trevor didn't have a good shot, so he held fire.

Since I was sitting in the middle, I should have technically passed the shot at the big tom on to Cam, who was seated to my right. However, only because I knew that the day's main objective was to lift my spirits did I opt to kill the biggest and baddest gobbler of the bunch myownself. No; really! I wouldn't lie! We all got a good laugh out of me "meat-hogging" the long-spurred old tom from Cam, so I guess the day's intentions had been fulfilled, after all. And it's true…I did feel a little better.

Me, Trev, and Cam on a New York goose/turkey hunt.

With one of my New York toms now in the cooler and another tag in my wallet, I drove Trevor and Evan Walsh up north to Lewis County, where they had a couple of friends with access to lots of good turkey hunting ground. Dave is a state trooper and a real good feller, and his best friend Twiggy is a hard-charging character that's a ton of fun to be around. We stayed with them for three days and every minute was a blast. Well; almost...

The first day we started in a field where our hosts had been seeing multiple toms for weeks. We'd scouted there on the afternoon prior to this hunt and watched three toms for an hour as they hung out to the left side of a brushy section of old fence along a drainage ditch that protruded 90 degrees out into the field for about 75 yards. The next morning we arrived early enough to build a blind capable of hiding all five of us in that fence line, and when gobbling commenced, it was loud, often, close, and almost violent in nature. It was indeed an auditory display worthy of attending, but the toms wouldn't come into the field and eventually faded off a bit deeper into the woods.

Much too early (in my opinion), Trev and our hosts decided to vacate that spot and go find turkeys elsewhere. Personally, I would've stayed right there all day, because my eyes and ears had already told my brain exactly what we needed to do in order to kill a bird or three right there where we were at. All we needed to do was *be* there, and wait. However, you never guide the guide, so off we went. Arriving back at the truck parked 400 yards away, we were throwing our gear in the back when a bird hammered hard from just inside the tree line and right beside the spot we had just vacated. He then repeated his challenges three times Oops. So much for leaving the initial setup before 6:30 a.m.! The rest of the day was a series of failed attempts and driving around a lot. We had fun, in a comedic sense, but no turkeys were harmed in the process.

Day 2 was a shit-show. It started badly when we only heard one distant tom and then spooked him out of his roost while moving in. Twiggy was off hunting elsewhere with his son (who did manage to kill a bird), so that left Dave, Trev, Ev, and me to conduct the day's shenanigans. In all fairness, we did occasionally find turkeys. However, we made a mess out of every opportunity. The biggest screw-up of all occurred when we spotted a strutter up on a long side-hill disked field and stopped to gain access from the farmer to hunt him. "No problem. Do what you need to do."

While Evan sat in the truck observing the fiasco, the other three of us closed in, and then Dave held back while Trev and I snuck in the final hundred yards through three-foot-tall grass which terminated on the low end of the plowed dirt. The tom had several hens with him, and with the nearest tree line on either side of the field being a hundred yards away, we were hoping to get close enough by making like snakes and then working the birds while lying prone in our grassy cover.

Well, did I ever mention that Trev tends to project a feeling of pressure to perform up to his expectations on those people hunting with him? As we neared the tom I was in front on hands and knees. Trevor was following close behind me. When I first saw the tom he was probably 60 yards away, so I felt like I could easily make up another ten yards or more and get closer to the edge of the bare dirt, which was still 30 yards away. The grass was well above my head, so there was no way that we could be seen. Even still, Trevor kept whispering out what I interpreted at the time to be "instructions" as we went that were fraught with panic in their tone. Hey; I knew what I was doing and didn't need or appreciate him prodding me on like a show pig, but suddenly, he hissed out, "You spooked him." Then, looking totally disgusted with me, he got up and walked away.

That didn't sit very well with me. Not only had he been pushing me into doing something faster than I really wanted to do it, but unbeknownst to me, he'd also had a stupid "reaper" decoy thrust up above us as we advanced through the tall grass. If anyone had spooked that damned turkey, it had been him! And, I wasn't at all convinced that the turkey was spooked anyway, because all of his hens were still pecking around in the dirt contentedly; some of them were even now less than 30 yards away. The tom had simply hustled uphill and exited the field, which Trevor interpreted as him being boogered. Afterwards, back at the truck, Evan confirmed my suspicions because from his position he could see that the tom had started strutting again once he'd gained the top of the hill. Trevor and I had been unable to see that detail because of the rolling contour of the field.

Well, after I'd had a few choice words with Trevor to try and make him understand that this wasn't a damned job and that he needed to relax and quit taking things so seriously, the both of us spent the next couple of hours pouting. We almost never argue or disagree, and there's nobody in the world that I'd rather hunt with (especially so when things are going right and according to plan), but the minute circumstances go off kilter the boy can get a little sour and quick to blame those around him. In all honesty, he's usually right about it being somebody else who screwed things up, because Trev is a top-notch hunter and guide and he doesn't error often.

That's only one of the many reasons why he's so good at what he does. However, on that day, and with me, his drive to succeed in as efficient a manner as possible served only to take some of the fun out of the hunt. Of course, I do know that this wasn't his intention. Hey; like any good dog, I think that he'll begin to mellow some as he ages, and will eventually become a really *great* pooch.

Anyhoo; the rest of the day was a continuation of the modus we had used to that point so far, which was to rush hither and yon from place to place while trying to make something positive happen. We did get a tom to gobble at 11:30 and thought things might work out before the closing noon whistle, but a neighbor across the street with a 2-stoke weed eater started trimming his driveway at the worst possible time and the tom quit gobbling. In driving back to Dave's house we once again swung by the first place we'd hunted on Day 1, and sure enough, there was a tom in the usual spot right beside our brush blind.

The final day to hunt was upon us. I was really tired of riding around and running and gunning, so I asked Dave if he would mind just dropping me off at the brush-blind spot while he and Trevor made a play on a tom that the three of us had watched for two hours the evening prior as he strutted in a dirt field for a single hen. I told him that I was more than content to sit all day, if need be. He said that would be fine, and with Evan scheduled to accompany Twiggy and another guy, the plans were set in motion.

The farmer had disked up my field during the afternoon of the previous day, and in doing so, he'd also plowed under our brush blind. I rebuilt a portion of it just big enough to hide only myself before daylight, then stuck a jake deke and three hens out in the freshly turned dirt before settling in to await action. It felt so good to be hunting solo again, and to be able to conduct the excursion at my own pace! The sunrise was glorious too, and I just had a feeling that it was going to be a very good day.

First gobble was early and way off to the north; across the highway from me. I knew that Trev and Dave were hunting another piece of this same farm lying on that side of the blacktop, but they were two miles to the west. I didn't think it was even possible that they could've heard that first tom's gobble, but as he and a buddy fired up and began going absolutely bonkers, I texted to let them know that they had other options if their initial plan didn't pan out.

Two days earlier the woods beside me had been alive and rocking with hard gobbling toms, but now I heard not a peep. That really surprised me. Especially since we'd seen a tom the previous evening standing easily within 30 yards of where my butt was seated. Then, finally, another bird gobbled, although he wasn't close by. Instead, he'd piped up on the same line as those other two toms, but on my side of the highway. The field between us was 300 yards long, and beyond it was a creek bottom. That's where the bird was located. He didn't seem interested in coming to the field initially, but at least he gobbled sporadically enough that I was encouraged to stay put. In truth, I never even considered getting up and going after him because I had every confidence that he would eventually come to me. I was bound and determined to stay right where I was at and show my "young-gun" protégés that patience pays!

It wasn't long before I got a text from Trev saying that their bird had indeed put the screws to them and they were on the way to find the ones I'd heard. This made three mornings in a row that the boys were rolling out of the first spot before 6:30 a.m., which was pure silliness, in my opinion. Within the hour they had messed up the pair of birds which I'd heard, too, and were again tearing around the country in search of another hot tom. Me? I continued to sit tight right where I was at, confident as a cucumber, even though my tom had gobbled no more than 15 times in total before shutting up.

Around 8 o'clock a pair of hens popped out of the woods beside me and came over to get real aggressive with one of my fake hens. Then, they went right back into the woods and vanished. A short time later my tom gobbled two or three times and finally stepped into view at the far end of the field. He was with a jake, and after answering a couple of my calls, the big boy got all fuzzed up and began slowly making his way down the plowed rows in my directions. Then, he suddenly slicked up and turned to run back in the direction from whence he'd come, followed closely behind by his jake buddy. I still have no idea to this day what they were running from, but it didn't take them long to disappear. I felt a bit dejected, but remained sure of myself and the plan.

An hour later they came back out. I didn't even bother to call at first, because this time the pair were simply walking on a direct line towards me and only occasionally pecking at the turned dirt as they came. They weren't in a hurry, though. When they got to about 150 yards I yelped once, lightly, before setting my call down on the ground. I was confident that I wouldn't be needing it again. The tom stood tall for a long moment, just looking hard in my direction, and then I would swear that I could actually see a change in his attitude. He hadn't done anything different; it was more about his overall posture and the brightening colors of his head. Then, after gingerly covering another 25 yards like he was tiptoeing on broken glass, he assumed a slightly ruffled look to his feathers. Within a couple more steps the head came down and the shoulders rose up as he began the steady walk of a tom turkey with trouble-making on his mind.

As this grand and glorious tom was forthwith kicking and flopping his final death throes in the dirt, I could easily see from my blind with the naked eye that his spurs were long and hooked. That didn't really surprise me any, as by his actions and mannerisms I'd already judged him to be an old boss gobbler . Dare I say that it was what I was hoping for, too!

Trevor and Evan also got their birds that morning, but the story of the day among the northern NY crew was how I had toughed it out and killed a great tom with patience and a can-do attitude. That's not how they do it, and I was told repeatedly and in no uncertain terms how impressed they were. Listen up, here: there are all kinds of ways to go about killing turkeys, but the older I get, the more I appreciate hunts like that one, where you're not running around in a panic and forcing the issue, but rather, simply using brain power, logic, and accrued knowledge to best a particular tom. I headed back to Pennsylvania with a renewed sense of confidence and a good attitude.

Me, Dave, Evan, Twiggy, and Trev show off our toms.

My patience-produced tom in the field he had walked to reach me. I killed him at the old fenceline barely visible to the left of my right shoulder.

Five days later I was right back to my humbled old self, having been beaten up and battered by every turkey that I'd encountered. Once again I had been handed my ass on a platter. The birds had bested me. The toms were victorious. But, I'd hunted well, with dignity and honor. I'd enjoyed every single minute of my time afield, and I'd also spent precious good times with great friends. I'd kept my eyes open, my ears attuned, and my mouth generally shut in learning more about myself and my fascinating opponent. Despite the inevitable setbacks and heartaches, I was still looking forward to the next battle. Furthermore, I was still alive and the season had been a rousing success. However, it wasn't over, just yet. I could continue hunting in Michigan until the seventh of June.

I rolled into Michigan at about four in the afternoon. It had been raining ever since I'd crossed New York's western border two hours earlier, and the rain continued to fall until sometime after midnight. Fortunately, I had an ace-in-the-hole spot to hunt. Trevor had introduced me via phone to some fine folks who allowed me access to their property in his absence, and when I'd driven up their driveway, nine very wet turkeys were standing around in the middle of the 250-acre crop field directly behind their house. I could hunt all of that ground, and even though I wasn't there at dusk to confirm it as so (having gone to town for a hot meal), I logically assumed that the birds flew to roost on the far side of said field, in the hardwoods of a moderately narrow creek bottom. Mike told me that's what they did all the time, and he even pointed out the spot where they could often be seen entering or exiting the field. I hadn't got a good look at the birds to confirm age brackets or sexes before they'd disappeared behind the undulating contour of the field in the rain, but I was fairly certain that at least two of them were gobblers: whether toms or jakes, I did not know.

My initial morning setup along the treeline didn't pan out. The only turkey sound I heard was the softest, quietest little hint of a tree yelp, but even that bird was silenced after some raucous crows moved in and carried on for a good half an hour. If even those obnoxious pests couldn't get a turkey to gobble, then I considered chalking up the day to the lull that sometimes follows an extended rain event, when turkeys sometimes need an extra day before they get over it and start gobbling again. Fifteen minutes later I heard the turkey behind me fly down, but it sounded like a hen pitching away from the field and back through the creek bottom.

For another hour or more I heard/saw nothing else. Eventually, I felt the need to stand up and stretch, and when I did so, I spotted turkeys that were already out in the middle of the field. I still have no idea where they came from, or how they got there without my noticing them earlier. There's a big water pivot system out in the middle of that field, and they were now feeding beside its long arm and headed in the direction of the base. Every one of them completely ignored my calls and showed no sign of interest in anything other than feeding, and when I glassed them over real good with the Swarovski's, I could understand why: the flock was comprised of two toms and five jakes.

By dropping back into the creek bottom behind me and then moving 150 yards to my left, I could sneak out into a sort of "point" that projected 40 yards further out into the field than the rest of the woods edge. That put me as close to the turkeys as I could get, although they were still approximately 300 yards away. It was the best that I could hope for, considering the circumstances.

After successfully conducting this maneuver, I stood well-concealed inside the brushy wood line and studied what the flock was doing. In watching them for about a half-hour, I could see that they were still just milling about and pecking around…no gobbling, no displaying; just a bunch of drab turkeys showing no color or emotions other than an interest in filling their craws. The good part is that there was just enough undulation in the field so that occasionally most or all of the flock would disappear from view. I watched until such time as every turkey was out of sight and then I quickly hands-and-knees'ed it 20 yards into the dirt and stuck up a strutter and a hen DSD's. Once I'd crabbed back to my protective tree line I slowly stood up to see if I'd spooked anyone, but as all of the turkeys filed back into view, they were still calmly pecking along. Even better yet, they'd altered their path a little bit and were now coming back down along the length of that pivot arm. If they kept to their current heading, they'd pass by me at about 175 yards. I got seated and comfortable, with the limb of a tree in front of me forming the perfect gun rest.

When the lead turkey in the group reached that closest point I called loudly on the glass, twice, and although I got no answers, I did notice a couple of heads crane up to full height. Soon thereafter, one of the jakes casually broke free of the flock and began easing over in my direction. Others took note and followed behind him, and before long every turkey in the field was headed my way. As they closed in I could finally see some color brighten up on the heads of two birds, and then one of those cotton-topped toms

My final tom of the year was a fine Michigan gobbler who didn't utter a sound.

picked up his pace and overtook the first jake that had shown interest. At that point the tom's body assumed the position that I most wanted to see… what I often refer to as the old "head down, shoulders up, attach bayonets and charge" posture. It didn't take long after that before I had two adult toms and three jakes trying to muscle-up against my strutter, and after some shoulder thunder erupted from the old Benelli, only one tom and three jakes retreated towards the two other birds which had been lagging behind.

So ended the 2024 season, and in looking back afterwards, I could unequivocally say that it had been a year of grand accomplishments in epic proportions! Although there had been the inevitable miscues and low points expected from spending so much time in quest of a creature as unpredictable as the wild turkey, for the most part everything had gone off without a hitch. I'd greeted the dawn while wearing camo a total of 66 times stretched across 10 states during the months of March, April, and May, plus that one day of June, and called in 110 gobblers to under 40 yards (the standard which I refer to as, "in camp"). An unheard-of to that point in my life and surreal 51 of them had come home in the coolers of either me or my friends. My new (old…a 2014) van had also served me well for over 16,000 miles as I traversed the country from its southeastern corner, all the way to its southwestern one, and then almost all the way back to its northeastern edge, plus a multitude of destinations and unheralded pit stops along the way. Furthermore, I had finished up the final two states (AZ and WY) needed for completion of my fifth (and final) U.S. Super Slam. After all the miles, and all the trials, and all the tribulations, and all the effort, and all the strife, and all the joys, and all the sorrows, and all the glorious days spent along the turkey trails of this amazing country, I could finally boast (at least, to myself) that I was over and done with hunting where goals dictated my path. I felt free!

Then, I thought back to a year earlier, on May 15th specifically, when I was being wheeled into the operating room for a partial nephrectomy to remove a tumor from my kidney. At that point I was full of uncertainty about my future, or whether I would even have one. Death was a very real possibility. They say that it takes a close call with eternity to make a man fully appreciate what he has and the life he's been given, and as someone who's now been there and done that, I couldn't agree more. Not only is my mind free and at peace, but in the immortal words of Lou Gehrig, "I consider myself the luckiest man on the face of the earth."

2024

The year 2024 was certainly, by all measurable parameters, a rousing success, but as is always the case, I left it behind conscientiously aware that the true measure of achievement lay in far greater accolades than can ever be quantified by a yard stick or calculator. It had come in the sharing of good times with great friends; in the making of new ones; in seeking out and seeing new vistas and putting boot tracks on fresh dirt never before hiked; in the feelings felt in my heart and soul every time I heard a wily old tom rip out a resounding gobble, or in the chills rippling down my spine at the call of a Barred Owl or a coyote in the black of pre-dawn; in the peace and tranquility feeding my inner essence while traversing this great land and its wonderful and wild places; in every quickened heartbeat or anxious tremor felt when an unseen tom drummed from so close that I could feel it; in all the little things that mean so very much to me. This wondrous life that I've chosen as a traveling turkey hunter has given me more than I could ever hope to repay, and has truly served as a self-perpetuating inspiration and motivation in my own life to keep things going: always striving to achieve more, and experience more, and to *be* more. I hope that aspiration never ends.

This one says it all.

Chapter 8

2025

I'd originally intended for this book to end with the 2024 spring season. In fact, I was already claiming that the thing was "in the can" and ready for publication when I headed down to Florida to begin my 2025 shenanigans. However, as happenstances occurred and the season wore on, I realized that there was no way to end this book without including the season just passed. Too many things happened, of too much importance, and which will no doubt affect my life and any seasons to come. So, I've added in another chapter and a few more thoughts. Hang on; this one might get a little bumpy and convoluted.

As you will have by now taken note, I've dedicated this volume to my nephew Dan, who was the middle child of my elder sister's five. Even from a very young age Danny and I shared a strong connection. I remember when he was just a toddler and we took him and his twin siblings (Eliot and Cara…the final two kids wouldn't be born for a few more years) to a botanical garden in Florida, where they lived at the time. Danny had only recently begun to walk, but he latched onto the little finger of my right hand and followed me around that place for a couple of hours; all while constantly gazing up in wonder and amazement at the big old trees with their huge leaves and flowers. This little tyke was spellbound and smitten with the wonders towering before him, and his bright blue eyes sparkled in pure wide-eyed awe for the entire time we were there. I knew right then that this trip had left an indelible mark on my young nephew, and I was sure that I was witnessing the beginnings of a deep love of nature and the natural world blossoming in his little heart.

As Danny grew older he became an eagle scout and a gifted athlete, and later on, he aged into an adult who following a path unlike anyone else I've known. He was, in short, a true free spirit. Also: smart as a whip, kind and compassionate, loved by all who he ever encountered on the wild ride that would become his life, and simply a joy to be around. There was nobody else like him, and at his very core he maintained that love of wilderness which I'd seen bloom in him as a child. One of the reasons I identified with my nephew so much is because I recognized the way nature and the natural world were central to his true self. I'd felt those same feelings ever since my own father had taken me into the woods squirrel hunting at a very young age.

For a number of years Dan had been living out west while adventuring into untold places and honing his knowledge and expertise in the recently-legal marijuana farming trade. He'd also become a real good musician, and everywhere he went people gravitated to his magnetic personality and came to love him. Then, rather abruptly, he decided to come back home to Indiana with his three wolves, where he became one of (if not THE) first holders of a legal hemp farming license. I don't know; maybe he had a premonition of things to come, or perhaps not. It's just as likely that he simply wanted to come back "home" in order to be closer to his family, which always meant everything to my nephew. All I know is that it was great having him back around, and we began golfing together quite a bit. On most Sundays he would also stop by his Grandma's (my Mom) house, where she'd fix him huge stacks of her delicious waffles (that boy could *EAT*) while he did laundry and got a hot shower, since his abode out at the farm was pretty "rustic."

One day while we were golfing he mentioned that a lump in his groin had been bothering him quite a bit, and when he pulled up his shorts to show me, I was taken aback and left aghast at what I saw! The thing was an egg-sized knot, nearly an inch tall, and it had split open down the middle; oozing blood and gunk and looking absolutely hideous. I told him that I didn't know what was going on, but if he wouldn't go see a doctor the very next day, then I was going to drag him there myself!

Well, that damned engorged lymph node ended up being metastatic melanoma, and it was already at Stage 4 by the time the doctors began treatments. They told him the odds of beating it now were slim, but there was a good chance that they could at least keep it under control until a better treatment might come along. Danny was incredibly strong of mind and body, but nothing those doctors did could stop the progression of the inevitable, and we all watched helplessly over the next couple years as that heinous disease brought our precious Dan The Man closer and closer to his mortality.

Going into my departure date for Florida in the spring of 2025 I was particular worried about him, because despite all the different treatments, the disease seemed to be picking up speed, spreading, and getting worse. The best option now was to get him into some ongoing trials of new drugs, but he was also grasping at other alternatives like massive doses of vitamin C. We all still held out hope, but it was becoming more and more obvious that things were not going well. He'd become noticeably weaker, more gaunt, and in more pain. He'd even begun to lose his legendary appetite, which made me realize for the first time that the odds of his winning against cancer, or even playing it to a draw, were low. Despite the bad news, he continued to tough it out and smile through the pain.

Then, in late January I had surgery to repair a torn rotator cuff on my left shoulder. I shoot left handed, so that meant I would be unable to use a 12 gauge for the entire spring season. In fact, by the time I got to Florida I was still wearing a cumbersome padded sling, restricted to lifting no more than 15 pounds, and they'd set up physical therapy sessions twice per week in Zephyrhills. My shoulder was a mess, but my brain was also in a bad way because of the situation with my nephew. Thankfully, I had Trevor Bays there in camp to help me during the first part of the season. Otherwise, I'm not sure how things would've turned out.

Florida is a continual challenge for me as a guide anyway, since I never know exactly how much land I will have access to when the season starts, or what I might lose at any moment. That's because farmers sell out regularly due to unheard-of skyrocketing land prices. I try my best to pick up new parcels to take their place, but that's an especially difficult task seeing as how I'm a "Yankee" who lives in Indiana. I'm always battling a balancing act between how many birds I think my undulating amount of land can supply, and how many clients I should line up. The mental strain this puts on me is enormous; especially so because of the way I conduct my hunts by guaranteeing an opportunity for a shot at a tom. I never want to overbook clients *or* run out of birds.

Well, Trevor and I started off the season with a bang on opening weekend. My three clients that I personally took out killed four turkeys on Saturday alone, while Trev's five guys each killed one tom apiece by Sunday. That's *nine* birds in two days! On Monday the two of us then took Jeff Young to another great property, where Stephen Spurlock from Chasing 49 filmed the hunt. That endeavor produced a great tom and some incredible video footage! Following that, Trev and I took a pair of guys out the following day on what we call the "Love Boat Cruise," to a property only accessible by boat, and by 8:01 we had two stud Osceolas hanging by their substantial spurs from a horizontal limb…one of which measured 1- 11/16 of an inch!

That totaled 12 birds in only four days of hunting, and the rapid pace in which we'd gotten the first dozen kills freed us up for a few days before the next clients were due to arrive. It was a good thing, too; because I blew out a knee while climbing into my van, and after a trip to an Urgent Care clinic, I spent the next five days hobbling around on crutches. From that point on I was basically an invalid for the entire duration of the 2025 turkey season; incapable of walking downhill without excruciating pain. Going uphill wasn't much better. I can't emphasize enough how terribly that injury affected my entire spring!

Luckily, all of my Florida land is flat ground, and with Trev handling some of the clients and me toughing it out and working through the pain, we were able to create the opportunities for everyone to kill their Osceola. In fact, when it was all said and done, only two of our hunters needed a second day to get their bird! The season really couldn't have gone any more smoothly in that regard. The only hiccups along the way were a crippled and lost tom (I will never again guide another bow hunter!) and another fellow who missed a tom twice with his shotgun. Unfortunately for him, my guarantee is only good for the *opportunity* to kill a turkey….I can't guarantee the ability of my hunters to hit what they shoot at! There was also another "incident" that I'll mention here briefly, but only because of how much it infuriated me.

I took this guy out after a bird that had put the screws to me and another hunter two days earlier, and although we never heard a single gobble all morning long, at about 9:30 a.m. the tom came charging into our setup and the fellow killed him. This bird was *spectacularly* gorgeous, with real whitish leg feathers, several bright orange secondary wing feathers, and some pure black wing primaries on each side. Each wing also had a primary feather that was divided by the central quill: solid black on one side and mottled on the other…very unique! This turkey was a splendid specimen of his kind, and my knees began shaking just as soon as I realized what the guy had killed!

Everything was all good at that point, with smiles and lots of pictures taken, and then the guy put his bird in a cooler and drove 16 hours back home to the taxidermist. I don't know who the hell he talked to after that, but the next day I got a text message saying that he thought I ripped him off and planted a "tame" bird on the farm. Furthermore, he claimed that he was going to turn me in to the FWC, and wanted to know what I was going to do to make it right. Man, I was livid-mad, and could've bit through nails!!! He wouldn't answer my phone calls, so I told the damned fool in no uncertain terms via text that any turkey hunter (myself included) would've cut off a finger or two just for the chance at such a tom, and my only regret was that it had been him who brought this glorious bird to ground, and not a "real" turkey man who would feel proud and honored. What a f'ing moron!

He never bothered replying, and I still haven't heard from the FWC.

Well, after the second week of the season Trevor headed north with Bruce Hall to begin their epic swing of 15 or so states, but I stayed right there until the final day. First of all, I'd arranged my client list to drag out that long, but of even more importance was the fact that my shoulder and knee weren't going to allow me to hunt like I normally do every year once I leave Florida, so I was in no big hurry to head north. The situation with Danny was also getting worse and worse by the day, and to be honest, my mind was just in a very dark, negative place. I simply didn't feel that old familiar fire in my belly to get after turkeys with a passion unbridled.

This was a very odd sensation for me, and it was one that I didn't much like, but there was no denying how I was feeling. Heck; I hadn't even tried very hard to kill a Florida tom during the whole time that I'd been down there… due mostly to not being physically able to do so, but there was more to it. Yes; my knee was screwed up and my shoulder was so sore that the only gun I could've shot was a .410 (and I'd only been able to borrow one of those a couple of times), but where my head was at served as the real problem. In short, I was brain-boogered and spending a lot more time worrying about my nephew than I was thinking about turkeys. When Bill George bestowed upon me one of his infamous plastic monkeys given to anyone in our camp who doesn't kill a Florida bird, I simply stuck the danged thing in my vest with only mild protestations. There were more important things going on in my life.

Here are some Florida pictures of good times and special birds:

Bill George's "Camp Monkey."

Bobby Ostendorf and George Fant really enjoyed themselves.

Will J Parks on his way to completing a .410 Super Slam.

Father/Son Joe & Jarred Coffing from my home state of Indiana.

Sean Songer was the beneficiary of a coveted "Love Boat Cruise."

Will & Griff Moody were another father/son duet who shot great toms.

Mike Rexrode's bird never gobbled, but he was a stud!

Bubba and Rawlston Phillips were my final father/son set, and they stacked up three toms on a fantastic hunt.

Florida always produces some daggers!

Bill George lounging around camp in a chair I picked up alongside the road, but which everyone loves to sit in.

However, once the Florida season ended I had to go somewhere, so I drove back home and dropped off the trailer used for all of my camping and guiding gear down there, and then I spent some time with Danny. He was in lots of pain by then, shriveled into a scarecrow of his former self, and very, very weak. But, we went out looking for morel mushrooms one day and were able to talk for a while as he muscled through the hike using a walker. That was tough. There was still hope, but it was dwindling fast and we both knew it. The doctors were trying to culture some of his lymph cells to create another treatment, but to be honest, I wasn't even sure if he'd still be around for the five weeks that it would take to get that medicine manufactured and injected into his bloodstream. When I left his house that evening, I knew it might be the last time we would ever spend any quality time together, and my heart was breaking in two. Our goodbye took on a deeper meaning and our hug as I left was longer and stronger than usual. Neither one of us wanted to let go.

Feeling helpless and with nothing to do but hope, and care, and love, I decided to go hunt with my friend Ken Greene in Virginia for a few days. It had been a number of years since I'd been there, but I'd been looking forward to a return trip for quite a while. Besides that, Ken told me there was a giant tom on one of his properties that he was really wanting me to kill. I figured a short trip out there might help ease my mind and get me fired up about turkey hunting once again, but first I had to procure a gun. My old buddy Jim Spencer had offered to loan me a .410, but he lives in Arkansas and it would entail shipping the thing from there. Still, that seemed like the best option I had, so I began making arrangements to have his firearm received at a local gun shop.

Then, I got a call from a buddy in town who told me that he had a gun I could borrow without the wait or expense of getting one shipped to me. It was a sweet little TriStar semi-auto .410 with a pistol grip, which he'd bought as sort of a "project" piece. He'd patterned the gun extensively, killed a bird with it, and then put the thing away in the safe with no real intentions of using it again. I said that I'd sure take him up on the offer to borrow it if he really was ok with me doing that, but I would rather just buy the gun outright if he'd consider selling. That way I wouldn't have to worry about damaging someone else's firearm. Anyone who's seen my beat-up old 12 gauge Benelli M2 would certainly attest that I'm hard on my turkey hunting equipment!

Well, Jubal agreed to sell it, so now I had my gun. Ammunition, however, was going to be another problem altogether, as I couldn't find any of the Apex Nitro loads that he said this gun preferred. No matter whom I called, it didn't matter; not even a Cabelas along my route to Virginia had any in stock, and they were out of every other TSS load, as well. In desperation I called my buddy Brandon Ziegler and asked if he happened to have any .410 shells. Zieg was two hours into a road trip to NJ, but after rummaging around a bit while we talked on the phone, he confirmed that there were three Nitro .410 shells on his dashboard. He offered to stash them at a designated spot along Interstate 70 (the same path that I'd soon be driving to Ken's) so

I could pick them up on the way…sort of like a turkey hunter's geo-cache! Those rounds would at least give me a shot or two to check the gun's zero with the William's SLR Reflex sight that I'd put on it, while still leaving me one round for that big old VA gobbler. In reality, things weren't as bleak as I've made them out to be, because I knew that Ken had a selection of .410 shells on hand at his place. There was also a gun shop up in Greenwood, Indiana which I'd been told might have some of the shells that I was seeking, so I delayed my departure until the following day (it was Sunday afternoon). When I called that store just as soon as they opened for business the next morning, I was told that they had gobs and scads of the Nitro .410's in stock, so I hustled up there, bought two boxes of 10 rounds each, and headed out on the road. Then, I picked up the three rounds which Zieg had stashed at an old phone booth in a run-down gas station in West Virginia. I'm sure the two fellas curiously watching me grab a Ziploc baggy out of its hiding place thought they were witnessing some sort of clandestine drug deal, but I didn't stick around to discuss the matter and motored on out of there.

I still hadn't fired a gun against my recently rebuilt shoulder, but soon after my arrival in Virginia I took care of that at Stephen Spurlock's family cabin, where I met up with Trevor Bays and Evan Walsh. By only the second shot she was hitting spot-on to point of aim, so I decided to leave the boys to hunt the Spurlock grounds while I travelled on over to Ken Greene's place. The next morning found Ken and I set up at the property he calls "the shooting range," which was where we would hopefully encounter that big gobbler Ken had been watching and patterning carefully for me.

Our setup was along a treeline bordering a fescue field and backed by a fairly deep creek, where Ken had pre-cut some low-hanging limbs out from under a cedar tree to afford us a nice little natural hide. A DSD Strutter and a couple hens out front offered our adversary and a buddy whom he hung out with regularly the opportunity to come in looking for love or a fight; their pick. I had a good idea which one they would choose.

Initial gobbling was decent, but further downstream from us than I would've liked. However, Ken is always rather conservative in his approach to roosted turkeys…bordering on being overly cautious, even…but it's better to be that way than the opposite. You know what "they" say: the difference between setting up too far away from a turkey or too close is exactly one step. Ken had been watching these two gobblers for weeks, and he assured me that they would eventually head toward us. I know better than to question my old friend's turkey sense, so we settled in to await developments as a couple of hens began yelping loud and often from half as far as the toms. In my view, talkative hens are always a good thing…right up until they steal the tom away!

After flydown the two toms began gobbling even better, and they answered a call or two I sent out on an old, favorite Cane Creek Pro Custom Glass. Then, they began heading in our direction and it didn't take much time before we caught sight of them ass-grabbing a couple of hens in their company. But, as the toms drew close enough to see our decoy spread, they forgot all about the real girls who'd been adroitly avoiding them, to focus, instead, on our fake alternatives. Heads down, shoulders up; here they came on a hard march. One of them absolutely dwarfed the other, and I knew instantly that this was the tom Ken had brought me here to kill. He and I never even bothered to exchange a word between us…each of us knew that it was now "ShowTime."

Ordinarily, in this type of situation I like to sit and enjoy the spectacle for a bit. I've seen this same scenario play out so many times that I'm fully aware there's no real need to hurry or rush things. When toms are aggressively attacking a strutter deke they're going to be there for a while, and unless some unforeseen circumstance occurs (like other gobblers charging onto the scene, or a pterodactyl swooping in to attack), you can take your time and make sure everything is right before pulling the trigger.

Hence, I was calmly sitting steady, enjoying for the first time looking at a gobbler's head through the bright red circular reticle with crosshairs of that William's gunsight. Like I said, I had intended to wait a bit and enjoy the show, but when the monster gobbler separated a bit from both his buddy and the strutter decoy, and then thrust his head up high in the proverbial "kill me now" pose, I figured there was no real need in delay so I pulled the trigger.

Now, I've done a lot of shooting in my lifetime. And, when it occasionally happens that I "flinch," for whatever reason, I know it immediately. Trust me when I say this for all to read: *never* have I flinched *that* bad!! Did it happen because of a subconscious worry about my surgically repaired shoulder and whether I might be doing it harm while still under the doctor's care? I mean, I'd shot this gun twice just the day before, and the recoil was absolutely negligible. In fact, I'd quite frankly been shocked that it was so light. Surely, that wasn't the reason for the flinch.

Was it due to the oversized presence of the gobbler looming in front of my little "pew-pew" .410, and an inexplicable fear/worry/foreboding that this diminutive gun wouldn't have what it took to dispatch such a beast; thereby sending him charging over angrily to kick my ass for only annoying him with the "Pixie Dust" 9.5's that I was shooting? I've had a few hand-to-hand battles with gobblers over the years, but so far, I'm undefeated…so that scenario seemed a moot point, too.

Perhaps my spastic flailing at the trigger had been brought on by a case of "Sudden-Onset Tourette's Syndrome" and its accompanying physical "tics?" This was the only logical explanations that I could come up with in the nano-seconds following the errant trigger pull, while also simultaneously realizing that I had missed that danged gobbler by no less than a foot and a half due to spasming out like I'd been poked in the ribs with an electric cattle prod! Another vivid memory of that instant following the gun's repercussion was of hearing the crystal-clear voice of Ken hissing in my left ear, "God damnit, Doc!" That, as much as anything else, really sent my brain's synapses sparking out in every direction and flustered the heck out of me. The tom, after flying 10 yards, merely landed and began nervously walking away, so after I somewhat pulled myself together, I hurriedly took aim again and concentrated on holding steady as I squeezed the trigger. However, no matter how hard I pulled, the gun would not shoot. I couldn't for the life of me figure out why, but that did it…this unexpected mechanical snafu really threw my brain for a loop. From that moment onward I was, for all practical purposes, fried and done, and I simply gave up. Slumping down into the gobbler lounger chair dejectedly, I was reduced to watching that brute of a tom exit stage left.

For the next three mornings Ken and I tried various strategies and different setups to strike revenge on that tom. All failed. Maybe the old rascal was that good, but I really think he was just that lucky. One day we had him fired-up in late morning and pacing back and forth from 100-150 yards away, but there were also five hens sharing the field with us and every time I got the tom headed in our direction with my calling, those dastardly "ladies" would commence to yelping and promising all sorts of lewd and lascivious favors and the tom would capitulate to their evil intentions. It was certainly entertaining, and even rather comical, as well, to watch how he'd dance towards us to the point of our thinking that things were finally going to come together, and then the hens would aggressively yelp and he'd turn to strut towards them, instead. This same sequence repeated itself time and again, until finally, the real feathers won out and all the turkeys faded away across the field and out of our lives.

The weather pattern during this timeframe was horrendous, too: hot, hot, and then hotter still. The ground was already baked hard as a wedding dick, and it felt like rain was something that was only a faint remembrance from decades past. Finally, I'd had my fill of that particular tom, and of baking in the sun to try and kill him, so we decided to go hunt elsewhere. Late morning found us in a real pretty and relatively cool (i.e.: shady) creek bottom where Ken has enjoyed numerous successes throughout the years, and when a lone hen rapidly advanced on our position after my very first call, I felt pretty good about the possibilities. Then, that silly wench spent an hour pacing round and round my DSD feeding hen decoy, as she tried to figure out what that fake gal found so fascinating about the tiny spot of dirt below her nose. The real hen's behavior was a curious thing simply due to how intensely she seemed to be studying the situation, but eventually she lost interest and wandered away.

I can't say for sure whether it was this same hen who came back a half an hour later, but I tend to think so because she came straight to the same decoy and began acting similarly. However, there were now two toms tagging

Me and Ken Greene got a good'un in the shady creek bottom.

Virginia grows some big spurs, too.

along behind her! Rather surprisingly, they showed no interest in either the real hen, or the fake one, and kept on going like they were more interested in displaying for one another's benefit. At that point I decided to take the shot, even though the pair had actually been closer by a dozen yards when they first appeared on the scene. Now that the gobblers were obviously walking off for good, I had only one last chance. I'm not going to say how far of a shot it was, as I never give out such info in hopes of impressing anyone with what I would consider the "wrong" sort of data, but I will say that it was one of the longest shots I've ever let go at a tom…and the results were nothing less than stellar, both in the lethality and the number of pellet strikes in the tom's head and neck! The old boy also wore legitimate 1- 1/2" spurs on each leg, so I was thrilled by the first kill with my new pew-pew .410!

Now that I was officially "on the board" for the first time all spring long (the date already being April 27th), I was hoping that the ice had finally been broken and more good luck would soon follow. However, that wasn't to be the case as Ken and I continued to struggle. Oh, we heard turkeys gobble every morning early, but they would soon hush up and leave us panting and sweating in the heat and humidity of yet another blistering-hot day. Besides that, my left knee was really hurting bad, leaving me unable to cover ground like I ordinarily would. But, it was mostly the unbearable heat every day which kept us from hunting hard enough to make good things happen. The toms were also affected by the weather in a negative way: they refused to gobble at all after brief tree-bound flurries at dawn, and once on the ground they gave us *nothing* more!

What had originally been intended as a three or four day excursion had now stretched to seven days of torture when suddenly I realized that I needed to hustle home for a doctor's appointment regarding my shoulder. However, by then the pressure to kill another Virginia tom or two had been building by the day, and it had gotten personal. I wanted revenge, and I wanted it bad! So, after an eight hour drive home for a 30 minute evaluation by the surgeon, I turned right around and came back to Ken's. My gracious host insisted that my presence was still both welcome and enjoyed, although I quietly questioned his sincerity because I've always adhered to the old adage that two things in life start to stink after three days: fish, and house guests. But, Ken still acted eager to get after those old gobblers every morning, and another four days clicked off before we knew it. That meant I'd been in Virginia for 11 days in total, with only one tom and a miss to show for all the effort. It was time to admit defeat and pack my bags. I was tired and weary, my brain was baked, my body was trashed, and I was getting daily updates on Danny's condition that made me less and less interested in hunting. However, Doug Pickle and Bill George had recently arrived at Bill's camp near Tionesta, Pennsylvania, and they were reporting pleasant springtime weather with cool/cold nights and turkeys gobbling their brains out. That sounded too good to resist, so I pointed my van north.

Wouldn't you know it? Within twenty miles of leaving Ken's place I ran into a vicious rain squall that brought the temperature dropping precipitously. The weather station on my radio was suddenly calling for more of the same over the next week, even though up until that moment their predictions had been for continued hot and humid torture. I felt sure that rain and colder temps were just what those Virginia turkeys needed to start acting normal again, and I almost considered looping around and going right back, but after careful consideration I decided to maintain the plan and get out while I still had a little bit of dignity. In hindsight, I should have stayed put...

For six days in a row the turkeys of Forest County, Pennsylvania thumped my butt, and they did it with grace and aplomb! If I feigned right, they went left. If I went high, they went low. If I thought I had 'em figured out, they made sure to put the screws to me so hard that there was little doubt left of me being nothing but a blithering idiot. The steep terrain was certainly part of the problem, as my knee was giving me terrible fits. Level ground was ok, but there ain't a whole lot of that along the Allegheny River, and I found myself time and again severely limited in how, or even if, I could pursue my antagonists as they pranced merrily up and down; hither and yon. I'd never felt like an invalid in my life, but here I was at the tender age of 65 suddenly feeling like my turkey hunting glory days were in the past because of physical limitations. That sucked, and I was bummed out about it.

Then, I got the call that I'd been dreading for some time. Danny was going downhill rapidly and hospice had been called in to help with his care. Up to this point he'd been getting love and constant attention from his four siblings, his mother, my mother, my sister and her family, and a whole cadre of close friends, but now he needed round-the-clock assistance and major pain medications. For me, this meant that in all likelihood my turkey season had just ground to a halt, which didn't matter one iota and factored absolutely zero into my next move. It was simply time to go home and be there beside my friend and nephew as he completed his earthbound journey. The two of us had already said our love you's and goodbyes the last time I'd been in town, but now I considered it paramount that I get home as soon as possible. I dreaded that eight hour drive in ways which I can't even describe, and cried tears of sadness and despair the whole way.

For the next four days I spent nearly all of my daytime hours and up until they made us go home at night bedside with Dan at a Hospice House. Those amazing folks working there took great care of my beloved nephew, and I can't thank them enough. It was a terribly sad time, full of sorrow and heartbreak. However, during the whole stay there a strange feeling of vigor and positive energy enveloped his room...supplied and nurtured by a steady stream of Dan's friends and compadres, old schoolmates and fellow soccer players, ex-girlfriends and current love interests, our family members, and seemingly everyone else who had ever met my wonderful nephew. Guitars were played, songs were sung, and every one of the many kind folks who visited told us in great depth of how exceptional a person Dan was in their own lives, and how appreciated and loved he was as a friend. And, while he was unconscious or nearly so the entire time because of heavy morphine doses on the hour, person after person would sit with Dan for long periods of time, stroking his arms or holding his hand, rubbing his feet or cradling his head in their hands, whispering their goodbye's and love you's in his ear, and yes, crying a river of tears. It was an incredibly touching honor to be there with my nephew, and like I said, the volume of love that came into that little room further buoyed my soul and kept me from being swept away in grief.

When he died in the early morning hours of May 14, the outpouring of compassion and kindness shifted to a friend's house where his nuclear family had been staying, and all day long as people flooded to there in great hordes, stories were told and remembrances shared by people in Dan's orbit; many of whom I'd never met. Word of his passing spread rapidly, and people from all walks of life and all corners of the country rushed over to offer comfort and condolences. It was a very special day, with a wild mixture of tears, laughter, and love filling the air in an almost palpable hue. But, by dusk I was exhausted and overwhelmed by the envelopment of so many souls, so I decided to leave. I needed to get out in the woods and find my strength and spiritual uplifting in the place where I always turn to in times of trouble, turmoil, or heartbreak. I needed to head back to the beautiful hills of Pennsylvania, where I could stay at Bill George's camp while nobody else was there and grieve as I most saw fit. Dan, of all people, would've understood perfectly my need to get away, as we both shared a profound love of the woods and the sanctity for spiritual healing to be found there. The forest was calling us.

At 1 a.m. I pulled into camp. At 4 a.m. I awoke, and by 5 a.m. I was nestled into a comfy deadfall (Pennsylvania has a goofy law that says you can't construct a blind out of natural materials) where I'd come close to killing a tom back on May 10th and took note of its ideal location for a future hunt. Initially, I could hear turkeys gobbling down below me, near the highway, but about the time I was thinking about moving in their direction, a pair of toms opened up further out on the same shelf where I was set up. They were

I think my nephew had a hand in this victory.

Posing for yet another turkey portrait in front of the George family's camp in Pennsylvania.

probably 400 yards away, but soon began gobbling regularly and making steady progress in my direction. I didn't even bother touching a call, as I was sitting in the ideal "catbird's seat" and their path would bring them straight to me. I first caught sight of them at about 125 yards, and they caught sight of the DSD Posturing Jake decoy at about 70 yards. From that point on, it was just a matter of waiting for the perfect shot window after they rushed in, and that happened pretty quickly. Once the targeted tom began his final death throes and wing thrashings against the earth, his companion came over and spent nearly an hour more flogging and pecking at his dead buddy's head while regularly doing this weird purr-thing in conjunction with lifting his beak to the sky. It was another strange behavior that I'd never seen before, but which reminded me of the "grieving" tom that I'd shot in the San Carlos Reservation of Arizona back in 2024.

The hour I sat watching this show gave me plenty of time to contemplate the deeper meanings behind the hunt, and of life itself, and it didn't take much imagination to think that my beloved Danny had offered a hand in how everything turned out. I mean, I hadn't shot a tom in nearly three weeks by then, but this silky-smooth hunt came together just about 24 hours exactly after his passing. When I subsequently built my feather "shrine of respect" to the gobbler (and Dan) there was a much deeper significance behind it and tears fell freely on the forest floor.

The next morning I got on a bird that gobbled like his soul depended on it. He gobbled early, and he gobbled a lot. In fact, there were several times when he gobbled so often and so rapidly that I figured he might pass out from lack of oxygen to his brain, fall from the tree, and I could just walk down and pick him up before he regained consciousness. Unfortunately, most of that gobbling was directed at rumbling and cracking thunder, and while the day should've been growing brighter by the minute, it instead got progressively darker out and I knew that heavy rain was imminent. Rather than sitting there and getting soaking wet, I retreated 70 yards and stepped underneath a deer hunting tower stand just as the rain came down in buckets. I was actually dry as toast there and fairly comfortable sitting on an old milk crate, but the rain never let up a bit for three solid hours. By then the tom had either left the premises, or drowned, because I never heard another peep from him all morning.

The following day I snuck back into that same area early and was rewarded with not just one, but two toms gobbling very well. Not as good as the previous day, but good enough. The best part was that the stars were twinkling above and there was zero possibility of additional rain. Since they were each roosted on opposite sides of an old woods road, I was able to slip in quietly and pick a setup tree that was no more than a hundred yards away from either one, and when the right-hand bird flew down I yelped one time with a diaphragm and clicked off the safety just as soon as he gobbled back at me. Then, he moved steadily my way while clucking inquisitively.

When his bright red head popped up over the ferns at 29 yards I bowled him over and never gave it another thought…that is, until I was standing over his still-flopping body and saw the 3-inch beard and nub spurs of a *jake*. Up until that moment I'd shot a grand total of six jakes during my entire lifetime (three on purpose, and three by accident). Looking back through my records later on, I found out that the last one of those was killed in 1997. To say that I was disappointed would be a serious understatement, but truth be told, I never even entertained the possibility of either bird being a teenage turkey before pulling the trigger. They had both gobbled like adults and the one I shot came straight in to the call, albeit clucking, but that's something I've witnessed many times. The only thing I can say is that I should've waited and not been so anxious to get a bird on the ground. Oh, well. He would eat real good.

With my Pennsylvania bag limit now filled, I decided to venture on up to New York. This would be trip number 28 to one of my favorite destinations, and even though Trevor was out west and wouldn't be able to join me in the state where he grew up, I was looking forward to a return. In his stead, I invited an old friend from North Carolina, and we made plans to stay in the comfy deer hunting camp of Trevor's Dad, Jake Bays.

Earl Carpenter is a great turkey hunter of about my age who's been doing it since he was a mere youth, and he's hunted with or been around a long list of prominent turkey hunters from both North and South Carolina's storied past for all of his life. I think he was even there in attendance as a young lad at the initial meeting to establish the NWTF. Earl knows a million people and has two million interesting stories, and he's more than willing to share them at the drop of a hat…even during a turkey hunt, when a gobbler might be closing in! I've been trying to encourage him to write a book, because it would be pure entertainment for our fellow die-hard turkey hunting friends and comrades.

I got in town a couple hours before we were due to rendezvous at camp, so I stopped by Joe and Vinny's Pizzeria and ordered up a bunch of hot wings with celery and blue cheese dressing, plus a couple dozen garlic knots. That meal has been a staple during turkey season at Jake's camp for decades, and I look forward to maintaining the tradition for many years to come! This wonderful pizza joint in Sherburne is run by Salvatore Magro, who is a real "colorful" character, to say the least. Good as gold, an accomplished and acknowledged expert videographer in the outdoor industry, and a ton of fun to be around, he invited Earl and me to accompany him the following day to a sweet property that's full of turkeys. I've been there before with Sal, so he didn't need to ask twice!

When we pulled up to the Pizzeria early the next morning, Sal had already come downstairs from his apartment and was deciding which of the Corvettes he wanted to drive…his own maroon one, or the restaurant's delivery car which was painted up like an Italian flag. Laughing, I told him there wasn't room for all of us in either one, so we hopped in Earl's truck. Then, we drove to Sal's honey-hole and got settled into a blind tucked up tight against the wood line and overlooking a field grown up in fairly tall weeds. Oh… did I mention the weather? The wind was gusting, it was raining, and the temperature was in the very low 40's. Not exactly ideal conditions for a turkey hunt, but Sal assured us that we would soon be seeing birds and to not worry about it.

Despite the weather conditions, I thought we heard a single gobble not long after daylight wedged in, and even though I got no answer to a yelp on my pot call, it wasn't long before four turkeys arrived on the scene. Three of them were definitely jakes, but even though the fourth had a short, three-inch beard that stuck straight out from his chest, his head looked like an adult and his wing speculum did, too. We contemplated and debated that turkey's age status for quite a while, until Earl finally said he was 95% certain that it was a tom and he was gonna kill him, so he did. Sure enough, his bird had 3/4" spurs previously unseen by any of us due to the tall vegetation. In addition, he sported the smallest second beard that I'd ever seen…stretching to nearly half an inch! Then, an hour later Earl calmly (perhaps *too* calmly, as I thought he was kidding) said there were a half dozen toms standing in the dekes, and when I skeptically looked out the blind's window, I saw that he was right! It got a little hectic at that point as the gaggle of gobblers were pacing around and milling about en masse, unsure of how or whether they were going to attack my strutter decoy or exit the scene, and perhaps I rushed the shot (15 yards) a bit, because I missed. For the second time of the year, I heard very distinctly hissed into my left ear, by Sal this time, "God damnit, Doc!"

The rest of the day was fairly uneventful up close and personal, but we ended up seeing 12 different toms and several jakes at longer ranges. Only after exiting the protective cover of the blind at noon did we realize exactly how nasty the weather had turned, because I was soaking wet and cold to my core before we could reach the truck. Still, seeing that many turkeys on such a miserable day was an impressive accomplishment and we considered the event a rousing success. Besides that, Earl and I got to be entertained by the one and only Sal Magro for the entire time. That alone was certainly worth the price of admission!

The following day we drove an hour and a half to go hunt with Preston Reilly (Hambone) and his buddy Brandon Czepiel (Zeep). We had big fun, and I was able to atone for my performance the previous morning by smiting a tom at about the same range as the one I missed. Then, we spent the rest of the day trying to get Earl his second bird. Near noon we finally found a group of four toms with several hens. They were hanging out in a plowed field which sort of looked like a "bowl" atop a high hill. When they wouldn't leave their little "bailiwick" to search out the source of our calling, we attempted to move in tight and spooked the whole lot of 'em. After they were gone we then marveled at all the turkey sign in that disked up dirt, and when Hambone called that evening to ask if we'd like to come back and try them again, my response was a resounding, "Hell, yes!"

Two birds gobbled at dawn from about a quarter mile away, but only one

Hambone insisted on being the pack mule for Earl, Zeep, and me.

of those sort of cooperated by creeping in almost to killing range. His two hens, however, eagerly joined our flock of DSD's and felt so at home with them that they stood around preening for a while and then laid down. Their reluctant lover, however, merely strutted and stared at the happy flock from about 75 yards as he slowly circled around the lip of the bowl. Finally, after an hour and lots of pleading calls from me on a glass and Earl on his trumpet, that stubborn booger crept just close enough to be in killing range of Earl's 20 gauge spitting number 9 TSS pellets. Subsequent efforts at several of Zeep's properties to find another tom for me only resulted in a pair of skittish gobblers that swung by a little too wide. Even still; it had been a couple of real enjoyable days, spent hunting with a couple of real good guys, and we had lots of fun.

For the next four days the weather turned absolutely atrocious. Rain, wind, and cold temps made hunting a miserable endeavor. Every day I would get soaking wet and shivering cold by the noon cutoff, and only because we kept a constant fire in the woodstove was I able to warm up and dry out all of my gear every afternoon. However, there was a real nice tom hanging out close to camp, and it was only by the grace of the weather, the tom's good luck, and a couple of poor decisions on my part that I didn't get him killed. Earl hurt his back/hip on the second day and couldn't even go afield for the final two days of our stay, but I kept on fighting the good fight because I *really* wanted to kill this bird. I've been hunting the Bays' properties since 1988, and that obstinate gobbler was spending a lot of time in one of my old favorite haunts. That field is now owned by Trevor's Mom Janice following her divorce from Jake, but she welcomed me to try my luck there for as long as I wished. I was bound and determined to get it done and get that gobbler killed!

On the final morning I trudged out into a drizzling rain early and slipped into a blind that I'd put up the night before in the most strategic spot which the previous days had shown to offer promise, and as usual, the tom gobbled from across the road. I didn't care…he seemed to really like roosting over there, but would eventually work his way to the field where I was set up. Despite the scudding cloud cover and dreary weather, he gobbled fairly well. There was even another bird sounding off from about as far away as I could possibly hear a turkey sing. I called a little bit and was encouraged when my targeted tom answered a couple of times, but he didn't seem to be in any hurry to cross over the road between us. That was fine by me, too; I had a strong feeling that things were going to get good eventually, even though the rain was pattering steadily upon my blind's roof. I was sort of huddled up trying to keep warm (the wind was pushing a cold breeze directly into my face) when suddenly I heard the unmistakable sound of turkey wings slapping against plastic. Jerking my face up to look out the window, I saw four mad jakes trouncing my strutter and posturing jake decoys. I mean, they were really getting with it! I was a little chagrinned because I hadn't even seen them coming, but in fairness, I'd been more interested in listening to the distant gobbling and not focused on my immediate surroundings.

For fully 15 minutes the thrashing continued unabated, and all the while I kept noting that my intended bird's gobbles seemed to be getting closer. In fact, the final three shout-outs sounded like their maker was right down beside the road, and it wasn't long before I saw him in our field and jogging towards me and the jakes. At 100 yards out he fuzzed up into a full strut before continuing on to about 70 yards, where he did it again. A determined march followed, and when he was at 60 yards the jakes saw him and rushed out for a confrontation. Once they were all face-to-face the tom gobbled defiantly and the jakes gobbled in return and in unison. This was obviously the signal for a melee to commence, because they all instantly began jumping up in the air and trying to flog or kick the crap out of each other. Then, the tom began chasing them in circles. It was pure madness for a few moments and I feared that the Keystone Cops-style skirmish might take them across the field and out of the game, but the jakes finally got their act together and ganged up as one to turn the tables of the conflict around and chase after the tom, instead…who headed directly at me and my blind!

When only about 10 yards away from me, the old gobbler suddenly did an abrupt U-turn and raced straight out to my strutter decoy and began attacking it viciously. The jakes were right behind and piled into him from the rear, so he juked away from his tormentors and sprinted over to my posturing jake deke, which he basically tackled and began rapidly pecking at its head. I took that brief window of opportunity when the jakes were separated from the tom a little bit to promptly lay the old boy out good and proper, causing those teenage hooligans to all run or fly away. Then, I sat back, relaxed, and reveled in the memories made of a fine and interesting hunt for a worthy opponent, who weighed 22.5 pounds and sported *real* nice, hooked spurs from which he easily hung on a nearby horizontal limb. It felt great to once again find success in that old favored spot, and a sense of nostalgia warmed my heart against the chilly wind and rain as Earl timely drove up and helped me carry my gear and a very wet gobbler out of the field.

2025

*This one from New York didn't come easy,
but those are the best kind.*

Once we had a chance to dry out again at camp and get all of our belongings packed up, Earl and I said our goodbyes and thank you's to Jake and then we caravanned the seven hours to Bill George's Pennsylvania camp. I was already tagged out in that state, but Earl was eager to sample some of the fun that I'd told him happened there every year when a bunch of our friends would show up during the last week of the season. This year's crew included Bill, Doug Pickle from Virginia, Steve Torman from West Virginia, Bill Glasgow from Canada, and Craig Morton from the next county over from The Farm. Pennsylvania has a good turkey population, but it can be tough sometimes and this was one of those years. Hence; Earl and I struck out in trying to get him a bird or two. That didn't much matter, though. We weren't really there for any guarantees other than good times, laughs, and epic camaraderie. Earl ended up fitting in with that crowd like they'd been buddies all their lives, so I guarantee he will be coming back next year for more fun.

With Michigan once again offering a segment of turkey season ending on June 7th, I then opted to go give it a whirl. In 2024 I'd shot a tom the first day there without ever hearing any gobbling at all, and the landowner had told me that I was more than welcome to come back. However, upon my arrival this past spring he said that the turkeys on his place had completely vanished several weeks earlier. I was thus forced to seek out other options. Luckily for me, finding birds is *not* hard in Michigan, and after driving around the first couple days and seeing multiple toms, I finally caught at home the landowner of one particular farm where I'd spotted several birds, and when I asked him for hunting permission, he told me that I was welcome to "kill 'em all!"

On the first day while hunting there I saw two toms, 12 jakes, and four hens, but they mostly ignored my DSD strutter, jake, and hen decoys. The longbeards did come to about 60 yards late in the evening, but they seemed totally uninterested, or maybe even wary, of my fakes. After they left I decided to not put out the strutter again. The following day I set up where the flock had spent most of the afternoon hours of the previous day, and shortly after sunup an aggressive hen charged in and beat the crap out of both my hen dekes. Then, when another hen came into the field, the mean old hag raced over and trounced her, too. Right about the time I was expecting the toms to show up, a three-man work crew wearing bright orange safety vests and hardhats drove into the field in a golf cart and began spraying for weeds along the powerline which bisected the farm. Afterwards, they circled all the way around the field's edge and passed right by my blind at about five feet. At least the driver said, "Sorry" as they motored on. A few minutes later the neighboring farm began industrial spraying of their blueberry bushes, which took a couple of hours, and I saw no more turkeys until 4 p.m., when the entire flock except for the longbeards showed up. Every one of them ignored me and my dekes.

Rain began that night and was predicted to continue all the next day, so I felt absolutely sure of turkeys coming to the field. I was right, too, but the first one was a much larger tom than the pair I'd previously spotted, and he did not like the sight of my jake decoy even a little bit. He stayed way out in the field, and even laid down for about an hour, before eventually gobbling and chasing some real hens around. However, by late morning he and his girlfriends had all vanished from view. The original pair of toms showed up at about 2 p.m. and I really thought they were going to do it right when they eased over towards me, but once again, they got as close as 60 yards and then turned to leave. That was the final straw: these Michigan turkeys obviously wanted nothing to do with tom *or* jake decoys, so I removed them from the setup and put out only a couple of hens from then onward. Those same two toms came back at 6 p.m. and fed around for a while…right over beside my van parked by the owner's house on the opposite side of the field…and then they left to go roost on another property across the road from there.

During the next three days I sat in that blind for about 15 hours per day, and despite having jakes and hens within shooting range regularly, I never came close to killing either of those toms. I hate deer hunting, and I hated myself for using deer hunting tactics on these turkeys, but the landowner didn't own any of the woods surrounding his fields so that made sitting and waiting the only practical option. It was boring and pure torture for me. Besides that, I started feeling the old familiar pain of kidney stones. Maybe it was brought on by being basically immobile for so long, or perhaps it was simply from not drinking enough water, but there was no denying that I had a detested stone wanting to make an exit from my urinary tract. If you've never experienced that pain, count yourself as lucky and take my advice to drink way more water than you would think necessary. And do it every day, for the rest of your life! That's the only way to rid your body of the minerals deposits forming those heinous creations. Once they're too large to pass through your urinary system a doctor will have to go in and get them, and I can guarantee you one thing…that is *NOT* something you'll enjoy!!! I'd already experienced this horrendous procedure twice since the age of 50, as well as an operation to remove a tumor from my left kidney back in 2023, so it was with a feeling of extreme dread and foreboding that I toughed out the final few days of the season in pain and agony. I knew what was in my future after turkey season was over, and I most definitely wasn't looking forward to it!

My good friend Mathew Myers from Indiana was also hunting in the same general area, and after he quickly dispatched a tom on one of his accessible properties, he invited me to accompany him to a small field where there had been a strutter hanging out with a couple of hens. By then I couldn't stand the thought of sitting for even one more minute in that cursed blind, so I accepted his noble offer and on Friday we slipped in and set up 60 yards from an inside corner of the field, at the spot where he'd seen this tom for two morning in a row. However, like the dumbass I am, I then suggested that we put out some dekes, so I grabbed the posturing jake and two hens and stuck them in the dirt 25 yards from us. I'm nothing, if not stubborn, but after running off turkeys all week long by using decoys, you'd have thought I might learn my lesson. Wrong. Like I've often said, there's no dumbass like a hard-headed dumbass!

The tom gobbled early, and he gobbled a *lot* from straight back into the woods from that corner. Our setup was perfect, so I figured this hunt was going to be over quickly; especially when the tom hit the ground and headed directly for our field. His resounding gobbles rattled the woods and made my knees quiver. Then, the two hens coming along with him started yelping, and when the first of those old biddies stepped into the field, she took one look at my decoys and began putting. The tom couldn't have been more than five steps behind her, but when she turned around and retreated, he tagged along and away they went. For a while they stayed within a hundred yards of the field and the tom answered anything I said on a call, but eventually the group faded out of hearing range. Man, was I disappointed, as well as mad at myself for even considering the use of decoys. The dirt all around our dekes was trampled with turkey tracks upon turkey tracks.

When Mathew left late-morning to go spend the afternoon playing tourist with his wife, I returned to my blind for one last afternoon sit and was rewarded with the sight of my two toms and a dozen jakes chasing five hens around the field. However, they never even came close to me before going out of sight around the bend of the U-shaped 100 acre field as dusk approached. At least that told me which part of the farm they would be on the next morning, but when Mathew suggested that we return to Friday's claim of shame and hunt it like we should've done originally, I thought that sounded like an A-1 idea. We would sit there without decoys, or even calling, and see how the final morning of the Michigan season panned out. Confidence in the tom's return was strong, and we both felt very positive about the plan.

Unfortunately, nobody told that tom what he was supposed to do, and despite hearing probably 300 gobbles the previous day, on Saturday the only bird singing out was so far away as to only be a hinted whisper. Still, I figured that it was just a matter of time until that loudmouthed bird showed up. Maybe he'd simply gobbled himself out the previous day and now had a throat too sore for singing. For nearly an hour we sat there hearing and seeing nothing, until I eventually told Mathew that we needed to give up and go find another tom. Time was wasting. But, as we arose to leave a hen yelped in the distance, so we sat right back down and watched five hens fly into the stubble from the opposite side of the field. One of them was limping real badly. When I yelped on a glass call all of them immediately answered back, and then they began making their way to us, with the gimpy hen bringing up the rear. Soon thereafter, we had five love-starved hens standing around at ranges from five to 20 yards, where they continued to mill around cutting and yelping forlornly for another hour and a half. I just *knew* that their calling would eventually bring in the absentee tom, but time dragged on without the least hint of him being anywhere within our zip code. At last we decided to jump up and give the girls more than their daily allotted dose of exercise by flying off in five different directions, and then we headed over to the farm where I'd been hunting all week to make a final play on those two toms which had been successfully whooping my butt.

As I said, this field was shaped like a "U," so rather than coming in from the end of one long leg near the farmer's house (like I'd done all week), we used Michigan's 1-mile road grid system to drive over to the other leg and slip in that way. When I subsequently checked out the property lines on OnX, I discovered that the first 200 yards of it were actually forested, and as we made our way through the woods and towards the plowed and planted field, I saw enough scratchings and other turkey sign that I very much regretted not exploring the farm from this angle earlier in the week. Then, once I'd spotted the field ahead of us through the leaf cover, I almost immediately laid eyes on my two toms, a jake, and a hen out in its 3-inch tall soybeans. All of them were separated by at least 50 yards from one another and showed no interest in anything other than pecking around at the ground. The cover in the woods was thick, so that afforded me the opportunity to creep closer and after wading across a steep sided creek, I crawled up on the opposite bank and tucked in behind a leafy bush growing right on the field's edge. It afforded me a real comfortable place to lean in and support my weight while kneeling on my knees, and there was even a nice horizontal limb where I could rest my gun with its barrel guarding an opening from which I could see most of the field. I couldn't have dreamed up a better ambush spot, if only one of the toms might wander over…

The closest gobbler was 150 yards away, but he was, indeed, slowly working in my direction. The second tom was out past him, while the jake and hen were off to my right. Since the nearest bird seemed to be heading in my direction anyway, I didn't even bother calling, and as minutes ticked off the range between us shrank. Once in a while he'd veer off in the direction of the jake and hen, but then he'd turn to face me again and keep coming. Before I knew it he was at a hundred yards, then 90, 80, and 70. I started to get real excited and thought this might work out! Sixty yards, then 50, and at that point I decided one way or another the trigger was gonna get pulled on him, since I'd already seen what this gun could do at nearly such a range. Still, he kept coming even closer. Forty five yards, then 40, and at 35 steps I was just waiting for him to raise his head when he suddenly thrust out that long neck and gobbled! I took this as a sign to put an end to the hunt, so when he stuck up his head in that perfect "kill me now" pose, I squeezed the trigger. Nothing happened. I pulled harder; still nothing!

Well, this sudden and unexpected mechanical snafu caused my brain to immediately go haywire. I knew for a fact that the safety had already been flipped to "go" mode, because I'd checked the danged thing at least 40 times in the 20 minutes that it took for the tom to close the distance between us. The previous day in the small corn stubble field I'd accidentally triggered with my knee the switch which throws a shell from the magazine into the "ready" position underneath the chamber (this button was located on the bottom of the TriStar; unlike my old Benelli's side position), so I'd already taken the precaution of doing that when I loaded up after exiting the truck out of fear that I might inadvertently trigger it again at a crucial moment and spook a tom with the noise. Did this gun not fire if a shell was riding there? My Benelli sure did, but rational thoughts were now beyond me and my mind was racing as I cursed a lack of total familiarity with this new firearm. Should I jack out a shell and see if that fixed it? Surely such a move had nothing positive to offer and wasn't necessary, so I rejected the idea outright. Instead, while turning the gun over in my hands and trying to figure out what could've possibly gone wrong, I inadvertently slipped my finger onto the trigger and without even realizing I'd applied any pressure, the gun suddenly went, "BOOM." Of course, it wasn't pointed anywhere near the tom's head at the time, so after running for a couple of steps he launched airborne and flew, passing directly overhead at about five yards. I was so tangled up in the bush that there was no way I could have shot him anyway, so I watched brokenhearted as he sailed away.

As the reality of what had just occurred solidified in my brain like cold oatmeal, I couldn't even turn to look at Mathew, who was still sitting on the other side of the creek. I was so ashamed that all I could do was hang my head and stare at the ground between my feet; every ounce of self-confidence shattered by the sudden downturn of events, and my spirit crushed. Michigan had turned into my worst nightmare. I'd worked so hard, for so long, and now I'd blown an absolutely golden opportunity when it had been a proverbial "gimme" only moments earlier. The only thing lacking was someone whispering, "God damnit, Doc" in my ear, but I figured that I was simply spared this humiliation because Mathew was too far away for me to hear him say it.

Still fumbling with the gun in my hands in trying to find an answer, it suddenly dawned on me what had gone wrong. The TriStar has a very narrow trigger, with room on either side of it for a short, stubby fingertip like mine to rest on the frame of the trigger guard and feel like it was on the trigger, instead. Basically, I'd shortstopped the entire trigger and been pulling back against that metal! The realization of what I'd done in committing such a ridiculous error felt like a slap upside the head, and then like a flash I thought back to that first miss on Ken's monster gobbler and how I'd obviously done the very same thing when attempting a second shot after the initial flinch-miss. Wow; what an absolute moron!

Following a few hours of pouting and deep introspection, I finally had an epiphany of sorts and realized that this was really the only logical way for my season to end that made any sense. From the moment I'd left Florida the year had spiraled downward precipitously, and for a variety of reasons I'd had very little fun. In fact, for most of the time I was verging on being a miserable tired bitch (please excuse the rather vulgar language here…that is a term my dear departed buddy Zane Caudill used often, and I think it rather colorfully and succinctly illustrates the state of my mental outlook). If I had actually killed this bird on the final day, the victory-from-the-ashes-of-defeat would've left a rosy sheen on what had been, in reality, the worst turkey season of my life. I would've looked back on 2025 and thought, "That wasn't so bad."

Instead, missing this tom (and especially with *how* I'd done it) was not only appropriate, but it also adequately highlighted the feelings of anger, frustration, and hopelessness which had accompanied me afield for day after day throughout the entire spring. I earned that miss, just as I'd earned the season-long difficulties by not hunting hard enough, not hunting smart enough, and not having my head in the game often enough. In addition, there was no denying that I'd gotten out of shape, fat, and lazy over the last couple of years, and that had certainly been a contributing part of the equation, too. And that doesn't even account for my shoulder and knee issues; both of which were huge problems. However, the single biggest factor and the one that bothered me the most was that I'd simply let myself down by not giving it my all. In short, I deserved every last bit of the agony and misery that I was now feeling.

The only real positive to be taken from the season, other than Florida, was that I'd actually gotten in 64 days of hunting. Of course, this tally was boosted by those seven fruitless days of June spent in Michigan, but in hindsight I'd had a real solid showing so far as putting in some woods time. My goal every year is to accrue at least 60 days divided between guiding and hunting, and since I've always claimed that the truest measure of "success" is in the number of days spent watching the sunrise and listening for gobbling, I guess it could be argued that I had nothing to complain about and plenty of which to be proud. However, my five turkeys killed had set a low mark dating back to 1994, and the six states hunted were tied for the low from that very same year. That's a span of 31 years!

By looking at the tally of hunting days juxtaposed against a deeper dive encompassing all the negatives accrued, a synopsis of how I viewed the entire season as a whole developed in my brain. In summation: while there had certainly been some good times and great things accomplished, they were mostly overshadowed by lots of bad. Take, for instance, this: I'd called "in camp" 122 gobblers (my third highest total ever), and yet, the caveat here was that the vast majority of those came in Florida, and a large proportion of the others were jakes. Adult gobblers in gun range had been few and far between. That alone made for a tough year. In fairness, though, I do consider myself to be a "glass half full" kind of guy and try my best to look on the bright side of life, so I guess it would behoove me to point out how this many teenage boy turkeys should bode well for the next couple of seasons ahead. And I heard the same sort of observation from friends all across the country. Jakes were running rampant. Such a positive prognosis for the resource as a whole could certainly cancel out several of my personal negatives, so I guess it just depends on your outlook as to whether a given fact is good or bad. There's usually a silver lining to most worst-case scenarios if you only look hard enough to find it.

However, try as I might to put a shine on 2025, I still couldn't help but consider it a dismal failure overall, and although they alone don't define the reasons why I think this way, I'll submit two additional statistics which really stick out and are stuck in my craw. First; I'd missed three turkeys during the year. You'll have to trust me here when I say this, but I've blown opportunities at a rather large truck-full of birds over my lifetime. It's often been said that if you haven't missed any turkeys, then you haven't shot at enough, and I've shot at a bunch! However, the season's high number of miscues was totally unacceptable. I can live with an occasional one every other year or so, or maybe even two in the same season once in a blue moon, but three? That's ridiculous! I needed to tighten up my act. Secondly; for the first time ever, I'd failed to kill a bird in three different states. In fairness, I'd hunted only a single day in Indiana and come close to killing a tom while in the company of Brandon Ziegler, but I *had* been carrying a gun and fully intending to use it on that outing, so this counts against me. I don't enjoy eating tag soup, and I don't travel to other states expecting to return home "skunked." I'm there to kill turkeys. Yes; they call this sport hunting, and not killing, but that's why I almost always leave the schedule open-ended wherever I go, in order to allow plenty of time to get things done before moving on. This year the cards just didn't line up and I'd failed in half of the states hunted. Pitiful.

Well, those two items mentioned above had little to do with how I viewed the season in general terms, but they did hurt my personal pride quite a bit. I'll admit to that. However, what stung even worse was the disappointment and frustration I felt with myself. True; a good portion of my problems hinged around nephew Dan and all the thoughts, concerns, and worries over his pending death that pervaded my brain nearly 24/7. His whole ordeal had been a *huge* underlying current affecting my lack of motivation for getting after turkeys with the usual gusto. How could I focus on hunting when there were things going on of so much more importance? Besides all of that, the physical issues and limitations I was suffering through were substantial: from that rebuilt left shoulder, to a left knee so painful as to basically leave me no better off than an invalid. The truth of the matter is that I couldn't have hunted as hard as I wanted to, even if I'd wanted to.

Regardless of all those issues, I've made it a habit to set very high standards and hold myself accountable to lofty expectations, so in hindsight it felt like I'd not lived up to those. I hobbled away from the turkey woods on June 7th fully aware of every one of these things, and either because of that, or in spite of it, there existed in the core of my soul a burning which I knew needed to be addressed ASAP. Hence; I'd vowed to make changes in the months ahead to correct some of my shortcomings and alter the future. The status quo was no longer working for me. I'm a stubborn man, so you can be sure that once my mind is set on a course of action, I have every intention of seeing it through.

I *will* be back…

A few days after my return home the kidney pain reached critical mass level, and on June 13th Dr. Kitley removed a 9mm stone that was stuck in my urethra. I've described this horrendous procedure before, but here's a brief refresher course: they go in through the smallest orifice of your body to pulverize the stone into smaller pieces, and then they remove as many of those as they can, leaving in place a 12" long stent in your urinary tract to help fluids drain. They leave a few inches of string attached to the stent and dangling outside your body to serve as a pull chord for removing the stent once you're healed up. Then, you're supposed to drink copious amounts of water and urinate as much as possible. The main problem following this god-awful surgery is that for the first week or so you're pissing out blood, chunks of stone, and other assorted gunk, and it hurts whenever you urinate. It hurts a *lot*! Your body is also contracting against that cursed stent every time you pee, and that is not fun at all…ask your wife or Mother how child birthing contractions feel.

Well, all of that was bad, but eventually most of the pain subsided and the contractions had become tolerable. However, ten days after coming home from the hospital I started feeling like death itself, and two days later I was pretty sure that I was, indeed, going to die. I was running a high fever and sweating profusely for hours at a time, but then I'd get chilled and shiver so hard that I couldn't even turn on my phone. After a second trip to an Urgent Care clinic within three days, my urologist called and told me to go *immediately* to the Emergency Room of the hospital. Following lots of blood work and tests there, they informed me that I wasn't going home anytime soon, because they were admitting me. I was a sick boy, with blood and urine infections verging on sepsis.

Luckily for me, intravenous antibiotics knocked back the infections coursing through my body and after three days in the hospital I checked out just in time to make my appointment to have the stent removed. Believe me, there was no way in hell I wasn't going to make that appointment and have the very source of those infections pulled out of my body once and forever! I told the two pretty nurses set to perform the procedure that I was sorry, but due to being so sick I hadn't had a shower in a week and had spent the last few days hospital bound, and besides that, my string was only barely visible back inside my pee hole. They laughed and said it was ok, and then looked down towards my groin and told me that they thought they could see it. I responded, "You are talking about the string, right" Nothing like a little humor before someone pulls your intestines out through your penis (that's basically how it feels).

As I sit here a week later while finishing up the 2025 chapter of this book, I am finally starting to feel decent again. It's been a rough row to hoe for me so far this year, but I remain thankful of everything I have, of all the people who've cared for and cared about me, and for still possessing a strong desire to improve myself and learn from my mistakes. That's one of the defining characteristics of a turkey hunter, anyway…to always look forward and work towards the future. I can't wait to once again feel the crisp coolness of the coming day as barred owls hoot the night away and thunderous roars of the wild turkey stir my blood and invigorate my soul. The hope and expectation of hearing that sound is what drives me. It's what inspires me. And it's what I live for. The spring of 2025 may have been my worst season ever, but that just means 2026 has got to be better!

Back in February, at the NWTF Convention with a lot of my friends, things were looking bright despite having my arm in a sling.

Chapter 9

Recollections from a Turkey Hunter of a Certain Age

I just turned 65 on January 5th. As the old saying goes, "If I'd known that I was gonna live this long, I'd have taken better care of myself." Just kidding. All things considered, I'm doing pretty good, even though I'm beginning to doubt that I'll make it to my long-held goal of living to be at least 143 years old. I've noticed a tendency of late to look back upon my life in a more "reflective" manner, and I must say, in overall retrospect it's been one heckuva good run basically divided into two parts: before the wild turkey entered my life, and afterwards.

I only saw my first gobbler when I was 23 and already proud of being an outdoorsman with interests in a wide variety of pursuits....hunting many different species of game birds and animals, fishing in all manner of waters both fresh and salt, and generally immersing myself at every opportunity in the hills and hollers which so draw me to their wonders. Every single one of these endeavors was immediately relegated to the back seat of importance once a big, beautiful wild turkey tom came waltzing in out of a downpour to my poorly rendered attempts at imitating the calls of a timid girl turkey, and my life has not been the same since. How could it be? There is nothing else like these birds in all of nature, and I view the pursuit of wild turkeys during the spring season as the penultimate outdoor challenge. The sport has come to absolutely rule my very existence, and it's led to my spending on average nearly 70 days per spring in the turkey woods.

I've seen a lot of stuff in these thousands of outings afield. When I first ventured forth as a wet-behind-the-ears newbie, turkey numbers around the entire country were low. There weren't many turkey hunters, either. The sport itself was more legend than reality for most of us, with any supposed "knowledge" we possessed having come mostly from stories and tales told by what few actual turkey hunters we knew. These guys were held in high esteem and viewed as something special by us mere mortals, and their names were spoken of in whispered reverence. "Hush-mouthed" was a term coined to describe tom turkeys who didn't gobble much, but that moniker could have just as easily been used to define their old-school pursuers whom we were trying to emulate. Those guys didn't dole out a whole lot of information about either their exploits or their tactics, and so, the younger generation of up-and-coming turkey hunters (of which I was working hard to become a member) had to try and figure things out through the school of hard knocks. Trial and error were our teachers and main motivators: lots of trials, and lots and lots of errors!

The sport of turkey hunting held a great amount of mystique about it, and so did the birds themselves. They were said to possess uncanny and otherworldly powers of deception and escapism, and those of us inclined to fall under their spell treated each other as brothers and sisters of a common devotion should; sharing ideas and strategies while trying to help one another figure out these vexing birds. We did this while conducting ourselves under the strict code of never interfering with someone who was already working a bird, and willingly going elsewhere if we found out that another hunter had beaten us to "our" spot. In short, we treated one another with the same honor, dignity, and respect as that shown to our noble adversary.

Those bygone days were a simpler time in many ways, but one thing which we had going for us from the late '80's and onward was an exploding turkey population stemming from successful trap-and-transfer programs going on all across the country. It wasn't overly hard to find turkeys or places in which to hunt them back then...either on public land, or private property that could generally be accessed with nothing more than verbal permission and a handshake. State licenses were cheap, bag limits were liberal, and seasons were long. A hunter intent on maximizing his (or her) opportunities could easily hunt a dozen states in a single spring season if he was devoted and able to ignore responsibilities back home. I qualified as such in both regards, and many other folks did, too. A whole generation of pretty-darned-good turkey hunters "came of age" in the last couple decades of the 20th century and the first one of the 21st, as turkey populations thrived and continued to expand into practically every available acre of suitable habitat.

However, there were a few negatives to be found alongside the good, and an over-abundance of media saturation could conceivably be blamed for most of them. After all, the sport looked so easy on TV! That image drew people into the woods who were, quite frankly, unsuited to be called true turkey hunters. This new breed of outdoorsman didn't have any idea of the sport's history and its subtle nuances, nor an interest in learning about them. Furthermore, they didn't have enough respect for their fellow hunters; let alone for the wild turkey, itself. I mean, really; how else can you explain anyone ever referring to this magnificent bird as a "thunder chicken?" Comparing a wild turkey to a stupid yard bird? Sacrilege!

Turkey hunting isn't the equal of deer hunting, or duck hunting, or the hunting of anything else in the world, for that matter. It is a far superior pastime to them all, and should be conducted in an honorable manner and with the utmost dignity. I think the only comparable sport in terms of how its followers present a similar reverence for the game pursued might be those poor, tortured souls who hunt ruffed grouse. Unfortunately, there's been a marked change over the last three decades, or so, as shown by a steady degradation of etiquette and good manners, and coinciding with the exponential growth of the internet and Social Media. Coincidence? I think not! Those things, along with morals, ethics, and just being a decent person all around, seem to have gone by the wayside. And, I miss them.

So long as I'm picking scabs, I might as well address another elephant in the room by mildly insulting a few folks on the subject of decoys. Let's face the cold, hard facts here: the wide-spread use of decoys has quite simply made "turkey hunters" out of a formidable number of people who never would have been able to attain success on a regular basis without them. Of course, I would never go so far as to outlaw decoys, and often use them myself these days, but it sure does get tiresome to see how widely their influence has overtaken a sport which used to hinge solely around attempting to call a tom into close gun range by making him think that there was a hen in a place where one didn't exist. Since turkeys don't have the mental facilities to tell real from fake, and because he believes so strongly in what those incredible eyes of his can see, a tom turkey can quite easily be fooled with a lifelike decoy. And the dekes of today look like they could bend over and pick up a grasshopper at any moment! In short: using these things eliminates the traditional ruse and reduces the sport to one more comparable to duck hunting. Don't get me wrong here: I love hunting ducks, but I liken using decoys for turkeys to taking the easy way out and exploiting the bird's weakest attribute, rather than in trying to fool his strongest ones like sharp vision, acute hearing, and a strong drive to avoid all of earth's upper food chain critters who are trying to eat him during every day of his life. Decoy usage is almost universal when it comes to the video's which flood the internet on sites like YouTube these days, so I guess the proliferation of them was inevitable since everybody seems so hell-bent on becoming a movie star or an internet influencer and getting their 15 minutes of fame, but I think it's important to remind everyone that too much of a good spice can spoil the soup.

In total fairness and full disclosure, I think it's very important that I admit once again to using decoys fairly often and nearly always so when I'm guiding. I'm certainly not proud of their use when I'm hunting alone, though. Every time I pull the trigger on a tom over dekes it feels like I've sold out a little bit more of my soul, and like I've dishonored my worthy opponent. I look at decoy use as a crutch, and while there's truly no shame in admitting to oneself the need for help in winning a battle against an opponent so competent and challenging as the wild turkey, there also should be considered the honor and dignity gained in doing things the "right" way.

Like I said; I do use decoys quite a bit, but it wasn't always so. The older and more broken–down my carpenter's knees become as I age, the more I'm willing to concede that I ain't what I used to be. I sit more in one place now and let the turkeys come to me. That's not the way it always was, and in my physical prime I was a force to be reckoned with in terms of moving often, far, and over whatever terrain stood in my way. There's no questioning it: I've slipped a little. However, the day when I depend on decoy use to kill all of my turkeys is the day that I will hang up my vest for the last time. This isn't a criticism on how others should or shouldn't do things. Do whatever you want and hunt however you want so long as it's done in a legal manner, but please realize that the easiest and most efficient methods of killing turkeys take some of the wonder and magic away from a sport that was once based on those things alone. An incredible world is there to open up when you hold yourself to a higher standard.

Universal smart-phone ownership and their accompanying apps is another technological "advancement" that's denigrated our sport, in my own humble opinion. Folks who were once so scared as to never venture very far from the parking lot can now find their way back to the truck via any number of programs like OnX or HuntSmart, and that has resulted in boot tracks and additional hunters traipsing around in places where I never even dreamed other people might go. It used to be that a feller with a compass and a paper topographic map could get away from the crowds, but not now! I always counted on most of my successes coming as a result of working harder than other folks were willing to do and putting in the greatest effort. However, many of the younger generation these days see busting one's hump as nothing more than a character flaw. I may, indeed, have a dinosaur's thought processes going on here, but I think that the use of technology to take out all of the unknowns, guesswork, and intuition feels deep down in my soul like cheating in the worst way. And now, of late, we've got another of the latest-and-greatest technologies to contend with in the way of drones rising up on the horizon (both literally and figuratively) to further sully the meaning of "fair chase." Don't even get me started on their use, or the saturation of game trail cameras to keep tabs on the birds. I abhor them both.

Despite how this chapter might sound so far like an old codger shouting out, "GET OFF MY LAWN," I do not view today's situation as all doom and gloom. Quite the contrary! I still see the vast majority of turkey hunters as top-notch people, whom as a whole understand what this sport is all about and truly "get it." In all honesty, many of the negatives that I've mentioned here simply stem from the enthusiasm with which every one of us connected to this sport is possessed. Our legions hold an unabridged love for wild turkeys so great that it lights an eternal fire in our hearts, and that in turn propels us to do anything and everything within our competitive powers to win at the game. That's generally a good thing. However, what I'm saying here is that this drive to win can sometimes translate into carrying things a little too far and making a person overlook the real reasons for why we do what we do: i.e.; those thrills coming from the challenge and uncertainty of the chase, and all the personal benefits derived from operating in as moral and ethical a manner as possible.

This passion and love for the wild turkey is what propels us to carry on the traditions set down by the old-time hunters of yore, and it's that same devotion which causes us to speak out against anything that we feel might diminish the sport. The chess game that we play with turkeys is not a win at all costs proposition. If it was just about filling tags or putting meat on the table, we'd simply go around shooting our birds with rifles or stringing trot lines baited with corn, but instead, we set bag limits, season dates, and rules of fair chase so as to protect the resource at all costs. Those types of things are of paramount importance! All of us want others who follow in our footsteps to still thrill to the sights and sounds found only in the springtime turkey woods.

The good news is that once bitten by this turkey bug, the disease stays with us forever. We continue to give of our time, our money, and our energies to help the resource. We preserve, protect, and enhance our properties both public and private in order to optimize nesting and brooding habitat, and we raise monies at every opportunity to hire wildlife professionals and land/game managers trained to show us the proper way. We encourage and support youth, handicapped, and women's programs to provide more opportunities for those marginalized populations to get out into the woods. In short, turkey hunters are both the way and the means to keep this wonderful sport alive and going forward, and I applaud all the efforts of all the countless people who have made the sacrifices necessary to both get us to this point in time, and to give us possibilities for the future.

This last decade or so has definitely seen some challenges, such as a precipitous drop in turkey populations in many areas (particularly in the southeast, but elsewhere, as well). However, there is such a deep, profound, and heartfelt concern for the welfare of the wild turkey which rages so strongly in hunters' hearts nationwide that the efforts to find out what's going on and correct the issues is taking place even as you read this. I am quite confident that we will eventually get things figured out and turned around, and I'm equally sure that tomorrow's hunters will evermore thrill to that most magnificent of sounds found in nature....the gobble of the wild turkey!

I am continually humbled and encouraged when speaking with young people these days who exhibit the same bright-eyed excitement and enthusiasm which steered my course in the early years, and it warms my heart whenever I hear them describe the thrills and chills that calling in one of these glorious creatures creates. Turkey hunters old and young love telling their tales, and turkey hunters both young and old enjoy hearing those stories told by others. That hasn't changed since time immortal, and I don't think it ever will. My creaky old knees have undoubtedly slowed me down from the way in which I once pursued these birds, but the drive is still there in the center of my soul; it's a wonderment which will keep me chasing after wild turkeys for so long as I'm able to stand upright and venture forth. And when that time comes when I cannot, I know that there will be warm-hearted fellow turkey hunters willing to carry me out into the woods on their backs, if need be, just so I can once again experience the magic which has propelled me forward for all these years.

Tom turkeys can see right straight into the center of your soul.

Epilogue

Well, we've once again come to the point of closure; not of my life or anything so melodramatic as that, but rather, this book. In short, I've kinda run out of material due to this volume catching the reader up with my adventures as a turkey hunter to and through the 2025 season. Since this one covered the last seven annual spring sojourns, I don't foresee publishing another book until at least 2032, or later, and by then I'll be over 72 years old. Who knows if I'll still even be around, so the gist of it is that this might be my last book. I never thought that I would write even one, let alone five, so I guess that I should count my lucky stars...and I do! My time spent as a turkey hunter has been the greatest journey that I could never have even imagined early-on, with so many precious memories stacked up in my brain that it's almost filled to overflowing. That's one of the main reasons why I wrote these books to begin with: a simple desire to leave something of myself behind. If my words and tales have perhaps entertained or inspired others (and I am told regularly that they do both), then all of the hard work, time, effort, and money spent on the endeavor has been well worth it.

I want most of all to thank everyone who has purchased my books during these last few years, and I specifically would like to single out all those who have let me know personally through cards, letters, phone calls, or word of mouth that my stories deserve mention in their own life and have meant something special to them. In my heart, I regard the title of "Author" to be the equal or better of just about any other, and although I don't dare to include myself as worthy, simply seeing my name on the spine of a book about my favorite subject has been the honor of my lifetime.

Somewhere along this crazy pathway that I've chosen, I sort of stumbled into a desire to kill turkeys in every state except Alaska, and through perseverance and persistence, I eventually accomplished that goal. Once that was done I thought that doing it again would be kinda cool, so I did it. Since I had no intentions of quitting my state hopping spring turkey hunting lifestyle anyway, it was just inevitable that a third Slam might come to fruition, and from there I decided to go on ahead and finish up numbers four and five. Now that those rather ridiculous goals have all been reached, I'm entering into a whole new realm of focus...one that I haven't ever experienced before...whereby I'm content to just go where I want to go and hunt where I want to hunt, for as long as I want to be there and with no pressure or reason to move on elsewhere until I have satisfied the itch in whatever particular state I find myself. I can tell you right now that it's a refreshing feeling, and I'm really looking forward to the season(s) ahead!

Ok; that's it. Let's wrap it up. If perhaps you wish to purchase this or any of my other books, please order them directly from me. They are also available on Amazon and elsewhere, but the ones I sell from home allow me to personalize and sign them to the buyer, or to whoever is receiving them as a gift. The books in my own library most valued are definitely the ones signed by their authors, so I would be more than happy to accommodate.

Printing and shipping costs have continued to climb beyond the ridiculous level, so I've had to raise my prices a bit on the last two volumes in order to partially compensate. I apologize for that, but rest assured I will never make much money (if any) selling these books. If I were doing this with an eye focused on profit, then these danged things would need to be priced far beyond the reasonable reach of the common working man, of which I'm a proud member, and I just can't make myself do that. And so, the price schedule from here on out will be: $25 per copy for paperbacks and $35 per copy for hardcovers of Volumes 1-3, and $29/$39 for Volumes 4 & 5. I'll continue to pay all postage until such time as I can no longer afford it, or the post office straightens their act out.

The best and fastest way to transfer funds to me is via PayPal, using either one of my email addresses: tdocweddle@comcast.net, or tdocweddle@gmail.com. If you do order by this method, please utilize their "send money to friends and family" option, so they don't deduct fees on my end. And, don't forget to include your return address in the notes section, along with to whom the books should be personalized. Or, if you'd rather, send a check or money order to:

Tom Weddle
PO Box 7281
Bloomington, IN 47407

Thanks, y'all….hope to see you somewhere down along the turkey trails!

Oh: one final note. Since this might very well be my last book, I think it's important to firmly state exactly where I proudly stand in these times of polarized politics and a rapidly changing America. There is no solid ground on the wrong side of history. I love this country, Democracy, our Constitution, and the Rule of Law. I hate Nazi's, so FUCK Donald Trump!

www.ingramcontent.com/pod-product-compliance
Lightning Source LLC
Chambersburg PA
CBHW060552080526
44585CB00013B/542